MARK TWAIN'S
LANGUAGES

MARK TWAIN'S LANGUAGES

DISCOURSE, DIALOGUE, AND LINGUISTIC VARIETY

DAVID R. SEWELL

University of California Press

Berkeley · Los Angeles · London

University of California Press
Berkeley and Los Angeles, California

University of California Press, Ltd.
London, England

© 1987 by
The Regents of the University of California

Library of Congress Cataloging-in-Publication Data
Sewell, David R., 1954–
   Mark Twain's languages.
   Bibliography: p.
   Includes index.
   1. Twain, Mark, 1835–1910—Language.   2. Twain,
Mark, 1835–1910—Knowledge—Language and languages.
3. Language and languages in literature.   4. Speech in
literature.   5. Dialect literature, America—History and
criticism.   I. Title.
PS1344.S48   1987   818'.409   86-32632
ISBN 0-520-05702-3 (alk. paper)

Printed in the United States of America

1   2   3   4   5   6   7   8   9

That no one understands another, that the
same words do not arouse the same thought in
one man as in another, that a dialogue or a text
causes different trains of thought in
different individuals, was something I had long
realized all too clearly.

—Goethe

Even meanings born in dialogues of the
remotest past will never be finally grasped
once and for all, for they will always be
renewed in later dialogue.

—Mikhail Bakhtin

now thats also a model of human
understanding   sort of   though it no longer supposes that
you can penetrate to anybody elses experience

—David Antin

Contents

Preface

> "Why, Huck, doan de French people talk de same way
> we does?"
>
> "*No*, Jim; you couldn't understand a word they said—not
> a single word." . . .
>
> "Is a Frenchman a man?"
>
> "Yes."
>
> "*Well*, den! Dad blame it, why doan he *talk* like a man?—
> you answer me *dat!*"
>
> —*Adventures of Huckleberry Finn*

What impressed Mark Twain most about language was its diversity. Moving from the West to the East and on to Europe, living among boatmen, slaves, miners, journalists, and aristocrats, Twain heard the multiplicity of human voices that finds its way into his work. His concern with rendering speech accurately marks both his "Explanatory" note to *Huckleberry Finn* and his oft-repeated criticism of Bret Harte's inept literary dialect. But linguistic variety in Mark Twain's writing is not just an aspect of literary technique: it reflects a belief in the fundamental heterogeneity of human nature. Because this heterogeneity is always potentially threatening, we tend to deny or suppress it. Twain makes Jim, in arguing with Huck over the speech of Frenchmen, represent nostalgia for a single, undifferentiated, language that would immediately identify its speakers as "men." The irony is that the form of Jim's very words belies his argument. "Doan de French people talk de same way we does?" The "we" here begs the question: Huck and Jim speak dialects that unmistakably indicate different social and racial status. At the same time, there is something powerfully hopeful about Jim's naive "we," for Huck and Jim's friendship and their struggle to understand each other suggest that such differences may not be an insurmountable barrier to dialogue.

Mark Twain's *languages*, then. Each of the chapters that follow deals with one or more aspects of linguistic variety in Mark Twain's work: levels of grammar, the authority of Standard English, foreign languages, dialects, the politics of speech acts, technical jargons, misunderstanding. Although Mark Twain's direct statements about language often seem at best dated and at worst simply wrong, one of my theses is that he understood language more profoundly than is usually thought. A half century of sympathetic criticism has not, I fear, entirely absolved Twain of Van Wyck Brooks's charge of linguistic superficiality. According to Brooks, the largest component of Twain's literary criticism was

> his lifelong preoccupation with grammar. How many essays and speeches, introductions and extravaganzas by Mark Twain turn upon some question whose interest is purely or mainly verbal! . . . It is the letter-perfection of Howells that dazzles him; the want of it he considers a sufficient reason for saying "you're another" to Matthew Arnold and tripping him up over some imaginary verbal gaucherie. . . . Foreign languages never ceased to be ludicrous to him because they were not English. These are all signs of the young schoolboy who has begun to take pride in his compositions and has become suddenly aware of words; and I suggest that Mark Twain never reached the point of being more at home in the language of civilization than that.[1]

During the decades since Brooks published his criticism, many fine celebratory studies of Twain's style and vocabulary have made Brooks's complaints sound strident, but even supportive critics misconceive what it is to have a theory of language. At least since the publication of F. O. Matthiessen's *American Renaissance* in 1941 we have tended to champion Emerson and those writers most like him as our homegrown philosophers of language, the American equivalents of Coleridge or Goethe. Unquestionably the sophistication of Henry David Thoreau's etymological investigations, Walt Whitman's "language experiment," and Emily Dickinson's audacious metaphors was beyond Twain's grasp. But all Transcendentalist thinking about language is radically at odds with Twain's. Whereas the Transcendentalists sought above all a poetics that would explain how language might ideally mediate between individual and object, Twain was interested in language as it arises, functions, and changes as a medium of social relations. Twain's explicit comments on language are often disappointing because the vocabulary to express what he knew simply did not exist in the nineteenth century. A goal of my study, then, is to give a voice and names to ideas that are implicit in Twain's work, especially in his best fiction.

This goal explains why I have felt compelled to revise formulas that are by now almost standard in Twain criticism. The two critics who have written most keenly about language in Mark Twain are Henry Nash Smith (in *Mark Twain: The Development of a Writer*) and Richard Bridgman (in *The Colloquial Style in America*). Both stress the fundamental importance to Twain of a literary style based on speech. Smith sees the "vernacular" as a powerful instrument for deflating hypocrisy and pretension; Bridgman finds in Twain's "colloquial" the progenitor of modern American prose style. I find their methodologies limited, however, by the assumption that a single linguistic form corresponds to a single literary function. In the course of this study I seek to demonstrate that the value and significance of linguistic categories vary throughout Twain's work depending on the requirements of a particular context and the evolution of his attitudes.

The voice and names I provide for Mark Twain reflect a number of intellectual debts. A long-standing interest in sociolinguistics and discourse theory, and in literary criticism informed by their concepts and methods, will be evident in specialized vocabulary and unspoken postulates about the way language works. Mikhail Bakhtin has given the most direction to my thinking, for he speaks to Mark Twain's condition as a writer better than any other theorist of the novel we have. "The language of a novel is the system of its 'languages,'" Bakhtin tells us; "the novel can be defined as a diversity of social speech types (sometimes even diversity of languages) and a diversity of individual voices, artistically organized."[2] We need such a generic definition if we are to make sense of books like *Huckleberry Finn, A Connecticut Yankee, Pudd'nhead Wilson*. Nevertheless, mine is not an unalloyed "Bakhtinian" reading of Mark Twain, if only because Twain's own troubled investigation of language's shortcomings calls into question Bakhtin's utopian dialectics. If hardly as consistent or sophisticated as Bakhtin's, Mark Twain's understanding of language is ultimately more complex and less sanguine.

I have learned a great deal about language from Mark Twain himself. When I first conceived of this study, I was a graduate student wary of becoming a "Mark Twain scholar," troubled by Twain's lack of both high seriousness and literary "difficulty." Luckily, days on end spent reading Mark Twain teach a distrust of easy categorization and self-serving hierarchies. If Twain wrote, as he told Andrew Lang, for the belly and not the head, it is well to remember that in the belly Epicurus located the soul. Above all, Twain teaches respect for the plain style and clear writing. He could easily wield polysyllabic technical vocabularies, but for his own prose voice he chose the most accessible of styles. His lesson is that since we each bear ultimate responsibility for our language, we should not hide ourselves behind borrowed discourse in the hope that like some Wizard of Oz's screen, it will make us appear greater and more terrible than we are. I have often been aware that my own critical vocabulary confronts Mark Twain's language in a manner embarrassingly reminiscent of the parson's talk with Scotty Briggs. My consolation is that Twain, supremely among our writers, was catholic in appreciating the multiplicity of styles and voices in our verbal universe. Should Mark Twain, in spirit somewhere, be reading this study and stumbling over terminology assimilated from semiotics, sociolinguistics, and literary theory, I trust he will be kind enough to extend to me the indulgence he granted to a stretch of theology that he found rough going: "I do not know that vocabulary, therefore I laugh at the book by the privilege of ignorance, while quite well understanding that men with better heads than mine have learned it and stopped laughing" ("Fragment on Unfamiliar Texts," *WIM*, 517).

. . .

My scholarly career owes much to the influence and support of two teachers. From Craig Williamson's courses in Old English and stylistics at Swarthmore College I learned the *wundor* of words along with analytical linguistic method. Roy Harvey Pearce directed this study in its original form as a dissertation; the less cumbersome title it bears as a book was his idea. Roy taught me to temper my native formalism with a critical appreciation of history. Many members of the community of Mark Twain scholars will find their imprints here, but I wish to offer particular thanks to Everett Emerson, Victor Fischer, Forrest G. Robinson, and Thomas Tenney. Without Alan Gribben's *Mark Twain's Library* as a reference several chapters of this book would have been virtually impossible to write as they now stand. James Cox read the book in manuscript form; for his gracious and incisive comments I am especially grateful. Robert H. Hirst and the staff of the Mark Twain Papers at the University of California, Berkeley, helped me make profitable use of unpublished material in their collections. The Interlibrary Loan staff of Central University Library, University of California, San Diego, made accessible essential research materials from around the country. I wish to thank the Regents of the University of California and the College of Arts and Sciences at the University of Rochester for research and travel grants that facilitated my work at several stages. A version of chapter 4 originally appeared as "We Ain't All Trying to Talk Alike: Varieties of Language in *Huckleberry Finn*," in *One Hundred Years of "Huckleberry Finn*," ed. Robert Sattelmeyer and J. Donald Crowley (Columbia: University of Missouri Press, 1985). To Doris Kretschmer and Barbara Ras of the University of California Press go my thanks for their encouragement and patience; to Stephanie Fay, appreciation for her especially thoughtful copy-editing. Elizabeth Bennett and David Ames provided crucial help during the final stages of manuscript preparation. I owe most of all to those whose language has shaped and sustained me: my friends, my parents, my wife and daughter.

Abbreviations

MS   Manuscript

MTP   Mark Twain Papers, The Bancroft Library, University of California, Berkeley

TS   Typescript

PUBLISHED WORKS CITED

ATS   *The Adventures of Tom Sawyer; Tom Sawyer Abroad; Tom Sawyer, Detective*, ed. John C. Gerber, Paul Baender, and Terry Firkins (Berkeley: University of California Press, 1980).

CY   *A Connecticut Yankee in King Arthur's Court*, ed. Bernard L. Stein (Berkeley: University of California Press, 1979).

CofC   *Clemens of the "Call": Mark Twain in San Francisco*, ed. Edgar M. Branch (Berkeley: University of California Press, 1969).

ETS1   *Early Tales and Sketches*, Vol. 1, 1851–1864, ed. Edgar M. Branch and Robert H. Hirst (Berkeley: University of California Press, 1979).

ETS2   *Early Tales and Sketches*, Vol. 2, 1864–1865, ed. Edgar M. Branch and Robert H. Hirst (Berkeley: University of California Press, 1981).

FM   *Mark Twain's Fables of Man*, ed. John S. Tuckey (Berkeley: University of California Press, 1972).

FW   *The Forgotten Writings of Mark Twain*, ed. Henry Duskis (New York: Philosophical Library, 1961).

HF   *Adventures of Huckleberry Finn*, ed. Walter Blair and
        Victor Fischer (Berkeley: University of California
        Press, 1986).

HHT   *Mark Twain's Hannibal, Huck, and Tom*, ed. Walter
        Blair (Berkeley: University of California Press, 1969).

LE   *Letters from the Earth*, ed. Bernard De Voto (New York:
        Harper & Row, 1962).

LSI   *Letters from the Sandwich Islands*, ed. G. Ezra Dane
        (Stanford: Stanford University Press, 1938).

MSM   *The Mysterious Stranger Manuscripts*, ed. William M.
        Gibson (Berkeley: University of California Press,
        1969).

MTA   *Mark Twain's Autobiography*, ed. Albert Bigelow Paine,
        2 vols. (New York: Harper & Brothers, 1924).

MTE   *Mark Twain in Eruption*, ed. Bernard De Voto (New
        York: Harper & Brothers, 1940).

MTHL   *Mark Twain–Howells Letters*, ed. Henry Nash Smith
        and William M. Gibson, 2 vols. (Cambridge, Mass.:
        Harvard University Press, 1960).

MTL   *Mark Twain's Letters*, ed. Albert Bigelow Paine, 2 vols.
        (New York: Harper & Brothers, 1917).

MTN   *Mark Twain's Notebook*, ed. Albert Bigelow Paine (New
        York: Harper, 1935).

MTS   *Mark Twain Speaking*, ed. Paul Fatout (Iowa City: Uni-
        versity of Iowa Press, 1976).

NJ1   *Mark Twain's Notebooks and Journals*, Vol. 1, 1855–
        1873, ed. Frederick Anderson, Michael B. Frank,
        and Kenneth M. Sanderson (Berkeley: University of
        California Press, 1975).

NJ2   *Mark Twain's Notebooks and Journals*, Vol. 2, 1877–
        1883, ed. Frederick Anderson, Lin Salamo, and Ber-
        nard L. Stein (Berkeley: University of California
        Press, 1975).

NJ3   *Mark Twain's Notebooks and Journals*, Vol. 3, 1883–
       1891, ed. Robert Pack Browning, Michael B. Frank,
       and Lin Salamo (Berkeley: University of California
       Press, 1979).

PP   *The Prince and the Pauper*, ed. Victor Fischer and Lin
       Salamo (Berkeley: University of California Press,
       1979).

PW   *Pudd'nhead Wilson and Those Extraordinary Twins*, ed.
       Sidney E. Berger (New York: Norton, 1980).

RI   *Roughing It*, ed. Franklin R. Rogers and Paul Baender
       (Berkeley: University of California Press, 1972).

SB   *Mark Twain's Satires and Burlesques*, ed. Franklin R.
       Rogers (Berkeley: University of California Press,
       1967).

WIM   *What Is Man? and Other Philosophical Writings*, ed. Paul
       Baender (Berkeley: University of California Press,
       1973).

WMT   *The Writings of Mark Twain*, Definitive Edition, 37
       vols. (New York: Gabriel Wells, 1922–1925).

WWD   *Mark Twain's Which Was the Dream? and Other Sym-
       bolic Writings of the Later Years*, ed. John S. Tuckey
       (Berkeley: University of California Press, 1967).

1

Introduction:

The Problem of Variety in Language

(Shall I confess it?) I have never read Locke nor any other of
the many philosophers quoted by you. . . . So all these
months I have been thinking the thoughts of illustrious philosophers, and didn't know it.
> —Mark Twain, letter to Sir John Adams

"Mark Twain's philosophy of language": surely something
seems wrong with the phrase. It is pretentious, it claims too
much, it takes itself too seriously. Mark Twain was a novelist, not an academic philosopher. Yet we would not balk if
the name were "Melville" or "James," or if "language" were
changed to "history" or "religion." Novelists can be philosophical, and Mark Twain wrote at least one book, *What Is
Man?*, that claimed to be philosophy; the systematic determinism of his later years is notorious.[1] We readily grant him a
thorough amateur knowledge of European history but hesi-
tate to admit his expertise in the very medium of which we
claim he was a master. Why?

My question is partly rhetorical; I shall not maintain in this
book that Mark Twain had a formal philosophy of language,
not even to the extent that he had a philosophy of culture or of
morals. Van Wyck Brooks is right to complain that much of
his overt commentary on language is trivial or naive. His self-
education, wide in other domains, did not, in fact, extend to
linguistics (or "philology," the term he would have used): for
every book on language that we know he owned or read, we
can find dozens of histories, biographies, and memoirs.[2] I *will*
claim, however, that Mark Twain's understanding of language,

1

as evidenced primarily in his fiction, transcended its origin in public-school grammar instruction and moved toward an intuition of principles just beginning to appear in his day and fully enunciated only in our own.[3] Because Twain's principles are largely at odds with those of the Transcendentalists, the nineteenth-century Americans who, we agree by convention, *had* a philosophy of language, Twain himself has been denied title to that phrase. Where the Transcendentalists saw unity, Mark Twain saw variety: this is perhaps the most concise formulation of the opposition. David Simpson has identified exactly this difference between the Transcendentalists and James Fenimore Cooper, and his explication will serve for Twain as well:

> Instead of writing [as Cooper did] of the *kinds* of languages that are effective agents within variously diversified social contracts . . . [the Transcendentalists] write of language (in the singular) as a universal medium shared by all and enabling all to achieve the same access to God and to nature. In a system of doctrines that is, as Transcendentalism is, so completely mediated through the exemplary self and its utterances, the existence of languages as functioning to connect or divide *different* selves becomes so irrelevant as to seem impertinent.[4]

Mark Twain knew his Emerson—or at least what Emerson stood for—well enough to understand the impertinence of forcing the Transcendental voice into dialogue with others. So whereas Emerson, for example, sees quotation as the fundamental stylistic principle for appropriating the language of predecessors and asserting one's continuity with that language, Twain typically quotes parodically to assert radical difference. In his most impudent act of parodic quotation he put lines from poems by Emerson (and by Holmes, Whittier, and Lowell) into the mouths of drunken impostors in his Whittier birthday speech. In the midst of a tall tale, deprived of their original context, the lines become absurd; Twain punctures the poet's implicit claim to unchanging, authoritative meaning. He accomplishes what Mikhail Bakhtin defines as the purpose of parody: to shatter "the myth of a language that presumes to be the only language, and the myth of a language that presumes to be completely unified."[5] Mark Twain's philosophy of language can best be characterized as an intuitive rejection of these myths.

Jim's scandalized disbelief that there is more than one language proper to humans (see p. ix) has a long ancestry in Western thought. Before the nineteenth century, variety in language was most often seen as an evil.[6] In his *Cratylus* Plato has Socrates conclude that the Greek dialects are corrupted forms of a primary language whose names corresponded naturally to the essences they represented. The book of Genesis provides our myths of the single namegiver Adam, who creates an original language, and of a confusion of languages to punish sinful presumption. After Babel, to speak with the wrong tongue is to court death:

> Then said they unto him, say now Shibboleth: and he said Sibboleth: for he could not frame to pronounce it right. Then they took him and slew him.
>
> (Judg. 12:6)

> And after a while came unto him they that stood by, and said to Peter, Surely thou also art one of them; for thy speech bewrayeth thee.
>
> (Matt. 26:73)

Linguistic variety is redeemed at Pentecost, when the Spirit descends to speak through the many tongues of men; but Saint Paul reminds would-be glossolalists that tongues without interpretation are vain: "Except ye utter by the tongue words easy to be understood, how shall it be known what is spoken? for ye shall speak into the air" (1 Cor. 14:9). The multiplicity of tongues and the changeability of natural languages is a scandal, for the divine word, or Logos, in both Greek and Judeo-Christian wisdom literature is single and immutable. Nostalgia for an unchanging and primary language—and as late as 1760 Samuel Johnson was complaining of the "mutability" of human speech—partly explains why the major projects of premodern philology were normative grammar and etymology intended to derive European words from their divinely given Hebrew "originals." The Renaissance and early modern period saw thinkers like Descartes and Leibniz initiate a quest for universal grammars, as well as for philosophical languages, systems in which signs and referents, language and thought, would be maintained in precise and unchanging relationship. Mark Twain knew none of these philosophers of language at first hand, but their doctrines were part of the intellectual inheritance of nineteenth-century public grammar school students. "In the grammar of a *perfect* language," he would read in the first chapter of his schoolboy's grammar text, "no rules should be admitted, but such as are founded on fixed principles, arising out of the genius of that language and the nature of things." Only because language is imperfect must speech be regulated by *"custom"*—that is, the way people actually do talk.[7]

To think seriously about language in the nineteenth century, however, was to confront the problem of the One and the Many in a new and insistent form. By 1860 Continental philology had carried all before it, and speculations about language that ignored Grimm's law or the findings of the Vedic scholars could no longer receive a hearing.[8] Although the derivation of all languages from a single ancestor was still moot, comparative philology had shown that Hebrew could not have been the original tongue of mankind. The hierarchical ranking of speech, with the classical languages of Western Europe at the summit of human culture, was giving way to the relativism of scientific dialectology: philologists testified that rural and other nonstandard dialects were both legitimate objects of research and valuable enrichers of standard speech. The major philosophical shift, however, was a growing tendency to see variety and even discord as essential to language. The post-Kantian reinterpretation of reason as a dialectical process gave rise to a relativistic view of language as a dialogic phenomenon, impossible unless the viewpoints and experiences of the participants are nonidentical. To translate this into Twainian: language is more like Huck talking with Jim than like Adam talking to himself.

For German philologist Wilhelm von Humboldt duality is fundamental to language, and all speaking is founded in dialogue. Even in silent thought one speaks to oneself as to an "other," for "the very possibility of speech is conditioned by address and response."[9] Moreover, the Self can never use the language of the Other merely as a mirror, since there is always a gap between the language of the speaker and that of the addressee: "No one when he uses a word has in mind exactly the same thing that another has, and the difference, however tiny, sends its tremors throughout language. . . . All understanding, therefore, is always at the same time a misunderstanding . . . and all agreement of feelings and thoughts is at the same time a means for growing apart."[10] The Other who echoes one's speech with fully comprehensible language is not a true Other; to provide an escape from solipsism the Other must provide enough uncertainty and incomprehensibility to challenge the constructs of the speaking Ego: "Since the spirit which constantly reveals itself in the world can never be exhaustively known through any given number of views or opinions but is always discovered to contain something new, it would be far better to multiply the languages on earth as many times as the number of earth's inhabitants might permit."[11] Thus the myth of Babel is turned on its head, and multilingualism becomes a liberation instead of a punishment. Translating from one language or dialect to another or requiring speakers of different languages to express the same idea will *create* meaning rather than merely conserve it. But vital to Humboldt's vision of glossolalia is the faith that a hypostatic human nature unites the many varieties of speech as the hub unites the spokes of a wheel. This hub, this unity underlying multiplicity, prevents misunderstanding from becoming the *only* force in human communication and thus plunging us into an absurd universe where nonsense runs unchecked.

Similarly, despite its increasing reliance on historical and empirical methods, academic philology in England and America never entirely abandoned the eighteenth-century quest for an a priori universal grammar. William Dwight Whitney, the foremost nineteenth-century American linguist, gives the science of language a Janus face when he characterizes his own study, *The Life and Growth of Language*, as one that "strives to comprehend language both in its unity, as a means of human expression and as distinguished from brute communication, and in its internal variety, of material and structure." [12] Max Müller, for whom language itself was the primary evidence that human faculties had a divine origin, mythologizes linguistics as the secular analogue of Pauline "interpretations" of tongues:

> The idea of mankind as one family, as the children of one God, is an idea of Christian growth; and the science of mankind, and of the languages of mankind, is a science which, without Christianity, would never have sprung into life. When people had been taught to look upon all men as brethren, then, and then only, did the variety of human speech present itself as a problem that called for a solution in the eyes of thoughtful observers; and I, therefore, date the real beginning of the science of language from the first day of Pentecost. [13]

Whereas Müller's faith in the unity of language is theological, Whitney's is based on an optimistic construction of social cohesion as the centripetal force that counteracts the centrifugal forces of class and regional dialects. The desire to communicate necessarily limits potential incomprehension; over and over again Whitney equates language with communication.

> Mutual intelligibility . . . is the only quality which makes the unity of a spoken tongue; the necessity of mutual intelligibility is the impulse which called out speech. [14]

> Communication is the leading determinative force throughout [language]. . . . We speak so as to be intelligible to others; . . . we do not speak simply as we ourselves choose, letting others understand us if they can and will. [15]

Especially in this last sentence, Whitney's ostensibly descriptive language is powerfully normative as well. Language in society *must* be a homeostatic system if societies are to cohere, if *unum* is to be formed *e pluribus*. This had been Noah Webster's reason for desiring a truly common American language. [16] By the late nineteenth century a looser doctrine of independent but mutually tolerant varieties of speech has become an American ideal. It gives rise, for instance, to the enormous popularity of local-color fiction and nonhumorous dialect sketches in the last quarter of the century, with their obligatory attention to idiosyncratic speechways: differences between North and South, East and West, urban and rural are subsumed under the essential "Americanness" that is felt to bind us together in spite of superficial dissimilarities. Missing from this model of friendly heterogeneity is the sense that varieties of language can be in active conflict or that misunderstanding can be a deliberate social strategy.

In the nineteenth century, then, the two controlling myths about variety in language are Babel and Pentecost. Both assume an underlying unity in language, whether it derives from the divine origin of mankind, the Oversoul, or the universality of human nature; they differ principally over the question how much access speakers of a fallen language have to the power of an Adamic tongue. As we move into the twentieth century, and as we turn to the works of Mark Twain, we encounter two formulations of linguistic variety, heteroglossia and cacophony, that minimize or deny underlying unity. They too differ in their optimism about human dialogue and mutual comprehension. *Heteroglossia* is Bakhtin's term for the healthy, indeed essential, conflict of voices that destabilizes language, permitting change and preventing any one form of language from maintaining authority at the expense of others. *Cacophony* is my term for the condition of language in an absurd universe, where centrifugal forces are unchecked, idiolects tend toward maximum randomness and confusion, and multiplicity entails misunderstanding. In this thoroughly secular version of the myth of Babel God is dead and the Tower of Babel has fallen not through divine intervention but of its own weight. Mark Twain moves freely between these two characterizations of language throughout most of his life but he is pulled toward cacophony in the last few years. (Since cacophony is essentially a special, pathological, case of heteroglossia, I will reserve a description of that final movement until the last chapter of this book.) If Mark Twain discovered empiricism without reading Locke, he also looked forward to the particular interpretation of linguistic variety that we associate with Bakhtin.

As Bakhtin uses it, *heteroglossia* is a term not susceptible of easy definition. In its concrete sense, it refers to the multitude of small "languages" into which any single national language is stratified; abstractly, it suggests that no item of language exists in isolation, that meaning depends on all the forces that intersect in each word, including (but not limited to) its history, its speaker, its recipient, and the other words in its linguistic system. Bakhtin thus speaks of two phenomena that can be "differently voiced," the entire system of a given language and the individual word. At the level of the language, heteroglossia includes "social dialects, characteristic group behavior, professional jargons, generic languages, languages of generations and age groups, tendentious languages, languages of the authorities, of various circles and of passing fashions," and more.[17] As these varieties enter into conflict and dialogue with one another, they force the "standard language" constantly to renegotiate its centrality and authority. The single word itself is heteroglossic (or "double-voiced," or "internally dialogized") because in it all of these social varieties of speech intersect and take form. The result is a "Tower-of-Babel mixing of languages" that interposes itself between the speaker and the object to be expressed.[18] Bakhtin insists, as do current exponents of speech-act theory and sociolinguistics, that the context of a word contributes indispensably to its meaning. One person's word may resist or foil appropriation by another, or one may subvert an original word by borrowing it (as Twain did in his birthday-dinner parody). For Bakhtin, the major task of prose stylistics is to disentangle the skein of ideologies, beliefs, sources, and contexts (both literary and social) that runs through every word of novelistic discourse.

Mark Twain's unfinished novel *Which Was It?* provides a dramatic example of the mutual interaction of the two heteroglossias. George Harrison, a respectable white citizen, has committed murder in the course of a burglary. The only witness to the crime is Jasper, a free black who uses his knowledge to blackmail Harrison, forcing the white man to play the slave when no one else is present. Jasper parodies the language his white "superiors" use to compliment what they interpret as

Harrison's generous act of taking Jasper on as a personal servant, thus protecting him from banishment or seizure:

> People flocked to Harrison's house all day; partly to recognize his pluck and praise it, and partly out of curiosity to see Jasper, gardener, perform as a house servant. . . . Everybody was surprised and a little disappointed to find that Jasper did not seem very much out of place in his new office, and many were candid enough to say so, and fling him a compliment as well. . . . [One of these was Harrison's son Tom.] Tom said, heartily—
>
> "You are performing really well, Jasper, and I mean what I say. All you've got to do is to behave yourself, and show yourself worthy of what my father has done for you, and you'll have in him a protector that is not afraid to stand by you against the whole town."
>
> Jasper was so moved, and so grateful for these gracious words that Tom was quite touched, and gave him a dime, which he gave to Harrison that night, at the same time mimicking the son's manner and paraphrasing his speech:
>
> "You's p'fawmin' real good, Hahson, en I means what I says. All you got to do is to behave, en show yo'seff wuthy of what I's went en done for you, en I's gwyneter be a p'tector dat'll—yah-yah-yah! I couldn't scasely keep fum laughin to heah dat goslin' talk 'bout you p'tectin' *me!*"
>
> (*WWD*, 428)

The two dialogic conflicts in this passage correspond to the twin varieties of heteroglossia. First, Tom's standard language contrasts with the dialect into which Jasper transposes it. By itself, the language in which Tom's speech is cast might appear "neutral," but Jasper's paraphrase retroactively changes the significance of the original speech: the grammar and pronunciation of Black English, nonstandard and socially stigmatized, remind us that Tom is using the conventional grammar and rhetoric of the empowered class. His "really well" places him just as surely as Jasper's "real good" does Jasper. (George Eliot's Fred Vincy provides a livelier version of the same judgment: "All choice of words is slang. It marks a class. . . . Correct English is the slang of prigs who write history and essays.")[19] Standard English implicitly claims to be inclusive, but as Tom uses it here it is exclusive, drawing boundaries between master and servant. Second, Jasper's irony underlines the ideology in Tom's vocabulary. The word *perform* is a key to the whole passage. As applied to Jasper it means "carry out a task." When Jasper mocks Harrison with "you's p'fawmin' real good," we are forced to interpret the meaning as not only "act a (deceptive) part" but also "follow the master's orders," for Harrison has been doing both. If we now return to the first two instances of *perform*, we perceive that these meanings must always be part of the internal dialogue of the word when it is applied to a slave. That is, the slave is "functioning" (performing as a machine) from the master's point of view, but role-playing (performing as an actor) from the slave's. Similarly heteroglossic are Tom's words "behave," "worthy," and "protector." Tom means his speech to be congruent in register with "Well done, true and faithful servant"; Jasper hears it as tantamount to "Good dog." Analyzing the effect of Jasper's paraphrase helps us to see that even the narrator's language is double-voiced, exhibiting what Bakhtin calls "stylistic hybrid." The third paragraph of the passage consists of two parts, the first "belonging" to Tom and the second to Jasper. The reader knows Jasper is not genuinely "moved" or "grateful" for Tom's words, and "gracious" and "touched" cohere with the sentimentality of Tom's speech. Although syntax marks the first part as objective narrative discourse, semantic content forces us to read it as a form of free indirect discourse emanating from Tom. Likewise, if we return to the phrase "fling him a compliment" and filter it through Jasper's perception ("Good boy!"), the trace of "fling him a bone" is unmistakable. Even so apparently neutral a word as "gave" takes part in this dialogue: "Tom was quite touched, and gave [Jasper] a dime, which he gave to Harrison that night." In Tom's semantic world *give* connotes charity; in Jasper's, condescension or scorn. All of the dialogue that goes on around Jasper demonstrates that any language passing between the free and the enslaved is open to contention because it can be "possessed" by only one of the two parties. (In chapter 6 I will argue that an identical principle governs varieties of language in *Pudd'nhead Wilson*.)

At times heteroglossia nearly pushes upward from the substructure of Twain's fiction to become an overt theme. Twain, no more able than Bakhtin to imagine a state of language that precedes or transcends dialogue, relentlessly satirizes the quest for monologic speech that admits no one else's claims. To be sure, Bakhtin concedes that poetry can treat its relation to an object as unmediated, for in this discourse the speaker's consciousness is entirely immanent in speech that is "his language."[20] But this conception of poetry is ultimately an enabling fiction, for objects are always encountered already named: "Only the mythical Adam, who approached a virginal and as yet verbally unqualified world with the first word, could really have escaped from start to finish [the] dialogic inter-orientation with the alien word that occurs in the object."[21] Representing Adam as human, however, means endowing him with real human speech. Twain, who was all but obsessed with the character of his "poor dead relative," consistently embodies him in fiction as a man with all the foibles of his race, including verbal ones.[22] The opening of "Extracts from Adam's Diary" (1893) is a comic rendering of Humboldt's paradox: "Man is only man through language; to invent language, he would have to be man already."[23] The underlying thesis of the sketch is that left to his own devices Adam would never have invented language, never have broken the silence of a solipsist's paradise. Naming begins in dialogue, with the advent of Eve, much to her husband's displeasure.

Far from being either private or a monologue, "Adam's Diary" is a dialogue on two levels. The interlocutor physically present is Eve, whose arrival provokes Adam to record his thoughts. The latent interlocutor is Ralph Waldo Emerson, the major American expositor of the Adamic language that Twain is mocking. Emerson claimed that language had originally been poetry and that any poet who re-creates language is another Adam. The poet is "the Namer or Language-maker," who "nam[es] things sometimes after their appearance, sometimes after their essence," who gives each thing "its own name and not another's."[24] To name is to see the "soul of the thing," to hear the "pre-cantation," of the sea, the mountain ridge, Niagara. In "Adam's Diary" the running joke (a poor one, to be sure) is that Eden was located just north of Buffalo.

Eve has named it Niagara and its waterfalls Niagara Falls, as Adam complains: "Says it *looks* like Niagara Falls. That is not a reason, it is mere waywardness and imbecility" (*WMT* 24: 342). Poor Adam gets no chance to name anything, for Eve always jumps in ahead, and "always that same pretext is offered—it *looks* like the thing." We have leapt into a hermeneutic circle where essences bite the tails of appearances and are bitten in turn, where neither can precede the other. Trying to disentangle the logic of the paradox reminds us, as Twain's joke does less rigorously, that we cannot begin to imagine what it would be like to create names in a world devoid of them.

Names, words, come from other people. Adam, who would remain in blissful aphasia if he could, finds that to have an Other is to have another's word. "I wish it would not talk; it is always talking. . . . I have never heard the human voice before, and any new and strange sound intruding itself here upon the solemn hush of these dreaming solitudes offends my ear and seems a false note" (*WMT* 24: 343). Adam has evidently been reading *Nature*. (In the woods, says Emerson, after one has become a transparent eyeball, "the name of the nearest friend sounds then foreign and accidental. To be brothers, to be acquaintances . . . is then a trifle and a disturbance.")[25] Try as he will to keep away from the bothersome "new creature," Adam cannot help assimilating her voice: "Cloudy to-day, wind in the east; think we shall have rain. . . . [ellipsis dots in original] *We?* Where did I get that word?—I remember now—the new creature uses it. . . . 'We' again— that is *its* word; mine, too, now, from hearing it so much" (*WMT* 24: 342–44). "We" is a word that cannot exist in an imagined primal Adamic language; "we" is always an "alien word," a word that comes from without. It inevitably brings limitations with it, as Adam laments:

And already there is a sign up:

> KEEP OFF
> THE GRASS

My life is not as happy as it was.
                    (*WMT* 24: 343)

In Twain's earliest published fable of Adam, the voice of God is entirely absent. Instead, the first prohibition derives from a human agency. Eve "litter[s] the whole estate with execrable names and offensive signs"; Adam dares not ask their meaning because "she has such a rage for explaining" (*WMT* 24: 344). The semiotic puns that we cannot help hearing are entirely in accord with Twain's conscious intention: he means to show that acts of naming and assigning significance are resented as restrictive and even hostile by a being who has previously enjoyed the luxury of speechless communion with himself. In Adam's brief conclusion to the diary, a serious, sentimental paragraph headed "Ten Years Later," he admits that the fall into companionship and the Other's word was a fortunate one: "After all these years, I see that I was mistaken about Eve in the beginning; it is better to live outside the Garden with her than inside it without her. At first I thought she talked too much; but now I should be sorry to have that voice fall silent and pass out of my life" (*WMT* 24:356). "Adam's Diary" is a fairy tale whose happy ending is entirely dialogic: the conflict of two competing "words" is resolved by love, understood as a pair's mutual assimilation of each other's voices, a joint invention of the pronoun "we." ("He seemed pleased to have me around," Eve says in the sequel "Eve's Diary," "and I used the sociable 'we' a good deal, because it seemed to flatter him to be included" [*WMT* 24:364].) Eve, initially misunderstood by her helpmate, is finally incorporated as an inner word.[26]

Happy endings, though, rarely have the last word in Mark Twain's work. Variety in language would always remain for him both promise and problem. Against "Adam's Diary" we will have to set the pessimism of another Adam tale, "That Day in Eden," in which the Fall results directly from misunderstanding. In the following chapters I shall trace an often contradictory movement from one characterization of language to another as it develops in Mark Twain's works. Chapter 2 examines Twain's relation to one of the most powerful centripetal, unifying, forces of the language, the authority of standard grammar and usage, which Twain never consciously defied. Linguistically suspect as arbitrary prescriptive rules may seem in the age of Chomsky, the traditional grammarians served Twain the satirist well by showing him that language and social values are interconnected. Chapter 3 examines Twain's embodiment in *The Gilded Age* of a premise that descended to him from Emerson through the essayist Richard Grant White: corrupt language means a corrupt society. The remainder of the book focuses on Twain's encounter with variety: the shock of foreign languages, the heteroglossic mix of dialects and idiolects along the Mississippi seen in *Huckleberry Finn*, the role of language as a divisive tool of power in the racially divided society of *Pudd'nhead Wilson*. The final chapter documents Mark Twain's journey toward representing dialogue as mutual incomprehension, even as he paradoxically grew nostalgic for a transcendent metalanguage that might resist the centrifugal force of violent cacophony.

2

"A Lot of Rules":
Mark Twain and Grammar

Simple rules:
You must not use these forms: I done it, he done it you done it they done it
Don't you know. There is no such phrase; it is dontchuknow.
And so on—a lot of rules.
Don't say it *hain't* so, but it *ain't* so. The former is vulgar.
—Mark Twain, unpublished
notebook entry (†)

"Don't you reckon that the people that made the books knows what's the correct thing to do? Do you reckon *you* can learn 'em anything?"
—Tom Sawyer, in *Huckleberry Finn*

To the layman in nineteenth-century America, and even to most men or women of letters, the study of language meant grammar, and grammar meant rules. These rules were to be found in books written by—to use a favorite phrase of Tom Sawyer's—the "best authorities": Robert Lowth, Hugh Blair, Noah Webster, Lindley Murray, authors of the standard rhetorics, grammar texts, and dictionaries.[1] These men stand in relation to modern linguists as Hammurabi and Solon to modern political scientists; they were arbiters and lawgivers rather than researchers who followed an empirical method. Linguistics as we know it began with the German comparative philologists who established the taxonomy of the Indo-European languages in the first half of the century, but their work was little known in the United States before the Civil War. In the 1860s, almost simultaneously, Max Müller in London and

15

William Dwight Whitney in Boston would deliver two celebrated sets of lectures to introduce modern linguistic science to the English-speaking world. But these writers on language were unfamiliar to the American public, who instead read essays by amateur critics of verbal usage like Richard Grant White and George Washington Moon, legislators in the mold of the eighteenth-century grammarians and rhetoricians, whose books had been issued in dozens of editions by the turn of the century. Although Mark Twain owned books by White and Moon, there is no evidence that he ever read Whitney or Müller.[2]

The adult Mark Twain would rebel against the God, the political system, and even—as an ardent spelling reformer—the orthography he had been taught as a child to respect, but his iconoclasm never extended to the authority of the grammarians. He never abandoned or even seriously questioned the doctrines of the prescriptive grammarians whose texts he studied as a schoolboy. Although he poked fun at Tom Sawyer's devout submission to the "authorities" and their arbitrary rules, he did not realize that in accepting a conventional definition of good English he himself submitted to self-constituted authorities whose qualifications were perhaps not demonstrably superior to his own.

Twain's allegiance to prescriptive grammar should not surprise us. The late twentieth century is heir to H. L. Mencken's celebration of the American vulgate, Robert A. Hall's provocative admonition *Leave Your Language Alone!*, and the forceful advocacy of Black English and other nonstandard dialects, yet linguistic relativism has gained little adherence outside the academic world.[3] Twain's attitude was no different from that of literary acquaintances like William Dean Howells, Charles Dudley Warner, Bret Harte, and Ambrose Bierce.[4] I stress Twain's essential conventionality to balance an inaccurate view of him as a folk hero who championed, as Walt Whitman did, the customs and usages of socially marginal classes. Twain's relation to the colloquial or vernacular language was ambivalent throughout his life—even during the composition of *Huckleberry Finn*, the novel in which rules come under the heaviest attack. When a writer walks through life with George

Washington Harris's defiantly vernacular *Sut Lovingood's Yarns* in one hand and Samuel Kirkham's *English Grammar* in the other, it is of some interest to see just how he maintains his balance. Richard Bridgman has proposed that the United States as a whole moved from the formal pole to the informal in the course of the century, causing a redefinition of "standard" English: "For the aristocratic temperament, standard is prescriptive. . . . The democratic inclination, however, is to make the standard descriptive: . . . its features are understood to be the mass norm. . . . If the vernacular is not regarded as inevitably vulgar, but merely as ordinary, then it is clear that as the century wore on, ordinary language became increasingly identified with an ever-broadening middle class."[5] As a rough generalization this picture is accurate. But it leaves out anomalous trends and individual cases. One of the strongest backlashes from the purists, in England as well as in the United States, took place in the 1860s and 1870s. Among our nineteenth-century writers not Mark Twain but Walt Whitman, writing in the mid-1850s, comes closest to espousing a truly demotic standard; Henry James, speaking at Bryn Mawr in 1905, most proudly wears the aristocracy's coat of arms. Whitman carries a folio copy of *Sut*:

> The forms of grammar are never persistently obeyed, and cannot be.
> The Real Dictionary will give all words that exist in use, the bad words as well as any.—The Real Grammar will be that which declares itself a nucleus of the spirit of the laws, with liberty to all to carry out the spirit of the laws, even by violating them, if necessary.—The English Language is grandly lawless like the race who use it.[6]

James trundles a grammar book weighing a ton:

> I cannot but regard the unsettled character and the inferior quality of the colloquial *vox Americana* . . . as in part a product of that mere state of indifference to a speech-standard and to a tone-standard on which I have been insisting. . . . To the American common school, to the American newspaper, and to the American Dutchman and Dago, as the voice of the people describes them, we have simply handed over our [linguistic] property.[7]

It is possible to find isolated passages in Twain's writing that approach one or the other of these extremes. But Twain's habitual amusement at the awkward constructions of foreigners, the ignorant, and the young in no way resembles James's reactionary xenophobia. And when he plays outlaw—by going west, by wearing a sealskin coat, by speaking with the voice of Huck—he is not assaulting the standard codes, merely exploring alternatives ones.

In the 1840s, the period of Samuel Clemens's boyhood, American common school education sought to provide students with a uniform set of social and moral values. Grammar, as the very term *grammar school* indicates, was at the heart of this process. The "students' right to their own language" endorsed in the 1970s by the National Council of Teachers of English would have made no more sense to Mark Twain's schoolmasters than students' right to their own multiplication tables. The various spoken dialects that nineteenth-century schoolchildren brought into the classroom were thought to be literally lawless, ungoverned by any regularities, and they would have to be replaced with rule-governed "good English" before children could be expected to assimilate other formal systems of knowledge. "Over any fugitive colloquial dialect, which has never been fixed by visible signs, grammar has no control," wrote the most pedantic of the mid-century grammarians, "and in proportion as books are multiplied, and the knowledge of written language is diffused, local dialects, which are beneath the dignity of grammar, will always be found to grow fewer."[8] Throughout the nineteenth century, grammarians argued violently over the details of individual rules, but they never disagreed that correct English could be embodied in rules of syntax and morphology that in every case would allow one to judge whether a given usage was right or wrong. When Twain, in one of the Mysterious Stranger drafts, has a schoolmaster tell the new boy in class that to learn English he must memorize a "grammar [that] has about thirty rules," he is almost surely remembering one specific textbook, Samuel Kirkham's *English Grammar*, which he studied as a boy.[9]

The most striking feature of Kirkham's *Grammar* is an imposing summary of the parts of speech and rules of syntax, printed as a folio sheet, folded, and bound into the volume opposite the title page. Along the top it reads, "A Compendium of English Grammar, by Samuel Kirkham; Designed, not to be studied, but to be spread before the learner in parsing, previous to his having the definitions and rules committed to memory."[10] The body of the sheet is divided into two sections. Section 1, "Etymology," briefly defines the parts of speech and explains the cases and persons of nouns and the moods and tenses of verbs. Section 2, "Rules of Syntax," summarizes thirty-five rules that Kirkham explains at length in the text. These rules, most of them borrowed from Lindley Murray, clearly derive from the Latin-based grammars of the eighteenth century. They are concerned with matters like agreement between adjectives and nouns, and subjects and verbs; the cases of relative pronouns; cases governed by verbs and prepositions; and the functions of adjectives and adverbs. And they are guaranteed to convince a child that grammar has nothing whatever to do with everyday speech. Witness rule 16: "When a nominative comes between the relative and the verb, the relative is governed by the following verb, or by some other word in its own member of the sentence." It is probably this list of rules that Twain would remember in his 1898 "Comment on Tautology and Grammar": "I know grammar by ear only, not by note, not by the rules. A generation ago I knew the rules—knew them by heart, word for word, though not their meanings—and I still know one of them: the one which says—which says—but never mind, it will come back to me presently" (*MTA* 1:173). Kirkham claimed that his innovative *"systematic order of parsing"* would aid students to apply the rules precisely so as to understand their meaning;[11] unfortunately, Twain's teachers seem to have been indifferent to Kirkham's pedagogical idealism. Two recollections of early grammar classes indicate that in fact memory was valued more highly than comprehension in the school run by J. D. Dawson, Twain's Hannibal master. In Twain's own dramatization of *Tom Sawyer*, the lessons described briefly in chapter 20 of the novel are worked up into a full-scale farce. Ben Rogers, the "best grammar scholar in the school," makes a farrago of grammatical terminology when asked to parse the sentence "How many persons constitute a multitude?"

> R[OGERS]: How is a preposition, common preposition, third person, feminine gender, indicative mood, present tense, and refers to many. MANY is an auxiliary verb—
>
> D[OBBINS]: (*interrupting*) It isn't a verb at all, it's an adjective.
>
> R: Many is an adjective, possessive case, comparative degree, second person, singular number, and agrees with its object in number and person.[12]

An instance of Twain's lifelong delight in burlesquing technical jargon by scrambling it into meaningless combinations, this passage surely exaggerates classroom grammatical error in degree but not in kind. In "Schoolhouse Hill" Twain recalls a "grammar class of parsing parrots, who knew everything about grammar except how to utilize its rules in common speech" (*MSM*, 177); no wonder, since their instruction consists principally in constant repetition of the rules.[13]

Twain never faulted the rules of grammar themselves, only the instruction that made them impenetrable. Even when we discount its humorous exaggeration, the following encomium of "an excellent school" in Carson City indicates the mastery of language Twain expected of well-taught schoolchildren:

> There is a class in Mr. Lawlor's school composed of children three months old and upwards, who know the spelling-book by heart. . . . You may propound an abstruse grammatical enigma, and the school will solve it in chorus—will tell you what language is correct, and what isn't; and why and wherefore; and quote rules and illustrations until you wish you hadn't said anything. . . . There are youngsters in this school who know everything about grammar that can be learned, and what is just as important, can explain what they know so that other people can understand it.[14]

The science of grammar, then, studies "what language is correct, and what isn't"; in linguistically dividing sheep from goats, it relies on "the people that made the books."[15] Deference to these authorities was not merely for children, however. During his early career as a California journalist, Twain ridiculed the idea that adults could consciously defy the grammar books. When he accuses his own *Californian* of being too severe in criticizing the verbal shortcomings of other San Francisco newspapers, he is merely being ironic: "If the local of the *Call* gets to branching out into new and aggravating combinations of words and phrases, they [the *Californian*] don't stop to think that maybe he is humbly trying to start something fresh in English composition and thus make his productions more curious and entertaining—not they; they just bite into him at once, and say he isn't writing grammar. And why? . . . Why, merely because he don't choose to be the slave of their notions and Murray's."[16] The joke is to call adherence to the formal rules "notions." Murray does not have notions about grammar any more than an assayer has notions about the purity of gold in a nugget. To joke in this way requires the belief that grammar is as exact a discipline as mathematics, the grammar books as trustworthy as trigonometric tables. The humorist Mark Twain is hardly more sympathetic to linguistic mutability than was the lexicographer Samuel Johnson, who linked it to "folly, vanity, and affectation" in the preface to his *Dictionary.*

At times nineteenth-century grammarians justify their authority in almost theological terms. "Natural grammar," according to Kirkham, was as insufficient to linguistic salvation as natural religion to Christian redemption. Knowledge of the formal rules was indispensable, Kirkham told his young readers: "Doubtless you have heard some persons assert, that they could detect and correct any error in language by the ear, and speak and write accurately without a knowledge of grammar. Now your own observation will soon convince you, that this assertion is incorrect. . . . Without the knowledge and application of grammar rules, it is impossible for any one to think, speak, read, or write with accuracy."[17] At least Kirkham puts grammatical perfection on a democratic basis: the language of the text, not that of the court, is standard, and the schoolmaster's chance of mastering it is as good as the lord's—even better: impeccable speech preeminently concerned the Victorian middle classes, since it functioned as a belaying rope for the social climber. The crevasses of good society were filled with aspirants who had slipped on an "ain't" or a proscribed regionalism. (William Dean Howells's Silas Lapham would become the most notable American casualty.) Only the established gentry could afford to ignore the dominion of the schoolmaster or the linguistic self-help books intended for those who had been poor scholars in their youth.[18]

No, a man could no more wield the English language by ear than he could navigate the Mississippi by guesswork. Like Twain's "marvellous science of piloting," grammar required a prodigious memory and constant vigilance and correction at the hands of experts. Throughout his career Twain was wary of getting caught on snags. He was especially sensitive about the quality of his English when his work was first beginning to be read back East.[19] If Southern vernacular was Twain's "native idiom," he takes curious pains to distance himself from it when in *Life on the Mississippi* he describes his first trip to New Orleans in twenty years. It is safe to call the genteel Southern accent "music," but Twain's disapproval of grammatical and idiomatic "infelicities" suggests his conservative picture of Standard English in the early 1880s.

> There are some infelicities, such as "like" for "as," and the addition of an "at" where it isn't needed. I heard an educated gentleman say, "Like the flag-officer did." His officer or his butler would have said, "Like the flag-officer done." You hear gentlemen say, "Where have you been at?" And here is the aggravated form—heard a ragged street Arab say it to a comrade: "I was a-ask'n' Tom whah you was a-sett'n' at." The very elect carelessly say "will" when they mean "shall"; and many of them say "I didn't go to do it," meaning "I didn't mean to do it." . . . [Southerners] haven't any "doesn't" in their language; they say "don't" instead. The unpolished often use "went" for "gone." It is as bad as the Northern "hadn't ought."
>
> (*WMT* 12:360)

From the point of view of dialect geography and descriptive linguistics, this is a random assortment of casual judgments that are not uniquely true of Southern speech. Twain makes no allowance for context; apparently an "educated gentle-man" is supposed to speak by the book under any circum-stance. The substitution of "like" for the conjunction "as," for example, is anything but a Southern regionalism; as common in Twain's time as it is today in informal speech on both sides of the Atlantic, it was already one of the purists' favorite shib-boleths.[20] There is no hint that a first-person future with "will" may be the normal and proper American form; Twain un-hesitatingly labels it a "careless deviation" from the rules pre-scribed by the grammar texts, when in fact it was his own ordinary usage in speech and casual writing.[21] The super-fluous "at" and "go to" for "intend to," on the other hand, are valid regionalisms, as is "hadn't ought." "Don't" for "doesn't" in the South was not identical with the "infelicity" that was and still is found in general nonstandard American English. Here, as in England, the upper classes received a dispensa-tion to use the form in defiance of the grammar books. (Brit-ish gentlemen were allowed to use "ain't" and to drop their participial *g*'s as well.) Mencken, citing Twain's own frequent use of "don't" with a singular subject, notes that this usage "rises almost to the level of cultivated speech" in the South.[22]

Twain must have been relieved when in 1876 he learned from reading Henry Breen that "the grossest solecisms and the most palpable blunders" were "of frequent occurrence" in the English of the most respected British writers and that even the grammarians themselves were not sinless. (Rhetori-cian Hugh Blair had sinned against *every rule* of grammar, ac-cording to Breen.)[23] Breen's cheerful iconoclasm made his *Modern English Literature* one of Twain's favorite books.[24] Over the next quarter century variations on the maxim "Nobody speaks perfect grammar" occur over and over in his writing:

> Harris said that if the best writer in the world once got the slov-enly habit of doubling up his "haves" he could never get rid of it while he lived. That is to say, if a man gets the habit of saying "I should have liked to have known more about it" instead of saying simply and sensibly, "I should have liked to know more about it," that man's disease is incurable. Harris said that this sort of lapse is to be found in . . . almost all of our books. He said he had observed it in Kirkham's grammar and in Macaulay.

> We all have our limitations in the matter of grammar, I suppose. I have never seen a book that had no grammatical defects in it.
>
> No one in the world speaks blemishless grammar; no one has ever written it—*no* one, either in the world or out of it (taking Scriptures for evidence on the latter point).
>
> That Briton or American was never yet born who could safely assault another man's English; . . . the man never lived whose English was flawless.
>
> My grammar is of a high order, though not at the top. Nobody's is. Perfect grammar—persistent, continuous, sustained—is the fourth dimension, so to speak; many have sought it, but none has found it.
>
> There is no such thing as perfect grammar and I don't always speak good grammar myself.
>
> No one can write perfect English and keep it up through a stretch of ten chapters. It has never been done. It was approached in the "well of English undefiled;" . . . it has been approached in several English grammars, I have even approached it myself; but none of us has made port.[25]

The tone of these pronouncements ranges from straightforward to ironic, but Twain is perfectly serious about his central point. We all suffer from grammatical original sin, and if we are ashamed of our speech, it is a result of the Fall. The biblical echoes in Twain's remarks on grammar are not fortuitous. Like the Hebrew law, prescriptive grammar was so complex and troublesome that no one could hope to fulfill every commandment; by the law all are condemned. Yet perfection in grammar, as in deed, was treated as a moral imperative in early nineteenth-century education. Good grammar and good morals were thought to be inseparable.[26] At the beginning of an address "To the Young Learner" that prefaces his text, Kirkham takes pains to correct any "misguided youth" who think that "grammar is dry and irksome, and a matter of little consequence." No, grammar is "a study that tends to adorn and dignify human nature," a branch of learning capable of "elevating man to his proper rank in the scale of intellectual existence."[27] In the peroration to this preface, Kirkham warns his reader never to "be content to grovel in ignorance"; when he concludes with the injunction "Love God and serve him," he makes it hard for the young scholar to tell where the grammar leaves off and the prayer book begins.[28]

Mark Twain was perfectly capable of satirizing middle-class faith in the connection between grammar and morality. The vernacular of his good bad boys, Huck and Tom, serves as a running commentary on the moral inadequacies of the standard language with which social authority expresses itself. The obverse of Huck and Tom is the "child-missionary" Mamie Grant, whose gift of tongues enables her to speak like a tract: "I am but an humble instrument, yet I feel that I am like, very like, some of the infant prodigies in the Sunday School book. I know that I use as fine language as they do."[29] Mamie, like Sid Sawyer, is handled ironically because her "goodness" in fact renounces childhood's innocence for the linguistic self-consciousness of adulthood. Huck and other childlike vernacular heroes in Twain's writings walk naked of grammar and are unashamed.[30] But Twain expected men and women to put away childish things. In rejecting his own youthful adherence to Southern folkways and ideologies, he becomes critical of parochial idioms as well. Soon after his 1882 visit to Hannibal he recorded in his notebook a telling memorandum, "The atrocious grammar of Hannibal & the West" (*NJ*2, 480). This hint was expanded into two paragraphs that evaluate the vernacular of the gentleman who narrates the Darnell-Watson feud in *Life on the Mississippi:*

> [This] country gentleman . . . was a man of good parts, and was college-bred. His loose grammar was the fruit of careless habit, not ignorance. This habit among educated men in the West is not universal, but it is prevalent. . . . I heard a Westerner, who would be accounted a highly educated man in any country, say, "Never mind, it *don't make no difference,* anyway." . . .
>
> No one in the world speaks blemishless grammar . . . therefore it would not be fair to exact grammatical perfection from the peoples of the Valley; but they and all other peoples may justly be required to refrain from *knowingly* and *purposely* debauching their grammar.
>
> (*WMT* 12:222–23)

There is only the faintest patina of humor here. Twain is delivering a serious lecture on social propriety: it is the duty of an educated gentleman to speak the language appropriate to his class. In this instance the demarcation between abstract morality and the social code becomes hard to trace. The "highly educated man" offends not so much against the abstract structures of grammar, Kirkham's thirty-five rules, as against the unspoken rules that establish the social connotations of words, constructions, and pronunciations. In one sense prescriptive grammars are simply linguistic etiquette manuals. That is why it is difficult to classify the brief sketch used as an epigraph to this chapter. Does it parody Kirkham, or is it an addition to the burlesque etiquettes that Twain composed? "Don't say it *hain't* so, but it *ain't* so. The former is vulgar." Written in 1896, during a period when he was intensely questioning the relation of power to authority, this fragment shows Twain coming as close as he ever will to the realization that rules of usage may be arbitrary.

"Our linguistic opinions," wrote Brander Matthews, a professor of English at Columbia University and a friend of Mark Twain's, "are the results of habits acquired from those who brought us up, so that aspersions on our parts of speech appear to us to be reflections on our parents. To misuse words, to make grammatical blunders is an evidence of illiteracy; and to accuse a man of illiteracy is to disparage the social standing of his father and mother." [31] To propose, as Van Wyck Brooks did, that Twain's native idiom was Huck's is to make John Clemens out to be Pap Finn. This is both historically and symbolically wrong. The Clemenses classed themselves among Hannibal's "aristocracy," partly because of John Clemens's professional background, partly because of Jane Lampton Clemens's distant relation to the Lambtons, Earls of Durham. Always a "claimant" to whatever role appeared most exalted at the time, Twain must have taken naturally to the language of culture and breeding. Undoubtedly, correct English was spoken and actively encouraged in the Clemens family. Jane Clemens did not employ the local Missouri vernacular; when her son made her the basis of Tom Sawyer's Aunt Polly, he "fitted her out with a dialect" for the purpose (*MTA* 1:102). In 1845 John Clemens attended a series of lectures on grammar given by one Professor Hull and made a précis of "Rules for Parsing by Transposition," which he gave to Orion, then an apprentice printer.[32] The earliest piece of writing we have by Twain, composed two months past his fifteenth birthday, is prophetic of later work in its concern for language. Following the practice of contemporary Southwestern humorists, Twain puts his own first-person narrative in "fine language": "At the fire, on Thursday morning, we were apprehensive of our own safety . . . and commenced arranging our material in order to remove them in case of necessity." The humor comes from Jim Wolfe, the vernacular hero, who rescues a few valueless items, returns in an hour, "and thinking he had immortalized himself, threw his giant frame in a tragic attitude, and exclaimed, with an eloquent expression: 'If that thar fire hadn't bin put out, thar'd a' bin the greatest *confirmation* of the age!'"[33] Twain would often have met such utterly conventional dialect and malapropism in publications like the *Spirit of the Times* and the *Carpet-Bag*.[34] The only unusual feature of the sketch is that it is a fifteen-year-old author who so easily assumes the role of "gentleman" narrator and leaves implicit his own sophisticated awareness of the difference between *confirmation* and *conflagration*. (The humor of malapropism is by nature elitist, consolidating narrator and reader into a linguistic community whose verbal knowledge is necessarily superior to that of the error-prone object of the joke.)

The most memorable distinction between himself and the ungrammatical that Twain draws anywhere occurs in *Life on the Mississippi*, in the episode of his fight with the pilot Brown. In a previous episode Twain has associated linguistic ability with social rank. The mate on the *Paul Jones* swore and issued commands with bravura; the "humblest official," the night watchman, had bad grammar, worse construction, and profanity void of art (*WMT* 12:41–42). Visiting pilots, who wore silk hats and diamond breastpins, "were choice in their English, and bore themselves with a dignity proper to men of solid means and prodigious reputation as pilots" (*WMT* 12: 55). But the coarse vernacular of Brown, the hated "horse-faced, ignorant . . . tyrant," symbolizes his lack of moral and social authority over the cub pilot Twain. If the speech following young Twain's protestation that he has had no orders is based on biographical fact, Brown must have been one of the inspirations for Pap Finn's aggressive ignorance.[35] Brown mocks the cub pilot: "You've had no *orders!* My, what a fine bird we are! We must have *orders!* Our father was a *gentle-man*—owned slaves—and *we've* been to *school*. . . . Dod dern my skin, *I'll* learn you to swell yourself up and blow around *here* about your dod-derned *orders!*" (*WMT* 12:166).

A short time later Twain describes how he physically sub-dues Brown after the pilot has unjustly struck Twain's younger brother. The fight is unremarkable, but it is followed by a peculiar logomachy. Brown, having struggled to his feet, has picked up a spyglass and ordered Twain out of the pilot-house. "But I was not afraid of him now; so, instead of going, I tarried, and criticized his grammar. I reformed his ferocious speeches for him, and put them into good English, calling his attention to the advantage of pure English over the bastard dialect of the Pennsylvania collieries whence he was extracted. He could have done his part to admiration in a cross-fire of mere vituperation, of course; but he was not equipped for this species of controversy" (*WMT* 12:173).[36] Brown retires, muttering, to the wheel, apparently more daunted by the cub's words than by his blows. Twain, in fact or in fancy, has appropriated the ancient Greek and Irish satirists' weapon of deadly invective. (A fragment of Archilochus reads, "One great thing I know, how to recompense with evil reproaches him that doeth me evil.")[37] He asserts the dominating power of language, that power through which *grammar* turned into *glamour* and *gramarye*, archaic synonyms for enchantment or necromacy. But Twain draws his magical strength not from a volume of Hermes Trismegistus but from Kirkham's *Grammar*. The power he asserts is entirely secular and social. What he does, as Matthews insisted, disparages the social standing of Brown's father and mother, of the whole working-class Pennsylvania coal district of his birth.

The Brown episode does not appear in the original 1875 *Atlantic Monthly* series "Old Times on the Mississippi." In *Life on the Mississippi,* together with the narrative of Henry's death, it forms a transition to the new material that begins with chapter 22. Its structural position is therefore significant: it bridges the gap between Twain as cub pilot and Twain as writer, a gap summarized in four paragraphs of chapter 21 that describe how Twain became a "scribbler of books, and an immovable fixture among the other rocks of New England." Twain wants to call the attention of his Eastern readership, too, to his "good English," his "pure English," the guarantee of his social acceptability and of his right to join the literary "rocks" of the Eastern Establishment. If Howells did not pronounce "Tu es Petrus" loudly enough to suit him, Twain was perfectly capable of consecrating himself.

In Hawaii, in 1866, Anson Burlingame gave Twain some advice that long afterwards he would claim to have lived by for forty years: "Avoid inferiors. Seek your comradeships among your superiors in intellect and character; always *climb*" (*MTA* 2 : 125). Years later, he probably read in Thomas Lounsbury's *Standard of Usage in English* advice that confirmed his own course of action since leaving the river. Although grammar books may be helpful in learning good usage, "in no case can they ever be appealed to as final authorities. There is one way and but one way of attaining to the end desired as a theoretical accomplishment, and fortunately it is a course open to every one. Knowledge of good usage can be acquired only by associating in life with the best speakers or in literature with the best writers." [38] By creating him honorary *Litterarum Doctor* in 1907, Oxford University effectively proclaimed him one of those "best speakers and writers" who were supposed to promulgate the standard of usage for the rest. Despite his jokes about the literary "doctoring" he meant to do, he took the degree seriously. In an after-dinner speech at the Savage Club a few days after the Oxford ceremony, Twain objected to a newspaper interview that had put the adjective "bully" into his mouth. He *never* used slang, he claimed, to an interviewer or to anyone else; what he said was framed in good English. The typical humor that caps this portion of his remarks deflects but does not nullify the chivalric earnestness of his dedication to the language: "I have a great respect for the English language. I am one of its supporters, its promotors [sic], its elevators. I don't degrade it. . . . I have always tried hard and faithfully to improve my English, and never to degrade it. I always try to use the best English to describe what I think and what I feel or what I don't feel and what I don't think."[39] We know from his comments on Scott and Cooper, and above all from the beauty and suppleness of his own plain style, that he believed overrefinement and sentimentality were the most serious degraders of English. The "best English" he has in mind here, however, is not the vernacular poetry in which Huck describes a sunrise on the river but the pure and correct English of a Thomas Macaulay. He can enjoy breaking the rules because he is master of them; his "grammatical infelicities" proceed from neither ignorance nor careless habit but from calculated artistry. Twain's mediation between Whitman's lawlessness and James's obsessive obedience parallels the ordered license permitted by Alexander Pope's poetics:

> If, where the rules not far enough extend
> (Since rules were made to promote their end)
> Some lucky license answer to the full
> The intent proposed, that license is a rule.
> (*Essay on Criticism*, 1:146–49)

Like most of his contemporaries, Twain never realized that proscribed social and regional varieties of English are self-contained systems structured by their own rules. So he could never be satisfied to be known only as a great dialect writer, the creator of an Uncle Remus or a Sut Lovingood. He wanted to be judged by the exacting standards that Henry Breen and Richard Grant White had applied to serious writers and to be found pure in style and correct in grammar. He was delighted to read a biographical sketch that "contained praises of the very thing which I most loved to hear praised—*the good quality of my English*," buttressed by citations from "four English and American literary experts of high authority" ("Private History of a MS. That Came to Grief," *MTA* 1:175–76). Yet Twain's gradual recognition that he himself was a master of language led him from time to time after about 1880 to rebel against the restraints of prescriptive grammarians and arbiters of usage, to assume the function Pope assigned to Homer as the artist who creates the rules by following nature. Twain's essays and marginalia on English hint at an organic view of language, one that is tacitly at work in his best fiction. Twain almost manages to see school grammar as a humbug; had Kirkham's costume been slightly shabbier, Twain might have consigned him to the literary hell whither he had long since sent Sir Walter Scott.[40]

Almost manages, but not quite. Mark Twain's criticism of prescriptive grammar and grammarians is antipharisaic: he rebels not against the idea of a normative language but against those who presume to be its infallible legislators. Never is there a hint that as a writer he has come to abolish the law itself. When Twain burlesques the rules, as in the fragmentary "grammar" I have used as a headnote to this chapter, he merely inverts the norm: "Don't you know. There is no such phrase; it is dontchuknow. . . . Don't say it *hain't* so, but it *ain't* so. The former is vulgar."[41] (In his *Grammar* Kirkham explicitly proscribes both "ain't" and "hain't," along with contractions like "woodent" and "izzent" for "would not" and "is not".)[42] The humor here derives from the incongruity between the gentility of the generic form (etiquette manual) and the vulgarity of the content, exploiting without calling into serious question the dichotomy between genteel and vernacular. Contrast the more radically subversive humor of Gertrude Stein's mischievously titled *How to Write:* "A noun should never be introduced into a sentence. If it is it is because there is poverty poverty is at once and must be that they are anxious to kiss. A noun should never be introduced into a sentence. Also whenever should not be introduced into a sentence because without a leaf they imitate that without reason."[43] Stein's burlesque attacks the very categories of any grammar that offers rational guidance to language, whether prescriptive or descriptive. Rather than invert categories, she shatters them into unrecognizability. All we know for certain about the meaning of *noun* in Stein's context is that it is excluded from the domain of all possible meanings of *noun* in formal grammars. (In transformational grammar, the most basic definition of a sentence rewrites it as noun phrase plus verb phrase: S→NP+VP.) For her it is no disgrace that as Twain had said of the *Call* reporter, she "don't choose to be the slave of [Murray's *Grammar*]," instead "branching out into new and aggravating combinations of words and phrases . . . trying to start something fresh in English composition."[44] A writer's grammar is generated by his or her own individual work, or corpus: "It is impossible to avoid meaning and if there is meaning and it says what it does there is grammar. . . . Grammar is in our power."[45]

For Mark Twain, grammar, like grace, was out of our power. A perfect standard language is an abstract construct, not the reflection of anybody's actual usage; we are all born innocent of it and approach it as a curve approaches a mathematical limit that it can never reach. Our ultimate distance from perfection is determined by a combination of "training and temperament" (to use the vocabulary of *What Is Man?*). That we "all have our limitations in the matter of grammar" allows Twain in his 1880 *Atlantic Monthly* Contributors' Club column to minimize his inattention to adverb placement as the result of a constitutional defect. A "Boston Girl" had written him to complain about his putting "adverbs between the particle and verb in the Infinitive. For example: 'to *even* realize,' 'to *mysteriously* disappear,' 'to *wholly* do away.'" Twain responds: "I have certain instincts, and I wholly lack certain others. . . . I am dead to adverbs; they cannot excite me. To misplace an adverb is a thing which I am able to do with frozen indifference; it can never give me a pang. . . . There are subtleties which I cannot master at all,—they confuse me, they mean absolutely nothing to me,—and this adverb plague is one of them."[46] Even under the species of light irony, Twain's argument is a curious one. In essence the passage is an example of the mildly anti-intellectual humor that still flourishes in popular fiction and essay: the author or a character claims that the element of high-culture knowledge that he lacks is useless, pretentious, or effete and therefore unnecessary. But even as he slights the claims of formal English, Twain shoots back at his correspondent with a *tu quoque: I* at least can punctuate; *you* cannot. Nor does he deny, as he might have, that his adverbs and particles are misplaced.[47] Instead, the subtext of his column coincides with Pope's reason, in *An Essay on Criticism,* for advising the writer to

> Neglect the rules each verbal critic lays,
> For not to know some trifles, is a praise.
> (2:261–62)

This, in essence, was Twain's defense of Ulysses Grant against Matthew Arnold's strictures on his grammar. In 1887 Arnold set off a minor furor in the United States when he reviewed Grant's *Memoirs* (published by Twain's house); Americans overlooked Arnold's general commendation of Grant's "strong, resolute, and business-like" character and saw in Arnold's comments on the *Memoirs* only an apparent verdict of illiteracy: "I found a language all astray in its use of *will* and *shall, should* and *would,* an English employing the verb *to conscript* and the participle *conscripting,* and speaking in a despatch to the Secretary of War of having *badly whipped* the enemy; an English without charm and without high breeding."[48] James Barnet Fry at once issued a rebuttal from the authoritative pages of the *North American Review,* accusing Arnold of committing the very errors he had diagnosed in Grant's writing and patriotically championing Grant as the better writer of the two.[49] In the same month that Fry's article appeared, Twain, speaking at a military banquet held in honor of General Grant's birthday, seconded Fry's condemnation of Arnold. Twain plays Cicero to Arnold's Catiline in a masterfully rhetorical reworking of Fry, whose piece he had evidently just read. "What do we care for grammar," Twain asks in the peroration, "when we think of the man that put together that thunderous phrase: 'Unconditional and immediate surrender!'" (*MTS,* 227). Even in this speech, however, Twain does not attempt to refute Arnold's specific charges or deny the validity of the rules he invokes. Instead, he claims that grammar is a small virtue relative to the majesty of a man like Grant, so that the general's errors are no more than spots on the sun. Twain comes closest to a Whitman-like celebration of lawlessness in declaring that the style of the *Memoirs* is flawless and insisting that "great books are weighed and measured by their style and matter, not by the trimmings and shadings of their grammar" (*MTS*, 227). This assessment of Grant's writing would not deter Twain from using those "spots" to evaluate books in the future.[50]

Twain hated above all the critic who pretended to know more grammar than anyone else and who freely and clumsily corrected others' "errors." One of the autobiographical fragments, assigned to 1900 by Albert Bigelow Paine, is "Private History of a MS. That Came to Grief," a fifteen-page diatribe against a British editor who had presumed to edit for style and usage a piece on Joan of Arc he had solicited from Twain (*MTA* 1:175–89). Another fragment from 1898, "Comment on Tautology and Grammar," complains about a book reviewer whose "grammar is foolishly correct, offensively precise": "A person who is as self-righteous as that will do other things. . . . When a man works up his grammar to that altitude, it is a sign" (*MTA* 1:173–74). And the marginal comments Twain made in George Washington Moon's *Learned Men's English*, which he read in 1897, show that he had no patience with the internecine squabbles of self-appointed experts on usage, especially when conducted in a self-satisfied, smirky tone.[51]

Yet Twain could always take the very position he had just been denouncing. When he returned home in 1900 from nearly a decade of life abroad, the *vox Americana* jarred him just as it would Henry James five years later. Here is the opening of a talk he made at a New York Woman's Press Club tea soon afterwards:

> I was recently asked what I had found striking in this country since my return. I didn't like to say, but what I have really observed is that this is the ungrammatical nation. I am speaking of educated persons. There is no such thing as perfect gram-

mar and I don't always speak good grammar myself. But I have been foregathering for the past few days with professors of American universities and I've heard them all say things like this: "He don't like to do it." Oh, you'll hear that tonight if you listen, or "He would have liked to have done it."

(*MTS*, 346–47)

This is a protest against the *trahison des clercs*, the apparent unwillingness of "the people that made the books" to acknowledge the validity of their own rules. Raised on Kirkham's *Grammar* and the Presbyterian Bible, Twain retains to the end a Protestant conviction that the authority of the Book is to be taken on faith. The ghost of Kirkham's grammar walking always beside him prevented him from celebrating without reservation an ungoverned heteroglossia; even Huck Finn's language is meaningful only in relation to the rules it flouts.

Mark Twain would never believe that "grammar is in our power," and the extent to which he remained a prescriptivist measures how thoroughly he is after all a product of nineteenth-century middle-class American culture. But his deep respect for the authority of grammar, even when he kicks against it, leads him to an implicit formulation that in the end is sounder sociolinguistics than Stein's: grammar *is* power. This is true in the trivial sense that those who have mastered it can ridicule those who have not. More profoundly, however, Twain knew what in our day has best been taught by George Orwell: that authority over language translates directly into authority over other people and, conversely, that illiteracy means powerlessness—something equally clear to both Pap Finn and Hank Morgan, even though the practical consequences they adduce are different, Hank giving language to his foster son Clarence, Pap taking it away from Huck.

When the English radical William Cobbett dedicated his 1818 *Grammar of the English Language* to his fourteen-year-old son, the furthest thing from his mind was to suggest that the boy should free himself from the shackles of rules. Anybody can, "without rules or instructions, put masses of words upon paper," but to use language properly we must learn certain "principles and rules [that] constitute what is called Grammar." [52] But one learns these rules not for neutral or innocent purposes but to *"make use of words"* for political and social ends, chiefly to "assert with effect the rights and liberties of his country." [53] Because one corollary of this statement is that those already in power perpetrate the most dangerous abuse of language, Cobbett devotes an entire chapter to "Errors and Nonsense in a King's Speech." Faith in the authority of grammar ultimately allies itself with a reformist strain in nineteenth-century liberalism: purifying the language of the tribe ought to purify the tribe as well. In the 1870s Mark Twain still shares this optimism. Thus in his most carefully focused work of polemical fiction, *The Gilded Age* (written jointly with Charles Dudley Warner), social criticism and a critique of language are intimately allied.

3

The Gilded Age and the Corruption of Language

The nineteenth-century book on language that is most likely to have influenced Mark Twain's fiction directly is Richard Grant White's *Words and Their Uses*. Based on articles that had appeared in the *Galaxy* from 1867 through 1869, the book was published in 1870 and went through over thirty editions in as many years. The most prominent American verbal "shaman"—to use Dwight Bolinger's term—of the latter part of the nineteenth century, White retained his popularity well into the twentieth century, thanks no doubt to his unintimidating style and careful avoidance of anything resembling Germanic philology.[1] (In an essay on received notions about language, linguist Leonard Bloomfield recalled that his undergraduate instructors in the early 1900s "advised us to read Richard Grant White," while the immeasurably more important work of his contemporary William Dwight Whitney "was not mentioned.")[2] In White's own words, his book concerns itself "almost exclusively with the correctness and fitness of verbal expression, and any excursion into higher walks of philology is transient and incidental."[3] Like all prescriptivists, White contended that tradition and reason must temper the authority of common usage; in practice, this means a preference for the conservative rules of grammar and usage that had been handed down from rhetoric manual to rhetoric manual on both sides of the Atlantic for a hundred years. He offers a precedent for Twain's disapproval of both the adverbial *like* and the American confusion between *shall* and *will*, but Twain might have found similar proscriptions in any number of writers.[4] On the other hand, Twain would not have sided with White at his most reactionary, as when he spends an entire chapter in a futile rearguard action against the continuous passive "is being done" (pp. 334–63). But the linguistic arbitration that occupies most of *Words and Their Uses* is less relevant to the reader of Mark Twain than its chapters entitled "Newspaper English" and "Big Words for Small Thoughts," which vigorously attack the "corruptions . . . consequent upon pretentious ignorance and aggressive vulgarity" (p. 19). Mark Twain bought a copy of White's book in 1873; he and Warner composed *The Gilded Age* between February and April of that year. Thus it is probably more than coincidence that the excesses of language satirized in Twain's, and even Warner's, portions of the novel resemble those that White criticizes.[5]

Calling for a purified American diction, Emerson had written in *Nature* that "the corruption of man is followed by the corruption of language."[6] White goes a step further in his preface by claiming that the equation is commutative: "The influence of man upon language is reciprocated by the influence of language upon man; and the mental tone of a community may be vitiated by a yielding to the use of loose, coarse, low, and frivolous phraseology" (p. 5). If corrupt language is at once a symptom and a cause of social decadence, linguistic criticism is a form of social criticism. In a country with no Academy, no central authority over language, the only guardian against corruption is the independent, self-selected, elite judge of usage. Like the social ills of *The Gilded Age*, the diseases of language that White diagnoses are caused by abuses of democratic institutions and the distortion of laissez-faire into license. White's villains, like Twain's, are journalists, politicians, and advertisers, those who at once represent and create American mass culture.

White in his introduction implicitly equates social democracy with linguistic democracy, seeing both as dangerous. The fashionable philological doctrine that words are merely arbitrary signs of ideas is nothing new, White says, quoting Oliver Cromwell, who long since affirmed that words acquire their meaning "from the consent of those that use them, and arbitrarily annex certain ideas to them" (p. 13). But despite his apparent social-contract theory of semantics, Cromwell refused Parliament's request that he call himself king, because (says White), "*king* meant something that he was not," since "words have, like men, a history, and alliances, and rights of birth and inherent powers which endure as long as they live, and which they can transmit, although somewhat modified, to their rightful successors" (p. 14). Unlike eighteenth-century conservative language theorists (notably Samuel Johnson), White does not bemoan change in language; as societies change, so must languages. More important for White is who directs that change: "The changes of our day are mostly the result of the very superficial instruction of a large body of people, who read much and without discrimination, whose reading is chiefly confined to newspapers hastily written by men also very insufficiently educated. . . . The tendency of this intellectual condition of a great and active race is to the degradation of language. . . . Against this tendency it behooves all men who have means and opportunity to strive" (p. 18). Language must always be the product of the mass of language users, but "when that mass is misled by a little learning," license and corruption follow (p. 26). Hence the need for criticism, for a class of "trained and cultivated minds" to form the ranks of "those who are, if not the framers, at least the arbiters, of linguistic law" (p. 27). Granting that language cannot be controlled by an absolute monarch, White would have a republic whose elected representatives are the critics. One of his reviewers responded appreciatively to the political resonance of his verbal criticism: "In the introductory chapter . . . we are very glad to find Mr. White protesting against the heresy that *usage* is to be our supreme guide. This position has been stoutly maintained, and by persons who, moreover, understand *usage*, not as the practice of the *best* writers, but as popular custom, an average of Tom, Dick, and Harry, Tag, Rag, and Bobtail, Birdofredom Sawin, Hans Breitmann, and Miles O'Reilly."[7]

Mark Twain, too, was unsympathetic to a political system that allowed democracy to act as a leveler. In a political utopia he described in 1875, the "curious republic" of Gondour, the weight of one's vote is directly proportional to one's learning.

Gondour had "at first tried universal suffrage pure and simple, but had thrown that form aside because the result was not sat- isfactory. It had seemed to deliver all power into the hands of the ignorant and non-tax-paying classes." Under the new scheme, an individual was allowed extra votes according to his property and particularly according to the level of his edu- cation, and "the learned voters, possessing the balance of power, became the vigilant and efficient protectors of the great lower rank of society." [8] Twain here agrees with his later rival Matthew Arnold: to the educated falls the responsibility of political as well as cultural government in the best of repre- sentative systems.

White's antidemocratic bias is still more apparent in his chapter "Newspaper English," which blames corrupt lan- guage on the desire of the middle class for upward social mo- bility. In White's view, journalists, politicians, and advertisers gain social authority by pretending to knowledge. Whereas the lower classes are content with their humble ignorance and the gentry secure in their native attainments, the rising middle class is a brood of confidence men: "The curse and the peril of language in this day, and particularly in this country, is, that it is at the mercy of men who, instead of being content to use it well according to their honest ignorance, use it ill according to their affected knowledge; who, being vulgar, would seem ele- gant; who, being empty, would seem full; who make up in pretence what they lack in reality" (p. 28). [9] Against the ten- dency of "pretentious ignorance" and "aggressive vulgarity" to abolish "simple, clear, and manly speech," the educated must strive "almost as if it were a question of morals" (p. 18). White's major target is the popular press, which had already come under attack in both England and the United States for its partiality to "newspaper English," the euphemistic, Lat- inate prose style of "big words for small thoughts." Neither the fault nor the complaint is new, White admits; what *is* new in this chapter is his equation of the style with social insin- cerity of all sorts. [10] "Writing like this," White says, "is a fruit of a pitiful desire to seem elegant when one is not so . . .

which manifests itself in the use of words as well as in the wearing of clothes, the buying of furniture, and the giving of entertainments" (pp. 33–34).

Twain's sharpest attack on pretentious language occurs in *The Gilded Age*, in the brilliant parody of the conversation of Washington's "Aristocracy of the Parvenues." These *nouveaux arrivés* are confident that their wealth has purchased entry into fashionable society, but their awkward mimicry of fine language betrays their origins. The Honorable Mrs. Higgins, whose "English was fair enough, as a general thing," retains the New Yorker's pronunciation of "saw" and "law" as "sawr" and "lawr" (*WMT* 6:16). The O'Reillys stayed in Paris for two years "and learned to speak English with a foreign accent— not that it hadn't always had a foreign accent . . . but now the nature of it was changed" (*WMT* 6:20).[11] The parvenue aristocracy mistakenly believe that a few tricks of "genteel" pronunciation and vocabulary are enough to produce an elevated style of speech. But their speech is thinly gilded at best, and the tin underneath peeks through. White had complained about a policeman who, when asked about a neighboring building, replied, "That is an institootion inaugurated under the auspices of the Sisters of Mercy, for the reformation of them young females what has deviated from the paths of rectitood" (p. 30). This absurd mixture of elegant and vernacular styles characterizes the speech of Twain's parvenues, one sample of which should suffice to convey its flavor. (I have altered the original to highlight the clash of styles: markedly "genteel" expressions are in italics; nonstandard or regional usages are in boldface.) The speaker is Mrs. Higgins:

> *I should think so. Husband* says Percy'll die if he **don't** have a change; and so I'm going to **swap round** a little and see what can be done. I saw a lady from Florida last week, and she recommended Key West. I told her Percy couldn't *abide* winds, as he was *threatened with a pulmonary affection,* and then she said try St. Augustine. It's an **awful** distance—ten or twelve hundred **mile,** they say—but then in *a case of this kind* **a body cant stand back for trouble,** you know.
>
> (*WMT* 6:23)

Twain evidently shares White's feeling that whereas "simple unpretending ignorance" and genuine culture are respectable, the speech of "pretentious ignorance and aggressive vulgarity" (White, p. 19) merits only disdain. It is important to distinguish here between Mrs. Higgins's language and the superficially similar comic mingling of styles that characterizes the Mark Twain persona from the 1860s on. Mark Twain is in full *control* of his styles, and when in, say, a burlesque account of a San Francisco ball he lets the vocabulary of haute couture collide with mining slang, we recognize the effect as studied. So too with the author who has created Mrs. Higgins; but Mrs. Higgins herself is the victim of her own language, plainly incapable of the critical distance that would allow her to perceive its absurdity. Those who are pretentiously ignorant hypocritically disavow and attempt to hide a native tongue of low social origin; their superficial and purely instrumental interest in the genteel style shows that for them language is simply a material possession. Worst of all, they are not even skillful at their linguistic confidence game.

Laura, on the other hand, wins our (perhaps horrified) respect because she assimilates so successfully the manner of the society in which she desires to move. Her aims are no more honorable than those of the parvenues, but she pursues them with more skill. To prepare for her encounter with Washington society, she had entered upon a "tireless and elaborate course of reading. . . . The quality of her literary tastes had necessarily undergone constant improvement under this regimen, and . . . the quality of her language had improved, though it cannot be denied that now and then her former condition of life betrayed itself in just perceptible inelegancies of expression and lapses of grammar" (*WMT* 6:30).[12] When Laura flirts with Congressman Buckstone to win his vote, she shows herself a master of the badinage of Victorian romantic comedy. Laura reminds Buckstone of his promise to tell her about his trip to Egypt:

> "Why, do you remember that yet, Miss Hawkins? I thought ladies' memories were more fickle than that."

"Oh, they are not so fickle as gentlemen's promises. And besides, if I had been inclined to forget, I—did you not give me something by way of a remembrancer?"

(*WMT* 6:56)

The perspectives on Laura's language are complex. Buckstone takes her speech as serious evidence that he has charmed an accomplished coquette. Laura herself has no doubt that her speech is part of the strategy of a "desperate game" (*WMT* 6:58). For the reader this language is simultaneously part of Twain and Warner's parody of sentimental romantic fiction and a realistic mark of Laura's skill at altering her discourse to suit the occasion. But Laura and Mrs. Higgins represent opposite dangers: Laura grows to be *too* accomplished a rhetorician, too successful at aiming her language entirely toward her audience. Being wholly other-directed, she has no voice of her own. It is thus appropriate that after her murder of Selby has destroyed her career in Washington, she should seek her living as a lecturer. "She would array herself in fine attire, she would adorn herself with jewels, and stand in her isolated magnificence before massed audiences and enchant them with her eloquence" (*WMT* 6:295). (Note, again, the conjunction of language and material display.) She will exist only as reflected in the response of her hearers. But when her first and last lecture audience consists of a handful of coarse, jeering men and women, she loses her speech and therefore her self. Debating whether her ensuing death is suicide or "natural" is misguided: Laura is effectually dead from the moment her opportunity to speak is denied.

"Language," according to White, is "perverted in this country chiefly in consequence of the wide diffusion of very superficial instruction among a restless, money-getting, and self-confident people" (p. 39). For him the money-making spirit can lead to verbal simony, the mercenary use of sacred language, as when a real-estate agent in a newspaper ad urges prospective buyers to "come unto me" (echoing Matt. 11:28). A murderer works less *"diffusive"* evil than a man who publicly mingles sacred and profane styles, a man who is "the representative of a class of men which increases among us year by year—men whose chief traits are greed and vulgarity, who often get riches, and whose traits, when riches come, are still greed and vulgarity, with the addition of purse-pride and vanity" (p. 41). White's meditation on the etiology of corrupt language leads him to blame the "money-getting spirit," and the socioeconomic forces that create it, because his own insistence on standards that establish the real value of different forms of language presupposes the "monetary metaphor" of language that has underlain Western semiotic thought for over two millennia.[13] Words are tokens of exchange valuable only insofar as they stand for, or are guaranteed by, the ideas that lie behind them. "Newspaper English" is "inflated" language, verbal currency that does not possess the worth its circulators mistakenly ascribe to it. White notes that scholars have adduced as evidence of richness the thousand synonyms in Eastern languages for *sword* and the hundred for *horse*. "But this, unless the people who use these languages have a thousand kinds of swords and a hundred kinds of horses, is no proof of wealth in that which makes the real worth of language" (pp. 80–81). Language creates floating symbols that like paper money have no material value of their own. Language and economics meet in the word *speculation* if baseless ideation and worthless investment are seen as twin manifestations of a single phenomenon. And at this level *Words and Their Uses* and *The Gilded Age* meet most profoundly. For the fundamental theme of at least Twain's portions is deceitful elimination of the distance between appearance and reality, symbol and referent—a crime far more serious than the pretentious use of genteel idioms. To the social climbers who populate the novel, money and language are interchangeable means of speculation, of promising, of bribing. Both an issue of worthless stock and a hypocritical Sunday-school speech are symptoms of a society whose favorite activity is to get something for nothing.

The three basic images in Twain's part of *The Gilded Age*, and especially in the first eleven chapters, are inflation, facade, and creation *ex nihilo*. As embodied in characters like Squire Hawkins, Washington Hawkins, and Colonel Sellers, these images have both linguistic and economic significance. Language is necromantic; it "enchants," creating the illusion of value where none exists in reality. Inflated language in the novel characterizes a society that blindly rushes to expand, exploit, multiply, climb. To vary the metaphor, language is a stimulant that overexcites the metabolism of the body politic to the point of apoplexy.

"I *must* talk or I'll burst!": Squire Hawkins averts psychic explosion by venting himself in a jet of language that expands until it no longer conforms to reality. The whole tract of his Tennessee lands, he tells his wife, "would not sell for over a third of a cent an acre now, but some day people will be glad to get it for twenty dollars, fifty dollars, a hundred dollars an acre! What should you say to . . . *a thousand dollars an acre!*" (*WMT* 5:7). Language is always potentially inflationary, since the mere substitution of one word for another increases the apparent value of the referent. In fact Squire Hawkins's riches are only imaginary. Arguing against Descartes's ontological proof for the existence of God, Kant appealed to a monetary analogy: "[The proof] that claims to demonstrate the existence of a Being through concepts is futile, and simple ideas make one no richer in knowledge than a merchant becomes if with the notion of increasing his wealth, he adds several zeros to his checkbook." [14] Wealth is the God, the transcendental signifier, of *The Gilded Age*, whose existence is "proved" by the sheer ability of language to project it. The Hawkinses in fact *prefer* the imaginary to the real. In chapter 6 Squire Hawkins is offered ten thousand dollars cash for his lands. About to ask fifteen thousand, he changes his mind and demands thirty thousand. The prospective buyer departs, never to be seen again. Squire Hawkins is shattered: "Too late—too late! He's gone! Fool that I am!—always a fool! Thirty thousand—ass that I am! Oh, *why* didn't I say fifty thousand! . . . Fool as I am I told him he could have half the iron property for thirty thousand—and if I only had him back here he couldn't touch it for a cent less than a quarter of a million!" (*WMT* 5:56–57). Twain is explicit about the theological significance of the Hawkins land, for the squire's thoughts turn to that land rather than to God as he lies on his deathbed: "A better day is—is coming. Never lose sight of the Tennessee Land! . . . There is wealth stored up for you there—wealth that is boundless!" (*WMT* 5:91).[15] Washington Hawkins is a direct inheritor of his father's apocalyptic hope. The capital city, a "world of enchantment" that "teemed with speculation," is "paradise" to him (*WMT* 5:241–42). He translates a tentative offer of forty thousand dollars for the land—a "little sum"—into "operations . . . that will increase it a hundredfold, yes, a thousandfold, in a few months" (*WMT* 5:247). Twain comments ironically on all this inflation in the imaginary realm in describing the effect of Colonel Sellers's turnips on Washington Hawkins's stomach, the material realm par excellence: the "dire inflation that had begun in his stomach . . . grew and grew, it became more and more insupportable" (*WMT* 5:110).

Inflation is a special case of creation *ex nihilo*, and Colonel Sellers is the Twain character who refuses most stubbornly to admit that "nothing will come of nothing."[16] As an "enchanter" whose tongue makes others' fortunes and raises cities in the wilderness, he is a parody of the Creator-Logos and the evangelical Savior. So we see him in his letter to the Hawkinses in chapter 1, his first directly quoted language in *The Gilded Age* and one of the most brilliant pieces of verbal characterization Twain ever wrote:

> "Come right to Missouri! Don't wait and worry about a good price, but sell out for whatever you can get, and come along, or you might be too late. Throw away your traps, if necessary, and come along empty-handed. You'll never regret it. It's the grandest country—the loveliest land—the purest atmosphere—I can't describe it; no pen can do it justice. . . . I've got the biggest scheme on earth—and I'll take you in; I'll take in every friend I've got that's ever stood by me, for there's enough for all, and to spare.["]
>
> (*WMT* 5:13)

This is stunning intertextuality, for despite the lack of direct quotation nearly every phrase resonates with Gospel overtones: Sellers is the Good Shepherd, the Way In, promising salvation to those who believe, Paradise to those who sell all they have and follow him. But the nub of Mark Twain's joke is the equivocal phrase "take in," which tips off the reader to the deception Sellers practices. The description of his fraudulent scheme not only satirizes ill-judged investment but creates doubts about the trustworthiness of any referential language. If faith is "the assurance of things hoped for, the conviction of things not seen," does not all speech require an act of faith, since we have no guarantee that the words we use are backed by corresponding objects? Beyond the obvious point that Sellers's Missouri is an illusion is the far more unsettling suggestion that the theological promises he echoes are deceptions as well. A latent suggestion, the merest hint: Mark Twain in the 1870s is not yet the Mark Twain of the Mysterious Stranger tales, and his targets in *The Gilded Age* remain social rather than metaphysical.

In his popularization of Alfred Korzybski's "general semantics," S. I. Hayakawa notes that major abuses of logic and language occur when a map is mistaken for the territory.[17] When in a wonderful scene Colonel Sellers creates a "map" of a proposed railroad line with the aid of every kitchen implement he can lay his hands on, it becomes clear that his particular form of insanity is to believe that the map *creates* the territory. An authentic map is a symbolic representation of the real; Sellers's maps are all symbolic representations of the imaginary, which he mistakes for the real. One specific linguistic correlate of this semiotic confusion is Sellers's (and the Hawkinses') conflation of present and future tense. Chapter 27 begins with a dialogue between Sellers and his wife, who as usual lack ready cash. Sellers reassures her: "It's all right, my dear, all right; it will all come right in a little while." The railroad appropriation will shortly bring in two hundred thousand dollars, he insists, and the railroad itself infinitely more. Since she is prospectively wealthy, Sellers chides his wife for her current uneasiness: "Bless your heart, you dear women live right in the present all the time—but a man, why a man lives—" "In the future, Beriah? But don't we live in the future most too much, Beriah?" (*WMT* 5:265–66). As his wife sees, Sellers constantly moves from a postulated "will" to an assured "is." The best description of this verbal speculation occurs in a passage written by Warner rather than Twain. Harry Brierly has been boasting to some new acquaintances about a "big diamond interest" in Arizona that certain "parties" want him to investigate. His friend Philip rebukes him for "going on" in such a style. "'Go on?' cried Harry. 'Why shouldn't I try to make a pleasant evening? And besides, ain't I going to do those things? What difference does it make about the mood and tense of a mere verb?'" (*WMT* 5:225). All the difference in *The Gilded Age*, where the ontological status of modal verbs is highly suspect. "I have two million dollars" is—if true—a statement convertible in full for specie. "I will/may/might/should have two million dollars" is a note on a wildcat bank. (Speaking of wildcat banks, one of Sellers's schemes is to buy up a hundred and thirteen of them whose notes are being sold at a large discount—"buy them all up, you see, and then all of a sudden let the cat out of the bag! Whiz! the stock of every one of those wildcats would spin up to a tremendous premium . . . [bringing] profit on the speculation not a dollar less than forty millions!" [*WMT* 5:78]. Between the wish and the reality falls the *would*.) To put it another way, the finite verb is "reality," which is corrupted by the addition of a modal into "appearance." "Will have" is like the colonel's stove that glows but gives no heat, the central metaphor of the novel. He keeps a lighted candle in it because "what you want is the *appearance* of heat, not the heat itself—that's the idea" (*WMT* 5:72). But "the idea," as Twain expects us to see, never fed anybody.

Mark Twain's portions of *The Gilded Age* exhibit abundant pessimism about the extent to which language is used appropriately. Like White, he believed that language could be corrupted, degraded, or inflated so as to create a gap between appearance and reality. J. Hammond Trumbull provided chapter 13 with a heading from William Caxton about a man whose speech "semeth vnto manys herying / not only the worde, but veryly the thyng" (*WMT* 5:122). Twain would have us underline the "semeth." *The Gilded Age* presents a web of words that create nonexistent "things." Obscure letters shadow forth Laura's real father.[18] Town gossip creates a "past" for her. Colonel Selby promises romance but delivers an invalid marriage. Congressional rhetoric turns a swindle into a philanthropic scheme for elevating the Negro. Language is never ideologically neutral: every variation in usage corresponds to a social fact or to an instrumental intent. There are offenses against linguistic rules that are more serious than mere errors of grammar, as both White and Twain are aware. The flexibility and internal variety of language can add richness and color to social intercourse, or it can provide handles for manipulators who know how to wield their words to others' harm.

One *"great abuse of words is the taking them for things,"* John Locke wrote.[19] Like Cobbett, Emerson, and White before him, Mark Twain in *The Gilded Age* judges the voices he hears every day against the standard of a pure language that might repair the rent between word and thing through a resolute honesty. His social satire at once measures how far we Americans have betrayed that ideal tongue and calls pragmatically for reform. The part of Mark Twain that believed in progress toward perfection necessarily had to conceive of a unitary language, that is, one whose unique standard could be formulated in rules of grammar and usage equally accessible and intelligible to all members of the speech community. The grammatical language, the pure language, would seem to be both the cause and the effect of a well-ordered and harmonious society. A central tenet of Lockean theory is that language should unite its users: "The chief end of language in communication being to be understood, words serve not well for that end . . . when any word does not excite in the hearer the same *idea* which it stands for in the mind of the speaker."[20] A curious republic indeed it would be, a world where all words meant the same to all speakers, where language could not say "the thing that is not" (the virtue, or defect, of the speech of Swift's rational horses). Such a republic could be built only in a utopia, no place, because physical and social place in the sublunary world entails an inescapable difference between speaker and listener, which makes meaning possible. Mark Twain hardly needed twentieth-century theory to tell him this; his own experience as he moved from state to state and country to country confronted him with what George Steiner has called *"the problem of Babel,"* and brought him to an intuitive awareness that *"inside or between languages, human communication equals translation"* (Steiner's italics).[21]

I have insisted in this chapter and the previous one on Mark Twain's debts and even subservience to traditional authorities over grammar and usage, partly to counter a widespread view that Twain's fascination with the vernacular signifies linguistic populism (a claim I will return to in chapter 5). Yet his conscious allegiance to rules and standards coexists with a radical awareness, sometimes joyous and sometimes fearful, of the irreducible multeity of human expression. Paradoxically, to create the defiantly monoglot Huck, Mark Twain had to learn to speak as many languages as possible. The route to his fictional St. Petersburg, Missouri, led him through Europe—and Babel.

4

"Babel Come Again":
Mark Twain and Foreign Languages

Five languages in use in the house . . . and yet with all this
opulence of resource we do seem to have an uncommonly
tough time making ourselves understood.
                                        —Mark Twain, letter from
                                                Florence, 1892

Of course it is a family that speaks languages. This occurs at
their table—I know it by experience. It is Babel come again.
The other day, when no guests were present to keep order,
the tribes were all talking at once, and 6 languages were
being traded in; at last the littlest boy lost his temper and
screamed out at the top of his voice, with angry sobs: "Mais,
vraiment, io non capisco *gar* nichts."
                                        —Mark Twain, letter from
                                                Florence, 1904

On perhaps no American author has the impact of foreign
languages been so great as on Mark Twain. This will seem a
curious statement to those who are thinking of traditional literary influence, of the wholesale scholarly or imaginative assimilation of a language and cultural tradition by a formally
educated author. Dante and Milton are unthinkable without
Latin; Carlyle without German; Ezra Pound without Italian, Greek, Anglo-Saxon, Provençal, and Chinese. Certainly
Twain's little German and less French had at most a superficial
effect on the form of his literary creation. But if the clash of
dialects and styles in a single language is the most memorable
index of linguistic variety in Twain's work, the confusion of
Babel runs a close second. Because he came to the study of

foreign languages as an adult, and because he was largely self-taught, Twain was painfully aware of the semantic and grammatical barriers that separate languages and the difficulties that communication in a foreign tongue creates. To study a foreign language was, paradoxically, both liberating and oppressive. On the one hand, a command of French and German provided entry into the "adult" world of cosmopolitan, educated society; on the other, it made him a "child" again as it limited his means of expression and forced him to rely on others for the satisfaction of his needs and desires.

Van Wyck Brooks's indignant comment that Twain found foreign languages "ludicrous because they were not English" oversimplifies a set of complex and evolving attitudes evident in the body of Twain's writing. William Dean Howells saw more keenly when he wrote Twain during the second month of his friend's first trip to Germany, "I could imagine the German going [hard] with you, for you always seemed to me a man who liked to be understood with the least possible personal inconvenience."[1] In Twain's early treatment of his struggles with French and German, "personal inconvenience" is a rich source of farcical humor at the expense of the Mark Twain persona. That variety of humor never disappears; after the turn of the century he was still using "The Awful German Language" in lecture appearances and turning his struggles with Italian into similarly comic essays. But increasingly he came to see Babel as fundamental to the human condition and the opacity of a foreign idiom as a special case of the perplexity that can interfere with any human communication. "We must be careful not to overrate the uniformity of existing languages," American linguist William Dwight Whitney wrote in 1875; "in a true and defensible sense, every individual speaks a language different from every other."[2] At the same time, only through confronting the language of the Other, by struggling to see from the perspective of another mind, can one transcend the limitations of a single and limited point of view. Babel was both curse and blessing. For a clergyman who was Twain's contemporary, the building of the tower, in light of the divine response, was a *felix culpa:*

The dispersion of nations has acted as a stimulant to the powers of humanity, and has been the direct cause of a beneficial
variety in thought and action; and in the same way the diversity of languages has proved to be . . . an indisputable advantage, by adding fresh lustre continually to those conceptions
which by long habit become pale and dim. Yet this dispersion
and diversity is but the accident of a fallen state, and in the
renovated earth . . . all men will perhaps speak the same perfect universal speech.[3]

The novelist's interest in Babel, however, is not necessarily
the theologian's. Mikhail Bakhtin proposes that the novel
would never have evolved as it did without the stimulus of
competing national and classical languages in medieval and
Renaissance Europe.[4] Juri Lotman goes even further, claiming
that the disruption caused by misunderstanding is crucial to
the evolution of all literary texts. A special case is the foreign
text introduced into another culture: "[Its] incomprehensibility and undecodability . . . (or, more precisely, the difficulty
of decoding it) is a form of energy; one which sets in motion
the semiotic mechanism of culture."[5] Certainly the energy of
foreignness in general and foreign languages in particular
often sets in motion Mark Twain's writing mill. *The Innocents
Abroad, Roughing It, A Tramp Abroad, A Connecticut Yankee, Following the Equator:* a half dozen long books generated by actual
or imaginative travel into alien cultures. But Mark Twain was
also apprehensive of any foreign discourse that was *too* ener-
getic, recognizing that it can overwhelm and silence one's
own, and from the Duke and King through Hank Morgan to
Mary Baker Eddy he will create or find characters who use incomprehensibility as a rhetorical weapon. (I return to the
overall topic of incomprehension in chapter 7.) This chapter
examines Mark Twain's experience with the specific problem
of foreign languages and the dialectic between the "good" foreign language that liberates the energy of creation and humor
and the "bad" foreign language that dominates individuals or
cuts them off from others.

The first of Mark Twain's surviving notebooks begins with several pages of French lessons, transcribed at the age of nine-

teen while Twain was traveling by steamboat upriver from St. Louis to Hannibal. Marshaled into two columns are French words and their English equivalents for the days of the week, the months of the year, the names of family members, and greetings and essential idioms. Twain's first literary encounter with a foreign tongue begins, typically, with errors:

Sur la langue Francaise [*sic*]

and ends

J'ai peur	I am afraid
Lentement,	Slowly.
Je n'aimie pas ça.	I don't like it.
	(*NJ1*, 17, 21)

As the editors of the notebooks observe, "misplaced accents and other foreign language solecisms would persist throughout his life" (*NJ1*, 21). A naturally confident English speller since boyhood, Twain never could or would master the orthographic systems of French or German. The eerily somber closure of the notebook lesson seems to reflect the difficulties he was having; here French is imposing not just a grammatical structure but also a mood on the young learner. But Twain's linguistic errors did not long remain mere lapses. He would discover that the intractability of the alien idiom, inherently funny, could be useful to a professional humorist. Gravity, the "enemy" responsible for the pratfalls of the slapstick comedian, is actually the ally that produces the humor; similarly the foreign language, when it baffles the "Mark Twain" who encounters it in *The Innocents Abroad* and *A Tramp Abroad*, is the agent of laughter. Both the physical and the linguistic comedy in these works reveal the gaps between body and soul, desire and performance; when adults are reduced to the incompetence of childhood, the sheer mechanics of walking and talking become problematic once again. Or, to use Henri Bergson's terms, the "illusion of life" that our fluent use of a native tongue creates is shattered when the foreign language reminds us that speech is a "mechanical arrangement."[6]

Even Twain's early notebooks hint at the comic battles of tongues that would generate so much of the later, published, humor. Thus when Twain in his third notebook (where he has learned enough French to be able to copy Voltaire) first sets sail on his own and tries to reproduce a humorous anecdote in French about a doctor prescribing to a patient, he stumbles onto the comic genre of macaronic prose:

> Allai au apotheke, et acheter trois sous de la longue epèce et le break en short pieces—et acheter trois sous de la short epice et le break en longue pieces et acheter trois sous de l'autre epèce et le break en square pieces—boil 'em down—donc allai à la barbière et causer le tête ètre razè—donce dormir sur la lit trois semaines—la première fait un plastre et le mit sur le tête—
> Cela—veut-il une mal de dent?
> Ah—je pensait que vous eu mal de tête!
> (*NJ*1, 59)

In the center of all this mangled French is the pithy vernacular "boil 'em down," and the voice of the Mississippi momentarily drowns out the language of Voltaire. This strategy will have become entirely purposeful by the time Twain "retranslates" a French translation of his "Jumping Frog" story in 1875. Once he has begun to learn German, macaronic burlesques of one sort or another will be his chief mode of linguistic humor.[7] The constant eruption of English in these burlesques is a comic sublimation of Twain's frustration in suppressing his own natural language to reproduce another's. Bakhtin has identified two modes of assimilating the discourse of others, "recitation" and "retelling." The former involves transmitting "authoritative discourse"—whether religious creed or grammatical paradigm—that has explicit social sanction. It "demands our unconditional allegiance" and permits no play, no "spontaneously creative stylizing variants."[8] Retelling, on the other hand, creates an "internally persuasive discourse," a word of one's own, that can grow and be given aesthetic shape. Twain's strategy for learning languages was clearly to "retell" them, playing games with their rules, thumbing his nose at the discipline of textbook lists and paradigms. Because he wished to assert his own authority over foreign discourse, he moved quickly to a defiantly macaronic, Twainian, form of both French and German tongues. His method was to create a dialogue between a given foreign language, taken as an amalgam of words, rules, and social attitudes, and the "American language"—or his idiolect of it—that he claimed was his sole tongue. In the process Mark Twain learned the foreign idiom, but it too had to bend and learn from him.

Only a few of the sketches that preceded *The Innocents Abroad* merit Brooks's charge that Twain found languages ludicrous just because they were not English. Twain's short-sighted prejudice against Indians, for example, permitted him to belittle their languages as subhuman forms of communication and to joke at the Pidgin English that served them as a lingua franca along the frontier. In one of the early letters he sent home from Nevada Territory, he transcribes a bit of dialogue between some Washoe women and a white friend of his:

> They examined [our] breakfast leisurely, and criticized it in their own tongue. . . . After awhile, the Gentle Wild Cat remarked: "May be whity man no heap eat um grass-hopper?" . . . and John replied, "May be whity man no heap like um grass-hopper—*savvy?*" And thus the Lark: "May be bimeby Injun heap ketch um sage-hen." "Sage-hen heap good—bully!" said John. You see, these savages speak broken English, madam, and you've got to answer accordingly, because they can't understand the unfractured article, you know.[9]

The joke here is largely on the American who is forced willy-nilly to adopt "fractured" discourse. It depends, though, on seeing pidgin as the linguistic equivalent of a pratfall; its form is supposed to be self-evidently silly. We can hardly fault Twain for dismissing Pidgin English as mere "broken English," since its structure and social function were poorly understood until the twentieth century.[10] But he was equally scornful of the native languages themselves. His distaste for the Indians of California and the Great Basin extended to their speech, as in his futile protest against replacing the name Lake Bigler with Lake Tahoe; first printed in the *Virginia City Territorial Enterprise* in 1863, the protest was incorporated into *The Innocents Abroad* six years later. "Of course Indian names are more fitting than any others for our beautiful lakes and rivers, which knew their race ages ago . . . but let us have none so repulsive to the ear as 'Tahoe.' . . . They say it means 'Fallen Leaf'—well suppose it meant fallen devil or fallen angel, would that render its hideous, discordant syllables more endurable?" (*ETS1*, 290). In *The Innocents Abroad* he maintains that the "unmusical cognomen" means "grasshopper soup"; "Indian and suggestive of Indians," the word is a product of the "degraded" Digger Indians (*WMT* 1:204–5). It is hard to see what exactly makes *Tahoe* any less musical than *Como*, the name of the Italian lake Twain has just been comparing unfavorably to its Californian counterpart, but the objective sound of the syllables is not at issue here. If the alien word comes from an antagonistic or despised race, it automatically sounds bad. "Inferior" races speak inferior languages. *Tahoe* cannot possibly mean something lovely like "Silver Lake" or "Limpid Water," Twain says, because only "Fenimore Cooper Indians" have ever had poetry (*WMT*, 205). In 1879, in a notebook entry attacking the French as "the connecting link between man & the monkey," Twain similarly abuses the French language in defiance of what he must have known about it:

> They have no poetry else we should have some in translations. Bayard Taylor said the F. language was an inadequate vehicle for the conveyance of poetic thought.
>
> The language is right for the people—it is a mess of trivial sounds—words which run into each other (by law)—& words which never end, but fade away.   (*NJ2*, 320)

Twain's late writings, as we shall see, show that he believed language firmly constrains thought. As early as his California days, however, he was interested in facts about any foreign language that seemed to "explain" characteristics of its speakers. Thus in 1864 he attributed the putative lack of conventional morality among Chinese immigrants to their native tongue: "It is asserted that [the Chinese] have no words or expressions signifying abstract right or wrong. They appreciate "good" and "bad," but it is only in reference to business, to finance, to trade, etc. Whatever is successful is good; whatever fails is bad. So they are not conscience-bound in planning and perfecting ingenious contrivances for avoiding the tariff on opium, which is pretty heavy." [11] In Hawaii in 1866, where he carried a dictionary and a phrase book of the native tongue and made some attempt to acquire the rudiments of Hawaiian, he noted that the language had "no word to express gratitude," could "but lamely express virtue of any kind," and was "prolific in epithets to express every degree & shade of vice & crime." The polysemy of *aloha* led him to suppose that Hawaiian had "no word to express farewell—or good-bye" (*NJ1*, 224). Only once he had traveled to Europe, though, did he begin to be seriously concerned with the problem of communicating in any language but English.

In *The Innocents Abroad* the relation of language to power is complex. It might seem that to be mute, or incapable of speaking native languages, would entail powerlessness, the inability to get things done; the more language, the more power. Paradoxically, it is often the case in *The Innocents Abroad* that *less* language equals more power. The reasons have to do with the sociology of language negotiations in a bilingual speech setting. The minimal components of any act of communication are often diagrammed thus:

SPEAKER — MESSAGE — ADDRESSEE

In the Saussurean model of communication, "SPEAKER" is active while "ADDRESSEE" is passive. But Saussure's model is oversimplified: the silent addressee exerts a continual influence over the speaker. [12] The speaker always intends that the addressee *act* in response to the message by *comprehending* it at the very least. But the addressee cannot comprehend by virtue of willpower alone: to frame a message that can be understood, the speaker must take into account the addressee's competence (linguistic, but also cultural, educational, and so on). In this sense the most successful communicators are rhetoricians and polyglots, people who can adapt to the widest range of addressees, thanks to mastery of their codes. Yet from another viewpoint adaptation to the needs and expectations of the addressee is a form of "giving in" to an implicit demand on the part of the other party. A speaker can refuse from the start to negotiate over language, register, or dialect, insisting that the addressee communicate for better or for worse in the speaker's own variety of language. This insistence is particularly likely when two separate languages are in question, since in most bilingual settings a tacit or even explicit rule requires that the speech of the more "important" social group be used. A speaker who adheres rigidly to a prestige language can blame any breakdown of communication on the interlocutor. If the speaker has enough social, physical, or economic power, the interlocutor cannot afford to complain about misunderstanding but must do his best to comply with the speaker's demands.[13] We might thus distinguish between two primary and opposing strategies for obtaining power through speech, craft and force. (The archetypal representative of craft is Odysseus, the representative of force, Achilles.) Through rhetorical jujitsu, the crafty speaker manipulates the listener's activity, deflecting its force to his own ends. Huck Finn, when he lies, tells people what they want to hear; Hank Morgan cleverly uses Socratic questioning to demolish his opponent in an argument over economics. The forceful speaker, on the other hand, overrides the "active" component of listening and insists on complete passivity in the addressee. Both "bad" characters like Pap Finn and "good" characters like Ned Blakely are forceful in this sense.

The "innocence" Twain examines in *The Innocents Abroad* is

in part linguistic incompetence. The Americans cannot speak a comprehensible sentence in any of the languages they encounter; unable to pronounce foreign names, they call every guide Ferguson and Palestinian cities either Jonesborough or Baldwinsville. Twain's satire is double-edged. He is of course mocking the naïveté of the American traveler, his lack of culture and learning. At the same time we recognize that the innocents' aggressive vulgarity, their insistent monolinguism, is a form of cultural assertion. "After nightfall we reached our tents, just outside of the nasty Arab village of Jonesborough. Of course the real name of the place is El something or other, but the boys still refuse to recognize the Arab names or try to pronounce them" (*WMT* 2:192). The apparently harmless linguistic imperialism of the "boys" is not far removed from the high-handed renaming of "nasty" Indian villages by Americans pushing westward across the continent. The innocents' refusal to comprehend is closely related to their tendency to destroy, manifested in vandalism of ancient monuments, and is treated with a similar ambivalent wavering between condemnation and ironic admiration. If "Mark Twain" is ignorant of foreign languages, the joke is on those who value them as attainments of a gentleman. Twain himself was perfectly aware of the seditious effect of his ignorance in *The Innocents Abroad*. When he composes what purports to be a criticism of his book by an Englishman who had taken the work seriously, Twain makes the pompous "reviewer" complain that "[the author] is vulgarly ignorant of all foreign languages, but is frank enough to criticize, the Italians' use of their own tongue" ("An Entertaining Article," *WMT* 24:283–84). This is true enough: at bottom "Mark Twain" does not believe that Italian is an authentic language.

When Americans must choose between craft and force in *The Innocents Abroad*, the latter tactic generally wins the day. Twain's description of confusion over a Portuguese restaurant bill in the Azores illustrates the crude effectiveness of forceful misunderstanding. The travelers have received a bill for ten dinners totaling twenty-two thousand Portuguese reis. Young

Blucher, the innocent from the Far West who has been the host for the meal, is aghast at the elevated sum but resolved to perform his duty:

> "Landlord, this is a low, mean swindle, and I'll never, never stand it. Here's a hundred and fifty dollars, sir, and it's all you'll get—I'll swim in blood, before I'll pay a cent more."
> Our spirits rose and the landlord's fell—at least we thought so; he was confused at any rate, notwithstanding he had not understood a word that had been said. He glanced from the little pile of gold pieces to Blucher several times, and then went out. He must have visited an American, for, when he returned, he brought back his bill translated into a language that a Christian could understand [that is, "$21.70"].
>
> (*WMT* 1:38)

The "language that a Christian can understand" is both "English" and "dollars," understood as two manifestations of the same underlying system. Blucher cannot calculate in reis, but his pile of American gold pieces speaks the universal language of economic power.

Here as elsewhere, most notably in *A Connecticut Yankee*, Twain simultaneously mocks the old order and the new order that is replacing it. In linguistic terms, the old order in *The Innocents Abroad* comprises the old prestige languages, Latin and the modern Continental tongues of Italy and France, whose cultural authority is a matter of tradition. The new order is English—specifically, American English—which is coming to assume political and economic authority. From the conflict between the two emerges a double bind: neither stasis nor change is tenable. Whether characters adhere to a single order or attempt to move from one to another, they are objects of humor in *The Innocents Abroad* and other works of the 1860s and 1870s. Foreigners make ludicrous mistakes when they try to speak English, but their own languages, with their irregular verbs and odd orthography, are also ridiculous. How the humor cuts both ways can be seen in a *Territorial Enterprise* sketch from early 1866, reprinted in the *Jumping Frog* volume the following year as "Among the Fenians":

Wishing to post myself on one of the most current topics of the
day, I, Mark, hunted up an old friend, Dennis McCarthy, who
is editor of the new Fenian journal in San Francisco, *The Irish
People*. I found him sitting on a sumptuous candle-box, in his
shirt-sleeves, solacing himself with a whiff at the national *dhu-
deen* or *caubeen* or whatever they call it—a clay pipe with no
stem to speak of. I thought it might flatter him to address him
in his native tongue, and so I bowed with considerable grace
and said:
    "Arrah!"
    And he said, "Be jabers!"
    "Och hone!" said I.
    "Mavourneen dheelish, acushla machree," replied The
McCarthy.
    "Erin go bragh," I continued with vivacity.
    "Asthore!" responded The McCarthy.
    "Tare an' ouns!" said I.
    "Bhe dha husth; fag a rogarah lums!" said the bold Fenian.
    "Ye have me there, be me sowl!" said I, (for I am not "up" in
the niceties of the language, you understand; I only know
enough of it to enable me to "keep my end up" in an ordinary
conversation.) [14]

The primary butt of this slight sketch is "I, Mark," who presumes to initiate a conversation in Irish when he has in fact
only a few tags of the language. The dialogue is a poker game,
and Mark is a bluffer who loses his bet: "anteing" with an
"Arrah," he continues to raise until the Fenian calls with the
spoken equivalent of four aces. Foolish "Mark Twain" has
blundered into terra incognita once again. Yet the Fenian
comes off no better than his opponent after this skirmishing
raid. The Irishman is caricatured as a subhuman who speaks a
language not far removed from primal grunting. (The original
title of the sketch, "Bearding the Fenian in His Lair," makes
the caricature even clearer.) His speech is neither Gaelic nor
Irish English but a hodgepodge of stereotypical Irish exclama-
tions and slogans from both languages of the sort that Twain
had found in burlesques by Bret Harte and Charles Webb. [15]
His concluding sentence resembles nothing so much as James
Joyce's representation of Neanderthal speech in *Finnegans
Wake*, an atavistic nonsensical jumble.

In *The Innocents Abroad* "Mark Twain" is once more a pretentious impostor whose claim to status as a speaker of foreign tongues is shown to be baseless. The running joke for several chapters is that Twain and the doctor, who pride themselves on their French and Italian while criticizing young Dan for his ignorance of anything but English, prove worse than incompetent as communicators. They ply the natives with questions in their incomprehensible French; Dan befuddles a boatman with "Oh, go to the pier, you old fool—that's where we want to go!" (*WMT* 1:84). In an Italian bathhouse Dan protests the lack of soap:

> "Oh, bring some soap, why don't you!"
> The reply was Italian. Dan resumed:
> "Soap, you know—soap. That is what I want—soap. S-o-a-p, soap; s-o-p-e, soap; s-o-u-p, soap. Hurry up! I don't know how you Irish spell it, but I want it."
>
> (WMT 1:186)

Dan is the apotheosis of the assertive, unapologetic monolingual. For him all referents stand in a univocal relation to English words—no "Irish" symbol system need apply. "I want it" is the slogan of the forceful speaker; we might recall the retired army officer whom Twain heard declare, "We are of the Anglo-Saxon race, and when the Anglo-Saxon wants a thing *he just takes it*" (*MTE*, 380). The American who attempts to gain his ends through craft, on the other hand, has little chance of succeeding.

"Mark Twain" and the doctor's confrontation with an old hostess at a Marseilles café becomes a model for subsequent cultural disillusionment on the part of the Americans. They pose a simple question, "Avez-vous du vin?" It is not understood; neither are two repetitions. Finally the doctor lapses into English, and the old woman says, "Bless you, why didn't you speak English before?—I don't know anything about your plagued French!" Twain's reaction expresses one of the many deflations of romantic preconception that form an important pattern in *The Innocents Abroad:*[16]

> Here we were in beautiful France—in a vast stone house of quaint architecture—surrounded by all manner of curiously worded French signs—stared at by strangely habited, bearded French people—everything gradually and surely forcing upon us the coveted consciousness that at last, and beyond all question, we *were* in beautiful France and absorbing its nature to the forgetfulness of everything else, and coming to feel the happy romance of the thing in all its enchanting delightfulness—and to think of this skinny veteran intruding with her vile English, at such a moment, to blow the fair vision to the winds! It was exasperating.
>
>   (*WMT* 1:86)

Two of "Mark Twain's" illusions have been pierced here. One is that he can pass as a cosmopolitan polyglot; Dan can now make fun of him, having received independent confirmation of his suspicions about the soundness of his friend's French. The second is far more profound, the illusion that cultural otherness is "romantic" and can be penetrated simply by an attitude of will, that differences of language and thought pose no major barrier to the sentimental traveler. "Mark Twain" has looked forward to speaking French in the same way he has looked forward to riding a camel or getting shaved by a Parisian barber. "Speaking French" will be part of a travel experience, allowing the innocents to feel "happy romance . . . in all its enchanting delightfulness" without their needing to alter their own natures or values. If French signs are "curiously worded," that is because their code is unfamiliar, but "Mark Twain" does not see that he cannot preserve the strangeness that delights him while at the same time "absorbing [French] nature to the forgetfulness of everything else."[17] The travelers' poor French is the shibboleth that betrays them as aliens; their attempt to disguise themselves as natives has failed, and their hostess's English comment on their "plagued French" is their unmasking and their rebuke. The hostess draws firm boundaries between varieties of language, boundaries that romantic philosophies of language had tended to obscure or deny. For Emerson, different languages were simply so many homologous transformations of the thought of the "universal soul"; because all language is the expression of spirit mediated by nature, "the idioms of all languages approach each other in passages of the greatest eloquence and power."[18] "Mark Twain" in *The Innocents Abroad* is continually being flung from the heights of eloquence into the hurly-burly of everyday speech and thought, where the "idioms of all languages" have little to do with one another.

The travelers set out to find the center of Marseilles, asking for directions now and then. "We never did succeed in making anybody understand just exactly what we wanted, and neither did we ever succeed in comprehending just exactly what they said in reply—but then they always pointed—they always did that, and we bowed politely and said, 'Merci, monsieur'" (*WMT* 1:87). The only universal language the innocents discover in Europe is the most primitive of all, sign language, whose simplest element is pointing—the "deixis" of semiotics. Once they are humiliated to this degree, their fascination with foreign languages begins to wane and disappears entirely by the time they reach the Near East. Back on the ship after traversing France and Italy, Twain exclaims at the comfort of once again being able to hold familiar conversation with friends in his own language: "Oh, the rare happiness of comprehending every single word that is said, and knowing that every word one says in return will be understood as well!" (*WMT* 1:260). In *The Innocents Abroad* incomprehensibility is a danger that remains "out there," like the lurking bandits in Palestine, not yet an essential part of human experience. Since it can be externalized, since it does not yet threaten the self, it remains an occasion for light humor.

In 1895, while Twain was staying in Paris, an interviewer asked him a question about the translatability of humor, suggesting that English speakers

> "perhaps . . . lose the quality of the French humor as completely as they lose the quality of yours."
> "Oh, unquestionably! . . . A man may study a language for

years and years and yet he is never inside the holy of holies. He must get into the man himself, the man of another country, and he cannot do that."[19]

In "How to Tell a Story" Twain distinguishes between wit and comedy, which arise merely from the *content* of an anecdote, and humor, which depends on the *manner* of telling. If the form of humor is part of its meaning, it is as untranslatable in principle as poetry. Twain's response to the interviewer shows that he was ready to generalize from humorous language to all language: the worldview that generates the form of a language is inaccessible to an outsider, who can therefore never use that language as a native speaker would. Jorge Luis Borges has played brilliantly with this problem in his short story "Pierre Menard, Author of the *Quixote*," about a scholar who seeks to re-create Cervantes's composition not by copying but, in George Steiner's analysis, by putting himself "so deeply in tune with Cervantes's being, with his ontological form, as to re-enact, inevitably, the exact sum of his realizations and statements"—entering the holy of holies, in short.[20] Twenty years before the Paris interview, Twain had written his own version of "Pierre Menard," the second, longer, version of his "Jumping Frog" story, which Twain criticism has almost universally ignored in favor of its predecessor.

In 1872 there appeared in the *Revue des deux mondes* a French translation of "The Celebrated Jumping Frog of Calaveras County" as part of an article introducing Mark Twain to a French audience. Author and translator Thérèse Bentzon had chosen to begin with Twain in a two-part series on American humorists and had nothing but praise for his work, barring reservations about the provincialism she found in *The Innocents Abroad*. But when Twain eventually read the piece two years later, he stumbled over Bentzon's claim that the humor in his most famous story was hard to find:

> *The Jumping Frog* de Mark Twain doit être cité d'abord comme un des morceaux les plus populaires, presque un type du genre. Il nous est assez difficile néanmoins de comprendre, en lisant ce récit, les éclats de rire (*roars of laughter*) qu'il souleva

en Australie et aux Indes, à New-York et à Londres. . . . On va
en juger par la traduction que nous en avons faite en nous at-
tachant à conserver le mieux possible le ton goguenard de
l'original.[21]

[Mark Twain's "The Jumping Frog" must be mentioned first as
one of the most popular pieces, almost a model of the genre. It
is nonetheless rather hard for us to understand, as we read this
tale, the roars of laughter that it provoked in Australia and the
Indies, in New York and London. . . . One may judge by the
translation we have made of it, striving to preserve as far as
possible the chaffing tone of the original.]

But Bentzon's translation signally fails to convey Twain's tone,
mainly because she renders the piece in consistent standard
French, even though she recognizes how important vernacular is to the effect of the original.[22] Twain's irritated response is
just: Bentzon, he complains, "has not translated [the story] at
all; he [sic] has simply mixed it all up; it is no more like the
Jumping Frog when he gets through with it than I am like a
meridian of longitude" (WMT 7:16). To prove it, Twain determined to retranslate Bentzon's French into an English version
whose absurd clumsiness would bear no resemblance to the
original tale.

At least one critic has called "The Jumping Frog" the "best
example of Twain's frontier humor."[23] For most critics, as for
the general public, the original version of 1865 is *the* "Jumping
Frog": Simon Wheeler's monologue about Jim Smiley's being
conned by a clever stranger who loads Smiley's champion frog
with quailshot. The story that created Twain's national reputation, it served as a title for his first collection of sketches in
1867, and it would receive place of honor as the first piece in
the *Library of Humor* that Twain later helped edit. But in *Sketches
New and Old* (1875) and thereafter, the story would officially
appear with a lengthy subtitle: "The Jumping Frog. In English. Then in French. Then clawed back into a civilized language once more by patient, unremunerated toil." It is a mistake to see the additional material either as inferior buffoonery
or as a husk that may be discarded to get at the meat of the
story. This new "Jumping Frog" is in important ways an or-

ganic outgrowth of the original. The problematic of framing, translation, and quotation that figures in "Frog$_1$"is extended and made more complex in "Frog$_2$." (Since both versions carry the same short title, I hope I may be pardoned this ungainly but brief notation to distinguish between the original story and the revision.)

"Frog$_1$," is a *quoted* story, a fact emphasized in the narrator's introduction. The "I" of the story is the persona "Mark Twain," an impatient and rather stuffy fellow, whose formal language contrasts markedly with the vernacular of Simon Wheeler, the narrator of the tale. The reader is meant to understand that in evaluating Wheeler's tale as an "exasperating," "tedious," "monotonous," and "interminable" narrative (*WMT* 7:17), "Mark Twain" shows himself deaf to the humor of its style and delivery. Moreover, "Twain" gives us the important information that Simon Wheeler himself saw nothing funny in the tale but delivered it as straightforward history. The humor of the story thus derives not just from Wheeler's manner but from the dialogue between Wheeler's unselfconscious garrulousness and "Mark Twain's" judgmental frame. We give "Mark Twain" credit, at least, for quoting Wheeler accurately: "I let him go on in his own way, and never interrupted him once," Twain says, and the direct discourse of Simon Wheeler immediately follows, uninterrupted until the exasperated narrator departs at the end of the story. The structure of "Frog$_1$" is thus (brackets indicate quotation):

"MARK TWAIN"   [SIMON WHEELER]   "MARK TWAIN"

"Frog$_2$" becomes a Chinese box of quotations because in it "Frog$_1$" is quoted entire. Mark Twain frames the sketch at both ends with an introduction in propria persona. In the middle are three versions of "The Jumping Frog": the original sketch ("Frog$_1$"), Bentzon's translation of the Wheeler narrative (the *Revue* version includes the "Mark Twain" frame, but Twain omits it here), and Mark Twain's retranslation of Bentzon. In the following diagram, MT = Mark Twain, SW = Simon Wheeler, $\{\ \}_F$ = French translation, $\{\ \}_E$ = English translation:

$$MT\ [\{Frog_1\}\ \{SW\}_F\ \{SW_F\}_E]\ MT$$

The core of "Frog$_1$" was Simon Wheeler's narrative; the core of "Frog$_2$" is Bentzon's gallicized Simon Wheeler. Like Wheeler, Bentzon had presented her narrative with "impressive earnestness and sincerity," without imagining "there was anything ridiculous or funny" about the translation qua translation. By framing Bentzon's translation with the original on one side and Twain's purposely wretched Englishing on the other, "Frog$_2$" asks the reader to find Bentzon funny as a story-teller just as we find Simon Wheeler funny. The most important general implication of the sketch is that Simon Wheeler—and therefore Mark Twain—*cannot exist in French*, because direct discourse can never be preserved in translation.[24] The quotation marks in Bentzon's translation are misleading, in a sense, because her "Simon Wheeler" is her own creation and speaks her own words. (Twain was not yet ready to affirm the more radical proposition that *all* quotation marks are illusory because there is no such thing as direct discourse, but he would approach this position in his latest works.)[25]

Twain's retranslation does not need the defense of a structural analysis to demonstrate its interest and its worth. Granted, the joke is carried through to the end with relentless thoroughness, but the reader who takes the trouble to read aloud will be rewarded with some of the funniest passages Twain ever wrote, like this one from the description of "André" Jackson, Jim Smiley's fighting dog: "When the bets were doubled and redoubled against him, he you seize the other dog just at the articulation of the leg of behind, and he not it leave more, not that he it masticate, you conceive, but he himself there shall be holding during until that one throws the sponge in the air, must he wait a year" (*WMT* 7:29). Twain's retranslation is not "fair" because he does not limit himself to parodying the formal diction and grammar of Bentzon's translation. Instead, he mocks the French language itself, purposely (or accidentally—the effect is at any rate the same) confusing tenses and pronoun genders and cognates ("the infinite misery" for *l'infinie miséricorde*—a blasphemous "error"), and perversely translating idioms word for word so as to make nonsense of them. Yet by making us stumble over the manifold awkwardnesses in an overliteral French-to-English translation, Twain forces us to ask whether authentic translation is ever possible. Clearly, American English and French semanticize the world differently—all the more reason why a French Simon Wheeler is an impossibility. Consider Twain's burlesque of the French narrative tenses: consciously or not, he seizes on an important difference between the English system and the French. English vernacular narrative has available a stylistic choice between definite past and historical present, the latter being freely used to convey a sense of immediacy and interest. It is important that Simon Wheeler never moves out of the past tense in telling about Jim Smiley (with the single exception of the colloquial narrative "says" for "said"). The reason is that he betrayed no enthusiasm for his story: "In his mouth this episode was merely history . . . he was drawing on his memory, not his mind" ("Private History of the Jumping Frog Story," *WMT* 22:101). French oral narrative, on the other hand, is much more likely to use the historical present, and indeed this is the tense Bentzon uses to recount the culminating frog-jumping contest. Simon Wheeler accordingly loses much of the deadpan quality that makes him such an effective narrator. Likewise, the cunning Yankee stranger loses his individuality in another idiom. The stranger's "I don't see no p'ints about that frog that's any better'n any other frog" rapidly became a national catchword after the "Jumping Frog" was published. So it is natural that the French version of this line drew Twain's particular irony: "What has a poor foreigner like me done, to be abused and misrepresented like this? When I say, 'Well, I don't see no p'ints about that frog that's any better'n any other frog,' is it kind, is it just, for this

Frenchman to try to make it appear that I said, 'Eh, bien! I no saw not that that frog had nothing of better than each frog'?" (*WMT* 7:34). Even a twentieth-century American, for whom the laconic Yankee has faded as a stereotype, may miss the humor in the stranger's assertion. In French, as a bare referential statement stripped of dialectal and social context, the stranger's phrase lacks all the irony that makes it the "nub" of the story in English.

A relatively minor result of Twain's interest in translation was his contribution to a genre that might be called language interference humor, the collection and publication of laughable errors by foreigners writing or speaking English. Each of his travel books contains examples: in *The Innocents Abroad*, a "notish" posted in an Italian hotel and a "placard fairly reeking with wretched English" in a Milanese museum; in *A Tramp Abroad*, excerpts from *A Catalogue of Pictures in the Old Pinacotek*, a German museum catalog "written in a peculiar kind of English"; in *Following the Equator*, specimens of "Babu English" showing Indians' "quaint imperfect attempts at the use of our tongue" (*WMT* 1:188–89; 9:128–29; 21:273–84). By far the most notorious example of the genre was José de Fonseca's *New Guide of the Conversation in Portuguese and English*, for which Twain wrote an introduction when it was reissued by Osgood in 1883. In all earnestness, Fonseca wrote a Portuguese-English language manual despite his wholesale ignorance of English grammar and syntax, apparently manufacturing English equivalents of Portuguese by translating word for word with the aid of a dictionary. First published in 1855, Fonseca's book had received widespread attention when "discovered" by English and American reviewers a few years thereafter. Twain's introduction celebrates the guide's "delicious unconscious ridiculousness" and "miraculous stupidities" (*WMT* 24:301, 302). Always for Mark Twain the fall of Babel was a *felix culpa* insofar as it made humor possible.

Often enough for Mark Twain, though, the curse of Babel was merely a curse. The beginning of his serious interest in foreign languages can be dated precisely: 1878, the year he and his family began the European stay recounted in *A Tramp Abroad*. Before that date he rarely gives any thought to his limitation as a monolingual; from 1878 on, his notebooks and letters are filled with accounts of his frustrations and minor triumphs as he studies German, calls upon his rusty French, and eventually learns enough Italian to get by. The biographical details of Twain's encounter with the "awful German language" are amply provided in John Krumpelmann's *Mark Twain and the German Language*.[26] Krumpelmann shows that although Twain was a competent reader and translator of German by the time of his last stay in German-speaking Europe (1897–1899), he was never comfortable with the give-and-take of conversational German. Krumpelmann's study, however, contains little assessment of the effect Twain's knowledge of German had on his creative life. Ultimately Twain's direct literary use of German in *A Tramp Abroad* and elsewhere is less important than the sheer experience of continual failure to make himself understood.

"How charmed I am when I overhear a German word which I understand!" he wrote to Howells not long after setting foot on German soil (4 May 1878, *MTHL* 1:228). His initial delight was not to last long. As he found that book knowledge of German was not enough to enable him to capture the living word in transit, his comments on German took a different tone: "Drat this German tongue, I never shall be able to learn it. I think I could learn a little conversational stuff, maybe, if I could attend to it, but I found I couldn't spare the time. I took lessons two weeks & got so I could understand the talk going on around me, & even answer back, after a fashion. But I neither talk nor listen, now, so I can't even understand the language any more" (27 June 1878, *MTHL* 1:237). Twain confided most of his frustration to his notebook. In the notebooks he kept from May through September 1878, alongside material that he would work up for use in *A Tramp Abroad* one finds a diary of his struggles with languages. Given the scarcity of overt attention to language in the preceding notebooks, the density of references now is striking:

John Hay attempting German with a stranger all day, on a dili-
gence—finally stranger (after trying for 20 minutes to frame a
sentence,) "Oh, God damn the language!" Hay—embracing
him—"Bless my soul, you speak English!" . . .

Eavesdropping at table d'hote, in eagerness to learn the
language.

(NJ2, 80)

Godam godam language with 16 THE's in it.

(NJ2, 83)

Be talking in foreign tongue & be suddenly let down by running out of words—hideous!

(NJ2, 98)

June 19–Dreamed Rosa & Esel-woman complained in German
of Fraulein Bühler—good, fluent German—I could not understand it all, but got the sense of it,—could hardly scare up
words enough to reply in, & *they* were in very bad grammar.
Very curious.

(NJ2, 102)

I wish I could hear myself talk German.

(NJ2, 117)

Am addressed in German [in Switzerland] & say I can't speak
it—immediately the person tackles me in French & plainly
shows astonishment when I stop him. They naturally despise
such an ignoramus.

(NJ2, 119)

Furious at breakfast (Beau Rivage, Ouchy, Sept 4) have read
French 25 years & now could not say "breakfast"—could think
of nothing but aujourdhui—then demain!—then—& so on,
tearing my hair (figuratively) and raging inwardly while out-
wardly calm—one idiot french word after another while waiter
stood bewildered.

(NJ2, 170)

Given entries like these, we understand why Albert Bigelow
Paine wrote that for Twain the study of German "became a
sort of nightmare."[27] His experience was by no means unusual; surely the diaries of innumerable travelers have contained similar plaints. But this struggling learner was Mark
Twain, by now a world-famous author. Although he could
manipulate audiences at will through the artistry of his oral

delivery, he was suffering petty humiliations because he could not understand or be understood. His immediate reaction was to sublimate his frustration by transforming it into the comedy of "The Awful German Language"; a secondary bene- fit was a practical lesson in the inferiority of traditional for- eign-language teaching. But the entries quoted above suggest the outlets through which his subterranean "raging inwardly" would finally vent itself. Both in imagination and in reality, Twain is feeling what it is like to become a deaf-mute, a stam- merer, a mysterious stranger who runs out of words or who is despised as an ignoramus.

Beginning with *A Tramp Abroad*, in the comedy based on foreign language two basic modes of humor reflect corre- sponding insights on Twain's part into the nature of language. First, the rules that govern language are always potentially repressive; second, to paraphrase Talleyrand, "Language was invented for the purpose of misunderstanding." The first insight, translated into comedy, produces Twain's diatribes against entire systems of natural languages, while the second underlies the encounter between speakers who cannot under- stand each other. I do not wish to magnify the importance of these minor comic works, which are not among Twain's fun- niest or most interesting pieces (and I include "The Awful German Language," which strikes me as less skillfully man- aged than some readers have thought).[28] But I believe that un- derlying their broad humor are the same concerns found in more substantial narratives.

We must come back once again to Howells's remark about Twain's wanting to be "understood with the least possible per- sonal inconvenience," because its implications are profound. What discourse would in fact permit the absolute minimum of inconvenience? Only an unimaginable, instantaneous, tele- pathic transfer of thought from mind to mind that would by- pass the mediation of symbols altogether (see pp. 151–53). All language, all semiosis, is inherently inconvenient. To commu- nicate, I must map on a continuum of interior thought the discrete units prescribed by the grammar and semantics of the language I am using; the desire for immediate self-expression is frustrated by the prior existence of the rules that govern signs. Twain's burlesque of the German language—toying with its paradigms, throwing happy chaos into its syntax—is a temporary victory of the pleasure principle over the reality that language is always an imposition.

Twain made his first literary use of German barely more than a month after arriving in Germany, in the form of a "Fourth of July Oration in the German Tongue" delivered at a banquet of the Anglo-American Club of Heidelberg; this speech is appended to "The Awful German Language," itself Appendix D of *A Tramp Abroad*. The prevailing tone of this address is cheerfully comic. Twain is not so much satirizing German as toying with it, proclaiming his own verbal independence, enjoying his ability to make puns and plays on words: "Hundert Jahre vorüber, waren die Engländer und die Amerikanen Feinde; aber heute sind sie herzlichen Freunde." Once again a chief formal constituent of the humor is macaronic "interlarding": "Sie müssen so freundlich sein, und verzeih mich die interlarding von ein oder zwei Englischer Worte, hie und da, denn ich finde dass die deutsche is not a very copious language, and so when you've really got anything to say, you've got to draw on a language that can stand the strain" (*WMT* 10:283). The authoritative rigors of standard German are not at issue in this brief speech. But the rest of "The Awful German Language" denies the authority of the language in any situation.

The tacit assumption of the essay is that there is, or ought to be, a language that expresses thought naturally, logically, and independently of troublesome categories of grammar. Twain's humor depends on the assumption that German more obviously than English violates these requirements. Thus German sentences are constructed "backward" because the verb appears at the end; the root and the particle of separable verbs are put at intolerable distances from each other; gender is assigned in total defiance of biology; and the wealth of case endings is a needless multiplication of meaningless forms. Facts about German are presented as if they were self-evidently absurd. It is supposed to be clear that the table for adjectival declension is horrifying or that no self-respecting word should have as many meanings as *Zug*. (The humor requires us to ignore similar complexities in English; *get* is no less tricky than *Zug*.) Twain is at his most penetrating when he explores, as he had in the revised "Jumping Frog," the incommensurability between the ways that two different languages slice up the world. In a hilarious literal translation, the "Tale of the Fishwife and Its Sad Fate," Twain shows what would happen if we preserved the gender of adjectives and possessive pronouns when moving from German to English. Grammatical gender in and of itself is not funny, but its incompatibility with the neuter universe of English is: "See the Flame, how she licks the doomed Utensil [a fish basket] with her red and angry Tongue; now she attacks the helpless Fishwife's Foot—she burns him up, all but the big Toe, and even *she* is partly consumed" (*WMT* 10:274). Suddenly we conceive how alien to our mode of thought a gender system is, how animistic its picture of the world; to translate a language literally is almost automatically to defamiliarize it. Twain's farcical lesson in determining the case of a noun suggests how incompletely even a four-case declensional system covers the gamut of possible relations between subjects and objects:

> *The* rain is *der* Regen, if it is simply in the quiescent state of being *mentioned,* without enlargement or discussion—Nominative case; but if this rain is lying around, in a kind of a general way on the ground, it is then definitely located, it is *doing something*—that is, *resting* (which is one of the German grammar's ideas of doing something), and this throws the rain into the Dative case, and makes it *dem* Regen. However, this rain is not resting, but is doing something *actively*—it is falling—to interfere with the bird, likely—and this indicates *movement,* which has the effect of sliding it into the Accusative case and changing *dem* Regen into *den* Regen.
>
> (*WMT* 10:268)

Unfortunately, Twain continues, the correct form is *des* Regens because *wegen* idiomatically throws its object into the genitive. Beneath this nonsensical attempt to apply pure logic to grammar is the realization that any mode of cutting up the continuum of potential meaning is arbitrary. Simply because it is *articulated*, language produces the effect of the mechanical that Henri Bergson identifies as the root of humor.

When Twain reworked similar material into a speech entitled "Die Schrecken der Deutschen Sprache" he assured his German-speaking audience that he had never desired to hurt their "noble language" (*MTS*, 317). That is doubtless true of his conscious intent, but "The Awful German Language" gives occasional evidence of a hostility that is not simply exaggerated for comic effect. Twain devotes a paragraph to showing that "a description of any loud, stirring, tumultuous episode must be tamer in German than in English" (*WMT* 10: 279–80). He makes the puzzling claim that words like *Schlacht*, *Gewitter*, and *Ausbruch* are less forceful than *battle*, *storm*, and *explosion*. The German aspirate *ch* is usually perceived as harsh by speakers of English, and the preponderance of consonant clusters in German nouns is anything but "tame" to their ears. It seems that Twain is manufacturing a quarrel out of thin air, as he had in asserting that *Bigler* was melodious and *Tahoe* only odious. Twain concludes his article with eight proposed "reforms," his comic revenge for the troubles German has caused him. The last of these is a humorous version of the explosion at the end of *A Connecticut Yankee* that obliterates Arthurian England: "And eighthly, and last, I would retain *Zug* and *Schlag*, with their pendants, and discard the rest of the vocabulary. This would simplify the language" (*WMT* 10:283).[29]

"Italian with Grammar" (1904) is for the most part a pale imitation of the excursus on German, with the difference that it uses the language and attitude of Twain's old Western vernacular persona to ridicule formal grammar. Learning that the verb is the troublesome part of Italian grammar, Twain decides that he must "intelligently foresee and forecast at least the commoner of the dodges it was likely to try upon a stranger . . . get in on its main shifts and head them off, . . . learn its game and play the limit" (*WMT* 24:244). The fifty-seven forms of *avere* are Twain's prime target, as he plays Scotty Briggs to an Italian tutor's parson: "Never mind explaining, I don't care anything about it. Six Hads is enough for me; anybody that needs twelve, let him subscribe; I don't want any stock in a Had Trust. Knock out the Prolonged and Indefinitely Continuous; four-fifths of it is water, anyway" (*WMT* 24:252).[30]

More interesting is the companion piece, "Italian without a Master," which had appeared several months earlier.[31] The title plays on the popular *French* (and German, and so forth) *Without a Master* manuals but also recalls Humpty-Dumpty's famous thesis concerning semantics. When *he* uses a word, he tells Alice, it means just what he chooses it to mean. The question is "which is to be the master—that's all."[32] For Twain's sketch celebrates the interpretive freedom he enjoys when he reads Italian without the aid of either teacher or dictionary, assigning his own meaning to words he is uncertain of. (The first illustration in the *Harper's* text shows Twain seated in an armchair, reading an Italian newspaper, using an Italian-English dictionary as a footstool.) The "master," then, is any authority figure who insists that the foreign idiom be received in a prescribed way. Twain creates a linguistic utopia where one can play at being the "master" of an incomprehensible foreign tongue without suffering any of the ill effects that such an arrogation usually brings. It helps that in Florence he is literally the master of his household domestics. The sketch opens:

> It is almost a fortnight now that I am domiciled in a medieval villa in the country, a mile or two from Florence. I cannot speak the language; I am too old now to learn how, . . . wherefore some will imagine that I am having a dull time of it. But it is not so. The "help" are all natives; they talk Italian to me, I answer in English; I do not understand them, they do not understand me, consequently no harm is done, and everybody is satisfied. In order to be just and fair, I throw in an Italian word when I have one, and this has a good influence. . . . To-day I have a whole phrase: *sono dispiacentissimo.* I do not know what it means, but it seems to fit in everywhere and give satisfaction.
>
> (*WMT* 24:229–30)

Of course Twain knows that *sono dispiacentissimo* means "I am most displeased," precisely the language of a master who knows how to make the servants jump. But he is posing here behind the persona of a "powerful speaker" who can dispense with worrying about the needs of his interlocutor.

The remainder of the sketch describes how Twain, ensconced in the "deep and dreamy stillness" of the villa, subscribes to the Florentine paper, which he always reads unhindered by the dictionary. "Often I do not quite understand, often some of the details escape me, but no matter, I get the idea." A knowledge of French helps him recognize cognates, as he shows by translating a few short items. The words that elude him are no concern:

> There is a great and peculiar charm about reading news-scraps in a language which you are not acquainted with—the charm that always goes with the mysterious and the uncertain. You can never be absolutely sure of the meaning of anything you read in such circumstances. . . . A dictionary would spoil it. Sometimes a single word of doubtful purport will cast a veil of dreamy and golden uncertainty over a whole paragraph of cold and practical certainties, and leave steeped in a haunting and adorable mystery an incident which had been vulgar and commonplace but for that benefaction.
>
> (WMT 24:238)

He illustrates with an Italian newspaper item, reproduced photographically in his text:

> Revolerate in teatro
> PARIGI, 27. - La *Patrie* ha da Chicago:
>   Il guardiano del teatro dell'opera di Wallace (Indiana), avendo voluto espellere uno spettatore che continuava a fumare malgrado il divicto, questo spalleggiato dai suoi amici tirò diversi colpi di rivoltella. Il guardiano rispose. Nacque una scarica generale. Grande panico fra gli spettatori. Nessun ferito.
>
> (WMT 24:240)

Twain gives a confident translation; only the word *spalleggiato* has baffled him.[33] But "this is where you revel," for the word is so obscure as to be susceptible to any and all interpretation. The word does "carr[y] our word 'egg' in its stomach"; perhaps it means "egged on." The "egg" in *spalleggiato* is Humpty-Dumpty, as it were, sitting in the midst of the alien word, coping with its otherness by reducing it to the lowly familiar. The humorist resists the constant insistence that the Other's word be understood according to the Other's rules, playfully subverting the purpose of dictionaries and grammars, to provide rules for mapping out a one-to-one correspondence between idioms. Carried to its logical extreme, the unruly semantic theory of Humpty-Dumpty and "Mark Twain" entails that every word can mean anything, since by following either a metonymic or a metaphoric chain one can make every signifier identical with every other. Adherents to this theory are either malaprops or misanthropes, willfully ignoring discourse communities when they assign their individual interpretations. So these people themselves as much as the idioms they burlesque are the object of Twain's humor: the Twain persona here, too lazy to look up *spalleggiato*; the aggressive monolinguals in the travel narratives blithely unconcerned about the reception of their English; Tom Sawyer casually misconstruing the vocabulary of romantic fiction while using it to show off.

Mark Twain's most substantive criticism of the grammar books and language manuals was that in teaching a language through formal grammatical analysis or arbitrarily structured dialogues, they themselves impeded the acquisition of the foreign tongue. From personal experience he had learned that the paradigms and exercises in the books were of little use in helping him to "get into the man himself, the man of another country":

> The idiotic fashion in America of teaching pupils only to read & write a foreign language—this *was* actually the case at Vassar, one of the first if not *the* first Female college in America. There may be a justifiable reason for this—God knows what it it is. Any fool can teach *himself* to read a language—the only valuable thing a school can do is teach him how to *speak* it.
>
> In the German gymnasiums they even compel the pupil to speak Latin & Greek.
>
> (*NJ2*, 184)

Twain's criticism of traditional grammar-based methods of teaching foreign languages would be increasingly echoed dur-

ing the last quarter of the nineteenth century. The most important advocate of reform in language teaching was the Frenchman François Gouin. Works on the methodology of teaching
language still refer to his *Art of Teaching and Studying Languages* (1880; English translation 1892).[34] Twain noted the title
and publisher of the English edition in his notebook in July
1892; if he did obtain the book, he must have appreciated the
horrific struggle with German that had led Gouin to formu-
late his own method of language instruction.[35] Wishing to
study in German universities, Gouin had set out to teach himself German via the traditional formal deductive method:

> For the study of languages I knew but one process—a process
> without any particular name—the classical process. My faith
> in the grammar, the dictionary, the translation from and into
> the foreign language, was entire and above suspicion. . . . To
> learn first words, then the rules for grouping these words, and
> of these to make up sentences, this seemed to me to include
> the whole art, the whole secret, the whole philosophy of the
> teaching of languages. Was it not thus that I had learnt Latin
> myself, and had afterwards taught it to others?[36]

So he "devoured" German grammar in a week, memorized the
irregular verbs in two days, and then attended his first German
lecture. He understood nothing. The problem, he concluded,
was vocabulary; so he bought a list of German verbal and
nominal "roots," memorized them in four days, and went
back to the lecture hall. Again he understood not a syllable.
Deciding he needed structured lessons, he bought a copy of
Ollendorff's German version of the "New Method for Learning to Read, Write, and Speak a Language in Six Months,"
which he managed to master in only a month. Then he spent
a week in Berlin attending lectures for eight hours a day—
understanding nothing. Finally he made the heroic resolution
to learn the entire German dictionary and memorized three
hundred pages—thirty thousand words—in thirty days.
(There is no reason to doubt Gouin's claim to a near-eidetic
memory.) At last prepared, as he thought, to understand German, he attended his lecture and "understood not a word—
not a single word!" He assures the reader that he means what

he says literally.[37] Gouin's mistake, of course, had been to think that knowledge of the written language would confer a knowledge of the spoken: the ear, not the eye, was the "receptive organ of language."

Gouin's experience moved him to devise the "Natural Method" of language instruction, which subordinated paradigms and memorization to dialogues anchored in a specific, practical, social context. Twain understood intuitively that lack of a context was a shortcoming of traditional language instruction, and in his humorous way he prefigures the work of serious revisionists of language teaching. In "Italian with Grammar" he complains to his teacher about verb paradigms: "They say *I have, thou has, he has,* and so on, but they don't say *what.* It will be better, and more definite, if they have something to have; just an object you know, a something—anything will do; anything that will give the listener a sort of personal as well as grammatical interest in their joys and complaints, you see" (*WMT* 24:248). But his most extended satire of language teaching is the comedy *Meisterschaft: In Three Acts,* written for and performed by friends in Hartford who were studying German with Twain in the 1880s. Margaret and Annie, sisters, have been required by their father to spend three months in the country studying German; they may have visitors on the condition that all conversation be conducted in German. Their beaux, previously ignorant of the language, decide to memorize the Meisterschaft books to conform to the injunction. Since the girls are also novices in German and can only parrot what they find in their phrase books, the four must court in the prescribed dialogues of the Meisterschaft. "What would such a conversation be like!" Margaret protests. "If you should stick to Meisterschaft, it would change the subject every two minutes; and if you stuck to Ollendorff, it would be all about your sister's mother's good stocking of thread, or your grandfather's aunt's good hammer of the carpenter" (*WMT* 15:343). The comedy of the second act consists in the constraint on the young people to make such sentences serve as love talk. Far from protesting their restriction, boyfriends George and William embrace it, for as George asks, "Suppose we wandered out of [the text] and took a chance at the language on our own responsibility, where the nation would we be?" (*WMT* 15:356). In fact the girls complain bitterly when William skips over fifty pages at one point, and the boys call "no fair" when the girls switch texts:

ANNIE: Welchen Hund haben Sie? Haben Sie den hubschen Hund des Kaufmanns, oder den hässlichen Hund der Urgrossmutter des Lehrlings des bogenbeinigen Zimmermans?

WILLIAM: [*Aside*] Oh, come, she's ringing in a cold deck on us: that's Ollendorff.

GEORGE: Ich habe nicht den Hund des—des— [*Aside*] Stuck! That's no Meisterschaft; they don't play fair. [*Aloud*] Ich habe nicht den Hund des—des—In unserem Buche leider, gibt es keinen Hund; daher, ob ich auch gern von solchen Thieren sprechen möchte, ist es mir doch unmöglich, weil ich nicht vorbereitet bin.

(*WMT* 15:362)

[ANNIE: Which dog do you have? Do you have the merchant's nice dog, or the bowlegged carpenter's apprentice's great-grandmother's nasty dog? . . . GEORGE: I don't have the dog of—of— . . . I don't have the dog of—of— Alas, there is no dog in our book; so while I would like to speak of such beasts, it is impossible for me, since I am not prepared.]

Twain's themes of foreign language as nonsensical, as incomprehensible, and as rule-bound all come together here. The "little language" of lovers ought to be at least a dialect shared by two, at best a wordless instantaneous communication. Here the lovers' language is alienated in three respects: it is foreign, its forms are prescribed, and its topics are arbitrary. Beneath the specific satire of the tyranny of the Meisterschaft and Ollendorff systems, however, is the implication that transcendent love talk is a fiction because *all* language is part of a language game, part of a "text" already given to its users, from which one deviates at the risk of not "playing fair." Slight as it is, *Meisterschaft* asks the questions of the Shakespearean love comedies after which it is patterned: how profound can "love" be if it is generated by superficial phenomena of language, looks, and social conventions that do not necessarily correspond to any inward reality? Substitute *Herz*—or even the English word *heart*—for *Hund* in the above dialogue, and would the lovers really understand one another better? Babel lurks, Twain would come to realize, in every word of every language.

5

Not All Trying to Talk Alike:
Varieties of Language in Huckleberry Finn

> In this book a number of dialects are used, to wit: the Missouri negro dialect; the extremest form of the backwoods South-Western dialect; the ordinary "Pike-County" dialect; and four modified varieties of this last. The shadings have not been done in a hap-hazard fashion, or by guess-work; but pains-takingly, and with the trustworthy guidance and support of personal familiarity with these several forms of speech.
>
> I make this explanation for the reason that without it many readers would suppose that all these characters were trying to talk alike and not succeeding.
>
> —Mark Twain's "Explanatory" note
> to *Huckleberry Finn*

STANDARDS AND VERNACULARS

Conventional wisdom makes *Adventures of Huckleberry Finn* a declaration of linguistic independence and Mark Twain the Dante of the American vernacular. In the novel's opening sentence, one critic has said, "the American language was first used as the medium of great fiction."[1] Mark Twain might have written, "You don't know about Huck Finn unless you have read a book called 'The Adventures of Tom Sawyer,' but that is unimportant." Instead he let Huck tell his own story, in his own language: "You don't know about me, without you have read a book by the name of 'The Adventures of Tom Sawyer,' but that ain't no matter" (*HF,* 1). From the perspective of Standard English, Huck's speech is riddled with errors. But that perspective is impossible to maintain during a reading of *Huckleberry Finn;* since Huck is the narrator, his speech becomes normative for the duration of the novel. Read his narrative aloud, and only with difficulty can you resist modifying your speech towards your best approximation of Missouri dialect. Indeed, the only successful resistance is to close the book and retreat into silence. (This much the Concord Library Committee conceded when they refused to circulate their copy of the novel, complaining that "it is couched in the language of a rough, ignorant dialect, and all through its pages there is a systematic use of bad grammar.")[2] In compelling readers to mimic Huck, Mark Twain implicitly asserts that the narrator's language is a valid literary dialect. It is one thing, however, to claim with Michael Egan that Twain's novel teaches us to "speak Finnian" and another to infer that Huck's "depart[ure] from the polite cadences of educated grammar" makes us "co-conspirators in his subversion of our language."[3] In fact, Huck Finn's vernacular proves in the end a staunch, if unlikely, ally of educated grammar. After Robin Hood's fashion, Huck's verbal outlawry victimizes only those who usurp authority unjustly; it is ever ready to bow the knee to a linguistic Richard the Lionhearted.

Henry Nash Smith has taught a generation of critics to perceive a bipolar opposition in *Huckleberry Finn* between "vernacular" and "genteel" language. By *vernacular*, Smith tells us, he means "not only the language of rustic or backwoods characters but also the values, the ethical and aesthetic assumptions, they represent."[4] This conjoining of thought or values and language runs into immediate difficulty when applied to the novel, however. Surely, to take the most striking case, Huck and Pap Finn do not share identical "vernacular" values, although they speak roughly the same language. George C. Carrington, Jr., observing this paradox, has suggested that the distinction between vernacular and official, although "good as taxonomy, is inadequate in terms of the dynamics of the novel."[5] Carrington's structuralist approach to the novel has led him to the essential insight that good grammar and bad grammar do not correspond rigidly to good and bad morality, that the force of an "ain't" depends on context. But his criticism of Smith needs to be inverted: the problem with the dualism of vernacular and genteel has less to do with narrative dynamics than with the taxonomy itself. A better one can be devised. There are, in fact, two different vernaculars and two standard languages in the novel. Twain creates a linguistic universe in which the purpose and moral coherence of varieties of speech are more important than their objective form.

In *Tom Sawyer*, where the "shadings" of dialect are much lighter, the normative standard language is the dialect of St. Petersburg's ruling institutions: the church, the law courts, and the public school. In *Huckleberry Finn*, however, the standard is virtually absent. Almost nobody speaks what linguists today politely call Standard American English, what the nineteenth century more bluntly called good English. Nevertheless, Standard English remains, for both Twain and his narrator Huck, the understood symbol or outward sign of social authority. In Twain's linguistic economy, Standard English, like paper money, has no inherent value: it is worthless unless issued by someone possessing the fund of social authority promised by his or her language. A character like Judge Thatcher is "as good as his word"; his verbal currency is backed by moral gold, authentic social worth. A Tom Sawyer or a Colonel Sherburn issues words that look the same but are like notes on a wildcat bank: when we try to redeem them for gold, we find there is none in the vault.

Several of the novel's characters speak what I call *authentic Standard English*, which indicates merited social, moral, and intellectual position. Chief among these is Judge Thatcher, the sole character in *Huckleberry Finn* whose represented speech is entirely free from grammatical error or regionalism. Properly speaking, Judge Thatcher is not so much a character as a function: he serves as a polar opposite to Pap Finn, with whom he disputes the fate of Huck and Huck's money. Where Pap's heavily shaded dialect and scorn for literacy mark him as "ornery," an occupant of the lowest rung of white society, the judge's correct and colorless speech guarantees his respectability. The opening of the novel sets up a sharp distinction between civilized and uncivilized modes of behavior, and the judge's language is a convenient shorthand for "civilized." It is further characterized by semantic precision, as befits a lawyer. After puzzling out Huck's motive for wanting to give away six thousand dollars, the judge says, "I think I see. You want to *sell* all your property to me—not give it." Then he writes "for a consideration" on a sheet of paper, has Huck sign it, and explains, "That means I have bought it of you and paid you for it" (*HF*, 20). Judge Thatcher's careful discrimination between words illustrates the value of literate culture: attention to the fine distinction between written "sale" and oral "gift" will safeguard Huck's money against Pap's greed.

Twain's need to express social relationships precisely explains the inconsistencies in the speech of another minor character, Doctor Robinson of the Wilks episode. When he first appears in chapter 25, where his function is to debunk the King's imitation of an Englishman, his speech is eloquent standard American except for a lone colloquial "somewheres" (*HF*, 219). His speech in this chapter serves two purposes. First, it contrasts his authentic learning with the exorbitant pretension of an "ignorant tramp," the King, who is attempting to pass counterfeit oratory and etymology for current coin. Second, it establishes his social distance from the rest of the audience, since he alone recognizes as fraudulent the King's imitation of English pronunciation, still the model for elegant American speech in the mid-nineteenth century. In chapter 29, however, when the morally outraged town shares the doctor's suspicion of the "Englishmen," Twain has him slip back into a comfortable Pike County dialect: "Neighbors, I don't know whether the new couple is frauds or not; but if *these* two ain't frauds, I am an idiot, that's all" (*HF*, 251). From the point of view of mimetic realism Twain has erred, but in its context the doctor's language is appropriate in each case.[6] Lawyer Levi Bell and the unnamed doctor in the Phelps episode both consistently speak a heavily shaded dialect, reinforcing the interpretation that relates Doctor Robinson's unique use of correct English to the constraints of the fictional situation rather than to the typical speech of the small-town Southern professional classes. (The "jedge" who attends the "Royal Nonesuch" in Bricksville and proposes that the rest of the town be "sold" also speaks Pike County dialect [*HF*, 197].)

The absence of Standard English at even the upper levels of society in villages along the Mississippi accords with Twain's conscious evaluation of speech habits in the West and South. In *Life on the Mississippi*—written while he was at work on *Huckleberry Finn*—Twain is severely critical of the region's grammatical laxity (see pp. 22–23). *Huckleberry Finn* is the product of an author for whom correct speech is still a moral norm. Huck's vernacular—and this point will be explored at length—is "good" partly because the rules of adult society simply do not apply to it. The vernacular of Pap, the King, and the Bricksville loafers is "bad" because it represents corruption and degradation, either the "knowing" and "purposeful" debauching of civilized values that Twain complains about (*WMT* 12:223) or an atavistic ignorance that is even worse.

The use of "correct English" to indicate moral authority explains what is otherwise a flagrant inconsistency in the speech of a major character, Mary Jane Wilks. At first she shares the dialect of her younger sisters. Redheaded and "awful beautiful," she appears conventionally genteel, but her speech betrays her origins: "Take this six thousand dollars . . . and don't give us no receipt for it" (*HF*, 219); "It ain't right nor kind for you to talk so to him, and him a stranger and so far from his people" (*HF*, 224). For three chapters Mary Jane is kindly and sympathetic, but she is not yet a heroine. When in chapter 28 she assumes the moral stature of Twain's beloved Joan of Arc, she undergoes an instantaneous linguistic transformation.[7]

As the chapter opens, Mary Jane is sobbing over the fate of the household slaves, separated when the King sold them in opposite directions. While she remains an object of pity, she is allowed to keep an index of her vernacular: "Oh, dear, dear, to think they ain't *ever* going to see each other any more!" (*HF*, 238). As Huck reveals the details of the King and Duke's con game, sorrow gives way to righteous indignation, marked physically by "eyes a-blazing higher and higher all the time" and a face "afire like sunset" (*HF*, 239–40). Her speech becomes that of a dramatic heroine, losing all trace of

grammatical impurity: "The brute! Come—don't waste a minute—not a *second*—we'll have them tarred and feathered, and
flung in the river!" (*HF*, 240). More than pure, it is elegant:

> "Stand by you, indeed I will. They shan't touch a hair of
> your head!" she says, and I see her nostrils spread and her
> eyes snap when she said it, too.
> "If I get away, I shan't be here," I says, "to prove these
> rapscallions ain't your uncles."

Mary Jane has deftly navigated the modal waters of "shall"
and "will," thus escaping the confusion judged in *Life on the
Mississippi* to be endemic among Southerners.

Doctor Robinson's protean dialect and Mary Jane's sudden
grammatical purgation result from a conventional, as opposed to a naturalistic, handling of character, which is not an
error but a deliberate strategy, one that Twain would have discovered in English novelists from Fielding to Dickens. In the
British novel, as Norman Page has shown, "dialect is a variable dependent on the demands of fictional situation rather
than on the probable behavior of an actual speaker."[8] Oliver
Twist speaks like a young gentleman despite his origins;
Lizzie Hexam in *Our Mutual Friend* rapidly loses dialect features as her moral education progresses. In general, Dickens
follows a "convention of dialogue which deliberately sacri-
fices realism to moral appropriateness."[9] For the American
novelist there was a closer model, James Fenimore Cooper,
whose young heroines in the Leatherstocking tales rarely
share the rough vernacular of their male companions. In *The
Deerslayer*, for example, Cooper repeatedly draws attention to
the gentility of Judith Hutter's speech, absorbed from her
mother and preserved despite her having grown up in the
woods with an uncouth, illiterate father. So powerful was the
literary convention that attractive young women speak correctly that it is followed even in Twain's unfinished "Huck and
Tom Among the Indians," which overtly attacks other aspects
of Cooper's romanticism. Young Peggy Mills might as well be
Judith Hutter's twin: the rest of her family are the "simple-

heartedest good-naturedest country folks in the world," but she herself has read "considerable many books" and talks just like a Walter Scott heroine (*HHT*, 99).

For the virtuous characters in *Huckleberry Finn*, then, the standard language is a sign of affiliation with a natural aristocracy whose membership qualifications are primarily moral. Another set of characters uses, or attempts to use, correct or elevated speech in support of claims to an aristocratic station for which they are not morally qualified. I classify their deceptive language as *misappropriated Standard English;* it corresponds to what Henry Nash Smith calls "genteel English." This is language as sheer instrumentality, a commodity valued entirely for what it can accomplish.

To the Duke, for example, Standard English is merely the sine qua non of a professional confidence man, and his ability to wield it distinguishes him from the King, who like Pap Finn has barely emerged from the lowest stratum of drunkards and villains in frontier fiction. While the King is firmly locked into his own strongly marked dialect, the Duke, as an experienced actor, can modify his lightly shaded Pike County speech upward to achieve a reasonable facsimile of hypergenteel sentimental diction. He shifts into his formal register to establish his "aristocratic" credentials shortly after he meets Huck and Jim. His performance is flawed by an "ain't" here (*HF*, 161) and an "I reckon" there (*HF*, 178), but on the whole he is convincing: he can fabricate the high style as easily as he can a patent medicine. Thus he represents what Erving Goffman has called the confidence man's essential threat to the reliability of social indicators: "Perhaps the real crime of the confidence man is not that he takes money from his victims but that he robs all of us of the belief that middle-class manners and appearance can be sustained only by middle-class people."[10] Twain wrote to Mrs. Fairbanks after his notorious Whittier birthday speech, wondering why "anybody should think three poets insulted because three fantastic tramps choose to personate them & use their language."[11] Goffman's definition of the confidence man gives the answer: by *using the language* of the respected classes the confidence man undermines the belief of those classes that their language is ipso facto a mark of respectability.[12]

We ordinarily think of dialect imitation as a unidirectional phenomenon: a performer of higher social status mimics a dialect with low prestige for comic effect. The Duke reminds us that so far as mimicry is concerned, Standard English is as legitimate an object as any other. Twain observed in the minstrel shows of his boyhood the capacity of the professional showman to imitate in either direction:

> The minstrel used a very broad negro dialect; he used it competently and with easy facility. . . . However, there was one member of the minstrel troupe of those early days who was not extravagantly dressed and did not use the negro dialect. He was clothed in the faultless evening costume of the white society gentleman and used a stilted, courtly, artificial, and painfully grammatical form of speech, which the innocent villagers took for the real thing as exhibited in high and citified society, and they vastly admired it and envied the man who could frame it on the spot without reflection and deliver it in this easy and fluent and artistic fashion.
>
> (*MTE*, 111–12)

When used by actors and charlatans, "correct English" is void of moral value; it is one of an array of tools with which any competent social "performer" may achieve an effect.

Twain's description of the manners and speech of the minstrel show straight man is a coat that will fit Colonel Sherburn with little alteration. He "was a heap the best dressed man in [the] town" (*HF*, 184); his speeches to Boggs and to the lynch mob are courtly and artificial; and the ignorant villagers of Bricksville are cowed and impressed by what is essentially a set piece. Sherburn's address to the mob is, in fact, a dramatic performance, no less theatrical than the "Balcony Scene" from *Romeo and Juliet* that the Duke and the King have just advertised.[13] The high style in Colonel Sherburn's speech is marked mainly by rhetorical structure rather than by grammar and diction, which, though far above the level of the Bricksville patois, fall short of perfection. Walter Blair argues that Twain revised to make Sherburn's character more sympathetic by eliminating the "excessively rhetorical" passages in the manuscript version: "Colloquial phrasing is in character for even the leading citizen of Bricksville. More important, as revised the speech loses the highfalutin diction which in the book is a mark of insincerity."[14] The revision, however, is not extensive enough to produce a difference in the stylistic pitch of Sherburn's oratory.[15] In fact, too great an increase in colloquialism would have reduced Sherburn to the level of the parochial Western gentleman who uses "loose grammar" out of "careless habit, not ignorance," and hence would have discredited his self-proclaimed cosmopolitanism and superiority to the mob. Some critics are disturbed by Sherburn's denunciation of mob violence and human cowardice because they feel that we hear too obviously the voice of Mark Twain speaking ex cathedra. Twain's language it is, but Sherburn has misappropriated it, his cold-blooded murder of Boggs having eliminated his right to pretend to any degree of normative speech. His address to the mob is the supreme example of the misappropriated standard in *Huckleberry Finn:* the heroic ethos he means to project is in truth a persona, a mask, a role. The veneer of *Murray's Grammar* that covers his Southern village speech is the verbal equivalent of whitewash on a sepulchre.

If standard or "genteel" speech in *Huckleberry Finn* is not inherently "bad," neither is the vernacular inherently "good." Three varieties of vernacular speakers in the work are distinguished not so much by the form of their speech as by the purposes it serves. First are the figures like Huck, Jim, Judith Loftus, Aunt Sally, and the raftsmen, whose vernacular functions as part of a positive characterization. Critics speaking of the "vernacular values" of the novel have these characters in mind. I call their language *folk speech,* a term from folklore studies that suggests appropriate parallels with folk art, folk music, and folk narrative. The second category is the *speech of pretentious ignorance* (a phrase I borrow from Richard Grant White). This is the speech of the King, the Grangerfords, and Tom Sawyer—of characters, that is, who attempt to assert the authority of an elevated social class but who are not skilled enough to mimic the genteel style, so that they superimpose a few learned borrowings on a substratum of the vulgate. Third is *ornery speech*, defined by the depravity of its users, their low social position, and their active hostility or passive indifference to rungs higher up on the social ladder. Pap and the Bricksville loafers are clear examples. Whereas the linguistic unconcern of folk speakers proceeds from childlike innocence, ornery speakers are adults who knowingly choose vicious language. This three-way structural division of vernacular speech reflects similar distinctions in the writings of nineteenth-century observers of language, in both England and the United States.

Folk speech is a product of the romantic movement. It is a thoroughly idealized version of genuine vernacular, understood to be morally and aesthetically superior; rural rather than urban, it is the Adamic language away from which civilized society has fallen. Had Twain been pressed to explain why his greatest novel should be narrated by an ignorant runaway, he could have done no better than to cite Wordsworth on the "language really used by men" in rural life, which

> has been adopted (purified indeed from what appear to be its real defects, from all lasting and rational causes of dislike or disgust) because such men hourly communicate with the best objects from which the best part of language is originally derived; and because, from their rank in society and the sameness and narrow circle of their intercourse, being less under the influence of social vanity, they convey their feelings and notions in simple unelaborated expressions.[16]

From this conception of folk speech comes the lyricism of many passages in Huck's narrative discourse, such as the long description of morning on the river that opens chapter 19. Romantic as well is Huck's innate sense of linguistic propriety; as narrator, he is his own purifier, careful to avoid occasion for "dislike or disgust." Huck and the other folk speakers are not gentlemen and gentlewomen, but they *are* gentle. Folk speech is the natural language of the family, an androgynous language that gives force to women's speech while tempering male discourse. The women characterized by folk speech—Judith Loftus, Aunt Sally Phelps, Aunt Polly (to whose brief appearance here may be added her role in *Tom Sawyer*)—are matrons who serve as stable centers of households that actually or symbolically lack men. (Aunt Polly is a widow; Silas Phelps is an absentminded, ineffectual man; Judith Loftus's husband is gone when Huck arrives.) The promise of strength and protection in their ungrammatical, coarse-hewn speech is absent from the sentimental dialogue of their genteel sisters. Here Judith Loftus speaks to Huck: "Set down and stay where you are. I ain't going to hurt you, and I ain't going to tell on you, nuther. . . . You see, you're a runaway 'prentice—that's all. It ain't anything. There ain't any harm in it. . . . Bless you, child, I wouldn't tell on you" (*HF*, 73). Similarly, the violence of little Davy's raftsmen's slang is directed, in a parental way, against anyone who would unjustly harm Huck: " 'Vast there! He's nothing but a cub. I'll paint the man that tetches him! . . . Come, now, tell a straight story, and nobody'll hurt you, if you ain't up to anything wrong. . . . Overboard with you, and don't you make a fool of yourself another time this way. Blast it, boy, some raftsmen would rawhide you till you were black and blue!" (*HF*, 121–23). An oath in form only, Davy's "blast it, boy" is identical in emotional force to Judith Loftus's "bless you, child." Beneath the gruff exteriors beat hearts of gold; Twain owed more than he cared to admit to Bret Harte's benevolent gamblers and harlots. That Twain's slave Jim does not speak the exaggerated farcical dialect of the blackface minstrels has misled critics into describing his speech as "realistic" black dialect. It is, in fact, romanticized folk speech, purified of any forceful hostility that might, coming from a black speaker, have seemed threatening to a white readership even in the postwar North. (As we shall see in the next chapter, black vernacular becomes progressively more threatening in the works that follow *Huckleberry Finn*.)

The distinction between folk speech and ignorantly pretentious speech is stressed frequently in Richard Grant White's *Words and Their Uses:*

> Language is rarely corrupted, and is often enriched, by the simple, unpretending, ignorant man, who takes no thought of his parts of speech. It is from the man who knows just enough to be anxious to square his sentences by the line and plummet of grammar and dictionary that his mother tongue suffers most grievous injury. . . .
>
> Simple and unpretending ignorance is always respectable, and sometimes charming; but there is little that more deserves contempt than the pretence of ignorance to knowledge.[17]

White's categorization also helps relate language use to the moral evaluation of characters in *Huckleberry Finn*. The birthright use of correct English by members of the natural aristocracy provides one standard and "simple, unpretending" use of the vernacular the other. But woe to those who presume to a cultural authority they have not earned. Twain reserves his special scorn, in *Huckleberry Finn* as elsewhere, for social climbers of all colors who attempt to pass off flawed and inflated language as genuine merchandise, relying on a mannered style to cover hollow thoughts. In *Huckleberry Finn* the line between the vernacular of pretentious ignorance and misappropriated Standard English is not sharply drawn. Instead, characters can be ranked along a continuum, according to their success in imitating prestige forms: the Duke and Sherburn at the top, followed by Tom Sawyer and the Grangerfords, with the King at the bottom. Tom, the King, and the Grangerfords fall into the category of pretentious ignorance because their speech is essentially colloquial, with fragments of the genteel style pasted over it at irregular intervals. The humor in the treatment of Tom and the King derives largely from their misuse of language they believe will make a good impression. Speakers of the misappropriated standard are too dangerous to be funny, but the vernacular of pretentious ignorance continually deflates itself with needles borrowed from Mrs. Malaprop. The King, eulogizing his dead "brother," tries to cover up his reference to "funeral orgies" by insisting that "orgies is the right term . . . it means the thing you're after, more exact," supporting his claim with a ludicrous mock etymology (*HF,* 218). Tom wants Jim's coat of arms to figure a "runaway nigger, *sable*, with his bundle over his shoulder on a bar sinister"; pressed by Huck for an explanation of the last term, he confesses his ignorance: "Oh, *I* don't know. But he's got to have it. All the nobility does" (*HF*, 322). Ostentatiously misused Latinate vocabulary traces its ancestry in English comedy at least as far back as Shakespeare's constable Dogberry, but the King's discourse probably derives more immediately from the grotesquely error-laden stump speeches of the minstrel show.[18] This broad humor is achieved at the expense of a fully engaged condemnation of hypocrisy. More bitingly ironic is the masterful description of the Grangerfords' sham gentility. Colonel Grangerford's pretension to aristocracy is a realistic double of the Duke and King's wild claims to special treatment. When the colonel and his lady came down to breakfast,

> all the family got up out of their chairs and give them goodday, and didn't set down again till they had set down. Then Tom and Bob went to the sideboard where the decanters was, and mixed a glass of bitters and handed it to him . . . and then they bowed and said "Our duty to you, sir, and madam."
>
> (*HF*, 143)

> [The King] said it often made him feel easier and better for a while if people treated him according to his rights, and got down on one knee to speak to him, and always called him "Your Majesty," and waited on him first at meals, and didn't set down in his presence till he asked them.
>
> (*HF*, 163–64)

For the pretentious ignorant, fine language and literature are worthwhile as symbols of social status; for the ornery speaker these objects do not possess even display value. Books in the Grangerford parlor are "piled up perfectly exact, on each corner of the table" (*HF*, 137)—for decoration, in other words, not for use—but when the illiterate Pap Finn brings "an old book and two newspapers" to his cabin in the woods, they are to serve only as wadding for his gun (*HF*, 32). "Correct English" is foreign to this class of speakers, an intruder regarded with all the xenophobia of Know-Nothingism. Moreover, the compactness, energy, and penchant for meta-

phor characterizing folk speech are absent from this vernacular. Instead, ornery speech is marked by its tedious repetition; it is the language of the verbally damned, condemned
to walk forever in the same conversational circles. The Bricksville loafers, for example,

> talked lazy and drawly, and used considerable many cuss-
> words. . . . What a body was hearing amongst them, all the
> time was—
> "Gimme a chaw 'v tobacker, Hank."
> "Cain't—I hain't got but one chaw left. Ask Bill."
>
> (*HF*, 181)

The loafers' language is entirely formulaic. Their social lies
are so old and worn out that they "don't fool nobody but a
stranger"; their insults and complaints never vary. Pap Finn's
dialogue is comparatively animated, but it too displays an
abundance of the reiterated formulas typical of authentic vernacular speech: "I never see such a son" (two times); "Hey?"
(three); "You hear?" (two); "Looky here" (three), all of these
in the space of two pages (*HF*, 24–25). Pap's "Call this a gov-
ment!" monologue is marked by similar formulas, this time in
a narrative context (*HF*, 33–34). He stresses his reported dialogue with a constant "says I" and a defiant "them's the very
words." (These same formulas are also the most distinctive
feature of the "extreme backwoods" dialect of old Mrs. Hotch-
kiss on the Phelpses' farm, where they typify the "clack" of
rural gossip. But her dialect is not ornery speech, since its ignorance is handled with humor and sympathy.) Although as
Richard Bridgman has stressed, repetition is integral to the
narrative poetics of colloquial prose, the purely phatic repetition in the speech of Twain's lowest characters is meant to be
read as a structural weakness.[19]

David Carkeet has pointed out that ornery speech shares
several traits with the "negro dialect" of *Huckleberry Finn*. "In
Huckleberry Finn, gwyne, palatalization, and *r*-lessness are—
for both blacks and whites—physical signals of low social
status, and—for whites only—physical signals of 'substan-
dard' morals."[20] The reason is not far to seek: slaves are not

responsible for their low social status and marked speech, whereas whites are not only allowed but obligated to educate out the "infelicities" of their language. Standard English, back-woods speech, and black vernacular in the novel, all of which vary in significance, provide good examples of what Meir Sternberg has called the "Proteus Principle" in discourse theory: "In different contexts . . . the same form may fulfill different functions *and* different forms the same function."[21] Standard English and vernacular English do not possess value independent of context; their meaning depends on their structural function in a series of oppositions. In *Huckleberry Finn* we have a schema like this:

Virtue:	Authentic Standard (natural aristocracy)		Folk Speech (idealized vernacular culture)
Corruption:	Misappropriated Standard (sham aristocracy)	(↔)	Pretentious Ignorance (social climbers)
			Ornery Speech (debased vernacular culture)

(The arrow between Misappropriated Standard and Pretentious Ignorance indicates that these two forms shade into each other.) The contradictions and oppositions between categories suggest the traditional logic square for modal propositions. Indeed, we can redefine the categories to fit it precisely ("SE" stands for Standard English):

SE must be spoken	SE cannot be spoken
SE can be spoken	SE need not be spoken

Each group of speakers can then be described in relation to the deontic statement "Standard English must be spoken." Huck and his fellows do not defy the linguistic code; they are merely incapable of following it, speaking as they do a language ordered by entirely different rules. Their failure thus carries no moral opprobrium. Far more severely judged are those who are able but unwilling to follow the normative code and those who follow it out of self-interest rather than out of a sense of obligation. In the world of *Huckleberry Finn* logical contraries ("must be" versus "cannot be") can coexist, and Judge Thatcher and Mary Jane Wilks, bearers of the authoritative culture, can form common cause with the innocent outcast Huck.

These schemata help clarify the confrontation of the vernacular and the genteel in the novel. Neither Twain nor Huck is mounting a demotic attack on genuine high culture. Instead, the major conflict is between an idealized folk better than its real prototype and a debased pseudo-gentility parasitic on its prototype. The model also explains why Mary Jane can jump instantaneously from folk speech to standard without inconsistency: a positive moral component sets these two varieties of speech together against the three corrupted varieties. Moreover—and most importantly—the only "characters" in the novel who simultaneously understand the systems of both the ideal standard and the ideal vernacular are the author and his implied reader. As a naive narrator, a folk speaker who is outside the standard system and the values it symbolizes, Huck is likely to mistake what Emerson called the "paper currency" of "rotten diction" for the "good writing and brilliant discourse" that make words one with things. Although Huck can see through the "tears and flapdoodle" of the King's oratory, he stands for the uncritical mass reading audience when he is impressed by the sentimentality of Emmeline Grangerford's funerary poems. Only the intelligent, sophisticated adult reader who brings to a reading of the novel the entire complex of values belonging to the high culture can evaluate correctly the inflated and pretentious language of a Grangerford, a Sherburn, a Tom Sawyer. Only the literary artist Samuel Clemens, speaking elsewhere in his own voice, could fuse the standard and the vernacular to form the tertium quid of his mature colloquial prose style.[22]

CONVENTIONS AND
ANTICONVENTIONS

I want to return to the second paragraph of Twain's "Explanatory" note, which has received less attention from scholars and critics than the first paragraph: "I make this explanation for the reason that without it many readers would suppose that all these characters were trying to talk alike and not succeeding." [23] Why, even in jest, would Twain offer this reason for his note? Overtly, of course, he is defending himself against the charge of mishandling literary dialect—a charge he himself leveled against Bret Harte in public and in private. Covertly, I think, Twain is alluding to the great nineteenth-century educational enterprise of prescriptive language teaching, which took for its text Noah Webster's pronouncement that our "political harmony is concerned . . . in a uniformity of language." [24] Linguistic prescriptivism ruled over three domains—orthography, orthoepy, and grammar proper. But "talking alike" also involves unwritten rules or conventions governing larger, less easily formalized types of discourse. Rules of paralinguistic behavior, conversational turn taking, the cases when truth should or should not be told: these make up the bulk of the iceberg of language that lies below the visible mass charted by formal grammars. In a century whose only tool for analyzing the pragmatics of spoken language was the classical rhetorical tradition, the closest thing to discourse analysis is found in the etiquette manuals, whose rules were of course normative rather than descriptive: "Never notice it if others make mistakes in language. To notice by word or look such errors in those around you, is excessively ill-bred." [25] Mark Twain was always fascinated by the mass of unwritten rules that govern social behavior in general and language in particular. In public he would flout the rules by writing burlesque etiquettes, but privately, as his notebooks show, he was keenly sensitive to the norms governing conversation:

> After you have rudely (but heedlessly & unmaliciously) interrupted a narrative by breaking in with a remark . . . addressed

> to the person to whom you are speaking, apologize, but don't insist on the story being finished—let the matter drop & the subject be changed—the head is gone from the story & it only insults & further aggravates the party to beg him to resume.
>
> (Notebook 5, 1866, *NJ1*, 161)

> In N.O. [New Orleans] they always *interrupt*—conversation is impossible. One soon loses confidence & doesn't dare begin anything, knowing he will be interrupted with an irrelevancy.
>
> (Notebook 20, 1882–1883, *NJ2*, 470–71)

Twain transforms his irritation at speakers who abide by conversational rules different from his own into the humor of Tom's attempts to reason with Huck and Jim in *Huckleberry Finn* and (more extravagantly) *Tom Sawyer Abroad.*

Throughout his life Twain was interested in strategies and rules governing conventional speech events like the tall tale, backwoods boasting, after-dinner speeches, swearing, and so on.[26] The "grammars" governing such events are highly sensitive to context: for example, the pause that made the "nub" of Twain's "Golden Arm" story so effective would have been death to a dinner-table conversation. The conventions and rules that govern dialogue and speech event in the world of *Huckleberry Finn* are no less important than the "number of dialects" to which Twain draws the reader's attention. It turns out that his characters are *not* all trying to talk alike, because the conventions by which they operate are mutually exclusive. Characters ignore, misinterpret, or else seek to manipulate each other's conventions. It is no coincidence that we remember best from the novel Huck's lies, the raftsmen's arguments, and the exaggerated oratory of the King and Colonel Sherburn. We remember Huck and Jim on foreign languages: "'Spose a man was to come to you and say *Polly-voo-franzy*—what would you think?' 'I wouldn' think nuff'n; I'd take en bust him over de head'" (*HF*, 97). The violent legacy of Babel, in the form of farce (as here) or of tragedy (as in the Boggs-Sherburn confrontation), governs the frequent misunderstandings that occur along the Mississippi. On the few occasions when there is perfect understanding between characters (notably Huck and Jim, and Huck and Mary Jane Wilks), we are in a realm of idealized convention, like that of the ideal vernacular, that verges perilously on sentimentalism.

Huck Finn is in every sense an *unconventional* character. His rebellion against the conventions of polite adult society is the kernel around which other layers of his personality have accreted, as critics of the novel have observed.[27] In an important early passage we are shown that middle-class conventions of language, physical etiquette, and religion merge almost without boundaries as they are wielded against Huck's behavior:

> Miss Watson . . . took a set at me now, with a spelling-book. She worked me middling hard for about an hour. . . . Then for an hour it was deadly dull, and I was fidgety. Miss Watson would say, "Don't put your feet up there, Huckleberry;" and "don't scrunch up like that, Huckleberry—set up straight;" and pretty soon she would say, "Don't gap and stretch like that, Huckleberry—why don't you try to behave?" Then she told me all about the bad place, and I said I wished I was there.
> (*HF*, 3)

Huck's "bad" rebels against the "good" or "right" conventions Miss Watson is imposing—literally, ortho-graphy, ortho-pedics, and ortho-doxy. Appropriately, Huck's language is thoroughly unconventional, breaking rules of discourse at all levels. His "bad" grammar and pronunciation, markers of a traditional literary vernacular, are finally less important than his refusal to follow or to understand the conventions of ordinary speech acts and of speech genres like riddles and playful make-believe.

In Huck's speech, for example, the limited range of styles typical of uneducated speakers is exaggerated beyond the bounds of realism. Huck is virtually incapable of altering his speech in the direction of a prestige dialect; moreover, his speech lacks a distinction between formal and informal registers. He speaks to Judge Thatcher and Doctor Robinson just as he does to Jim; he makes no effort to alter his Pike County dialect when posing as a British valet, though the fervor of his effort to lie indicates that he wants the imposture to succeed.

Such inability to adapt to the demands of different speech situations is hard to reconcile with Huck's real, if limited, exposure to the language of schooling and literature and his awareness of the difference between the "quality" and the "ornery."[28] But Huck's limitation has a clear literary purpose: folk speech in Twain is characteristically innocent, averse to the role playing that goes along with the shifts in style adopted easily by the Duke or Tom Sawyer. To a large extent Huck's language is dictated by his long-recognized role as an "innocent eye," a naive narrator whose perceptions of social hypocrisy create ironies that he misses but the reader is meant to catch: "The widow rung a bell for supper, and you had to come to time. When you got to the table you couldn't go right to eating, but you had to wait for the widow to tuck down her head and grumble over the victuals, though there warn't really anything the matter with them" (*HF*, 2). Literal Huck does not understand the concept of "saying grace"—objectively, the utterance sounds like grumbling. The humor resulting from such gaps between literal and conventional readings of words and events is part of the "making strange" that is a fundamental technique of satire.[29]

But Huck's lack of socialization extends far beyond the structure of his lexicon. In general, Huck does not or will not understand linguistic processes that permit a dissimilarity between content and form. To use J. L. Austin's terms, the widow at the dinner table performs the locutionary act of uttering mumbled words. The illocutionary (or meaningful) force of the act, however, is "prayer" or "thanksgiving," a conventional significance independent of the content or even the intelligibility of the words. (A standard illustration of illocutionary force is the question, "Can you pass the salt?"—not a query about capability but a request for action. Huck's reluctance to understand Tom's "Gimme a *caseknife*" [*HF*, 307] as the encoded form of "give me a pick-axe" plays on a similar relation between apparent and actual meaning.) Huck commonly rejects the mechanism that gives a statement a force different from that of its propositional content:

Mary Jane she set at the head of the table, with Susan alongside of her, and said how bad the biscuits was, and how mean
the preserves was, and how ornery and tough the fried chick-
ens was,—and all that kind of rot, the way women always do
for to force out compliments; and the people all knowed everything was tip-top, and said so—said "How *do* you get biscuits
to brown so nice?" . . . and all that kind of humbug talky-talk,
just the way people always does at a supper, you know.

(*HF*, 220–21)

Far more tolerant than Molière's misanthrope Alceste, Huck
nonetheless shares his disapproval of the minor insincerities
that make society go.

In his dialogue with Tom, Huck demonstrates his hostile
unfamiliarity with several oral and literary genres. At both
the beginning and the end of the novel, Huck fails to comprehend Tom's make-believe; he does not care to will the suspension of disbelief required for the success of both children's fantasy play and the literary play of the romances Tom enjoys.
The opposition between literal Huck and quixotic Tom has
long been a topic of critical commentary. Critics have not
noted, however, that Huck's pragmatism is "vernacular" only
in the linguistic form it takes as idealized folk speech; it is
otherwise anything but commonplace. Tom's enthusiasm for
varieties of make-believe is "realistic" insofar as it exaggerates
in degree but not in kind children's actual behavior. Huck, on
the other hand, shows that he is an outcast not only from
adult society but from the subculture of childhood as well. He
has no idea how to respond to Buck Grangerford's riddle:

He asked me where Moses was when the candle went out. I
said I didn't know; I hadn't heard about it before, no way.
   "Well, guess," he says.
   "How'm I going to guess," says I, "when I never heard tell
about it before?"
   "But you can guess, can't you? It's just as easy."
   "*Which* candle?" I says.
   "Why, any candle," he says.
   "I don't know where he was," says I; "where was he?"
   "Why he was in the *dark!* That's where he was!"

"Well, if you knowed where he was, what did you ask me for?"

"Why, blame it, it's a riddle, don't you see?"

(*HF*, 135)

Huck does *not* see, because he does not understand the conventions governing the genre "riddle." (Specifically, the riddlic question must not be interpreted as a request for information but as an invitation to either "guess" or "give up.") For Huck, a question ought to be a question; the sheer gratuity of riddling is beyond him, as is the language's general capacity for play.[30] His comments and his own speech activities demonstrate that he thinks language ought to be instrumental, which in turn explains why he (like Jim) understands magic but not religion. Spells work automatically so long as proper ritual is observed, but when praying for fishhooks fails to produce fishhooks, Huck rightly—according to his logic—discards prayer as useless.

Huck's most strikingly unconventional linguistic behavior is his lying. Like his ungrammaticality, it puts Huck in conflict with superficial social norms while establishing his loyalty to profounder values. Characters in the novel stand in precisely the same relation to truthfulness as they do to Standard English; the schema representing varieties of lies and truths in *Huckleberry Finn* turns out to be homologous to the schema of language varieties:

Virtue:	Authentic Truth	Innocent Lie
	(Truth must be told)	(Truth cannot be told)
Corruption:	Conventional Truth	Vicious Lie
	(Truth can be told)	(Truth need not be told)

As the objective absence or presence of dialect features in characters' speech does not correspond to "virtue" or "corruption," so the difference between "good" and "bad" statements in the novel is not their propositional truth-value but their intent and effect.[31] *Authentic truth* and *innocent lies* are both beneficial, both dictated by the heart, not the reason. Authentic truth is an ideal realized in the novel primarily by

Mary Jane Wilks, who "ain't one of these leather-face people" and so cannot play a false role. The ethos of authentic truth makes truth telling a categorical imperative. Huck's mytho-mania, like the tall tales and boasts of the raftsmen, is an ide-alized component of folk speech; his typical lie has "no harm in it"—in fact, it "smoothes people's roads" (*HF*, 242). Huck lies because he *cannot* tell the truth in a hostile society whose values are at odds with his own. He himself shows awareness of the gap between moral ideal and practical exigency when he pleads with Judge Thatcher, "Please . . . don't ask me nothing [about the money]—then I won't have to tell no lies" (*HF*, 19). Only when his interrogator is Mary Jane does he find "a case where . . . the truth is better, and actuly *safer*, than a lie" (*HF*, 239). (Almost immediately afterward, however, he must tell a white lie to cover Mary Jane's departure, something Mary Jane herself cannot do.) *Vicious lies* are the genuinely harmful, self-serving deceptions of confidence men—the Duke and King at the Wilkses' provide the best example. Characters whose lies are predatory reject the morality of truth telling altogether. *Conventional truth* includes what Twain calls "gigantic mute lies" (*WMT* 23:162)—socially dictated "truths" like the institution of slavery or the Grangerfords' code of honor. This variety of truth figures not so much in dialogues as in the novel's overall semantics. Thus, to conven-tional truth the proposition "Jim is a runaway slave" is false because he has been manumitted according to the formal legal procedure. To authentic truth, relying as it does on transcen-dental sanctions, the statement is false because the term *slave* cannot be predicated of a human being.

If Huck's unconventional language prevents him from par-ticipating fully in the discourse of his society, it paradoxically liberates him to move more freely in the domain of language itself. If we take Roman Jakobson's six functions of language as a convenient typology, Huck's discourse would seem to be limited to the referential and the conative functions: he is in-terested in the content of his speech and its pragmatic effect on a listener (particularly when his speech is a lie).[32] Tom, with his interest in "style," presumably values the poetic function of language, "focus on the message for its own sake." I would suggest, however, that Huck's beliefs about his own use of language are as inaccurate as those about his "guilt" as a proto-abolitionist. In fact, Huck and Jim are the only characters in the novel who freely and joyously embody all six of Jakobson's functions. Huck thinks he is merely pragmatic and literal, but we who read both his reported dialogue and his narrative know better. His descriptions of the river and his account of his attitude toward Jim are fully "emotive" and "poetic"—that is, Huck's own feelings and the texture of his language are foci of attention. Huck is sometimes even "metalingual," as when he evaluates the King's imitation of an Englishman or condemns the graffiti in the floating house as "the ignorantest kind of words" (*HF*, 61).

The limitations of other characters can be related to Jakobson's categories, although his scheme of six basic language functions must be elaborated by combining it with a moral axis. (Referential language can be true or false; emotive language sincere or insincere; conative language manipulative or empathetic; phatic language perfunctory or affectionate.) The language of the Bricksville loafers is stripped of all but its phatic function, "we exist" the sum of its referential content. Tom values the emotive and poetic functions to the exclusion of the conative; his delight in the "evasion" derives from a self-centered aesthetic, for he lacks Huck's concern about the effect of his words on his hearers. Tom is thus incapable of an apology, particularly one directed to Jim. The best he can do is offer a payment that substitutes for words ("Tom give Jim forty dollars for being prisoner for us so patient" [*HF*, 360]). The Duke and the King, on the other hand, value only the conative function, which allows them to manipulate others. For the Duke, Hamlet's soliloquy signifies money; so long as he "fetches the house" (*HF*, 178), it is no matter how Shakespeare's words are mangled.

These characters are not all trying to talk alike: Mark Twain's central linguistic insight in *Huckleberry Finn* is that the heterogeneity of language goes beyond surface features like pronunciation and morphology. Take, by way of contrast, Emile Zola's defense of vulgar slang in the preface to *L'Assommoir* in 1877: "My crime is to have had the literary curiosity to collect and pour into a carefully worked mold the speech of the people. . . . Nobody saw that my desire was to perform a purely philological labor, one that I believe to be of lively historical and social interest."[33] The naturalist Zola wants to transfer unchanged to his literary work speech that exists objectively in the working-class districts he writes about. Despite the apparent empirical pretensions of the "Explanatory" note to *Huckleberry Finn*, Twain's project was different; he created a literary simulacrum of linguistic diversity that exaggerates and stylizes the heteroglossic interweaving of speech types in real societies. In the process he created several pure types that never exist unadulterated in the world. Huck Finn, in particular, is a linguistic impossibility. He speaks an unfallen Adamic dialect that names objects as if they had never been named before.[34] His language is logically impossible, for it is a plenum, a fully functioning system, that is nevertheless innocent of the conventions imposed by the social roles that language must play. It is not, like that of Swift's Houyhnhnms, an idiom incapable of "saying the thing that is not," but it is one that speaks no evil. Roy Harvey Pearce has written of Huck as a boy who "exists not as an actuality but as a possibility . . . [an] ideal, perhaps never-to-be-attained type."[35] Huck is, in fact, an infinitely more human and humorous version of the Mysterious Stranger who was to haunt Mark Twain's later imagination, a figure whose transcendent nature makes him incapable of understanding ordinary human behavior. His speech reminds us that language, like any social institution, progresses only through the interplay between the fixed standard that crystallizes old visions and old voices and the grammarless voices, undergoing constant growth and flux, of the present historical moment.

6

Languages of Power and
Submission in *Pudd'nhead Wilson*

The decade between *Huckleberry Finn* (1884) and *Pudd'nhead Wilson* (1894) measures the difference between fundamental optimism and pessimism, between redemptive humor and tragedy. Mark Twain's turn toward gloom has been traced in many domains: increasing repugnance for human nature, despair of historical and technological progress, growing discontent with American civilization, fascination with deterministic philosophies. Only infrequently have analyses of this movement focused on language. The major exception is Henry Nash Smith's *Mark Twain: The Development of a Writer,* which documents a gradual loss of faith in the possibilities of vernacular values and the language that expresses them; after *Huckleberry Finn* Twain never regains Huck's voice because he has lost Huck's vision. To my mind, however, *Huckleberry Finn* celebrates linguistic variety more than anything else, and the "enemy" in the novel is whatever would repress that variety, whether straitlaced Miss Watson or unlaced Pap Finn, both of whom seek to cut off Huck's dialogue with important voices in his culture and his being. This celebration does not mean broad tolerance, of course; there *are* debased, misused, and immoral varieties of language. But Twain seems confident that language is a homeostatic system, that the free play of many voices will suffice to expose the inadequate ones, and that a character like Huck can listen to and record that multiplicity without losing his own integrity. This faith is principally what Twain loses in the years following *Huckleberry Finn.* In *Pudd'nhead Wilson* there is no central narrative consciousness, no Huck, to integrate the voices, because integration (in more than one sense) is impossible in Dawson's Landing. Dialogue has become a Manichaean struggle that must destroy one party or the other.

The tenuous moral boundary dividing "good" Standard English and vernacular from their "bad" counterparts in *Huckleberry Finn* was based on the assumption that some varieties of language can remain innocent of the corruption that affects others. Speakers of the authentic standard refrain from using their linguistic authority to suppress or exploit; the vernacular of folk speech is used in the interest of solidarity and companionship. In reality, as Twain knew, both the standard and the colloquial speech of the South were inescapably tainted by class and racial oppression. Compassionate though they are toward individual slaves, neither Huck nor Mary Jane Wilks questions the abstract institution of slaveholding. Jim retains the innocence of folk speech only by suppressing violent resentment against the slave-owning class and internalizing the categories that it uses to describe him. ("I's rich now, come to look at it. I owns mysef, en I's wuth eight hund'd dollars" [*HF*, 57].) While reading *Huckleberry Finn* we accept the hopeful premise that a sound heart can generate the sound dialect that, in T. S. Eliot's phrase, can purify the language of the tribe. Only when we back off from the world of the novel to judge it against historical and sociological criteria do we realize that a real Huck and Jim would have spoken languages more heavily influenced by the values and speechways of their society.

Pudd'nhead Wilson is *Huckleberry Finn* de-romanticized, a "dark mirror image" of Huck and Jim's world, as Leslie Fiedler says, without any "sentimental relenting."[1] Its Dawson's Landing is a town where idealized authoritative or innocent speech is so tentative and vulnerable as to be effectively nonexistent. The major oppositions between varieties of speech in *Huckleberry Finn* no longer obtain. Conflict between standard and vernacular has all but disappeared, at least so far as the white speech community is concerned, to be replaced by an infinitely less bridgeable split between white speech and black. Moreover, in the absence of significant moral distinctions among them, the major varieties of speech in *Pudd'nhead Wilson* struggle desperately for social power, with language a tool for preserving authority, mastery, or domination. As George Steiner has put it, "Where there is no true kinship of interests, where power relations determine the conditions of meeting, linguistic exchange becomes a duel."[2] Vestiges of authentic Standard English and folk speech survive in Pudd'n-head Wilson and Roxanna, but without enough force to create more than a potential alliance between the two characters; by the end of the novel they have opted for opposing forms of power, and they finish as adversaries. White speech is powerful by virtue of social sanction and becomes impotent only when an individual member of the white community is subjected to another's authority. Submission is the prescribed norm for black speech, which becomes powerful only when an individual black, through unusual circumstances, acquires temporary domination over an individual white.

In *Huckleberry Finn* Standard English was the prestige form of language whose authority was accepted as given by all who aspired to use it. In *Pudd'nhead Wilson*, on the other hand, the formal linguistic correlate of social authority is variable and open to negotiation. The "standard" language is that spoken by whichever social group or individual is uppermost for the time being. As the roles of master and slave, established citizen and "pudd'nhead" devolve on different characters, the expressive force of varieties of speech alters as well. Eberhard Alsen suggests that the mayoral election that raises David Wilson from marginality to power symbolizes "change from a society in which the power depended on property to one in which the power is based on popularity."[3] In Dawson's Landing, Standard English is a "property" without inherent value; its authority can be ratified only by the mass of citizens. The entire action of the novel is bracketed by two "elections," one that removes authority from David Wilson's speech, another that restores it. The power of authoritative language here derives not from outward form but from its acquired capacity to "elect," to choose, to define. Hence characters in *Pudd'nhead Wilson* do not, like the Duke or Tom Sawyer in *Huckleberry*

Finn, aspire to modify their own language but rather to have their language recognized as normative by others.

This major opposition in *Pudd'nhead Wilson* between languages of dominance and of submission, rather than between vernacular and genteel, has been prepared for in works as early as *The Prince and the Pauper* (1882) and as recent as *A Connecticut Yankee* (1889). In *The Prince and the Pauper* a beggar must learn to command like a king, and a king finds his royal peremptoriness useless. To achieve a semblance of authentic sixteenth-century English speech, Twain had read diligently in Elizabethan prose and practiced "finger exercises" in the form of phrase lists of archaic diction.[4] But he makes relatively little attempt at linguistic distinction between courtly speech and lower-class vernacular. (The major exception is his use of genuine rogue's cant for the speech of the band of thieves Edward meets with.) True, Tom Canty is able to pass for a prince from the start because he has, Quixote-like, become so infatuated with tales of noble life that even in Offal Court his "speech and manners became curiously ceremonious and courtly" (*PP*, 54). His major lesson, however, is in learning to give orders. At first the necessity of delivering commands is a nightmare to Tom, but as his usurped role becomes more and more attractive to him, he falls into a king's language naturally, as the fulfillment of the old daydreams in which he "did imagine [his] own self a prince, giving law and command to all, saying 'do this, do that,' whilst none durst offer let or hindrance to [his] will" (*PP*, 172). In contrast, Edward is incapable of abandoning his native kingly speech despite constant reminders that the rest of the world takes him for a beggar, and his inflexibility provides comic relief. Twain returns to this motif when in chapter 28 of *A Connecticut Yankee* Hank Morgan tries to teach the king the manners and speech that will allow him to pose as a serf. How would Arthur, clothed in peasant's garb, request hospitality of the master of a thatched hut? "Varlet, bring a seat; and serve to me what cheer ye have" (*CY*, 321).[5] One's habitual speech results from "training," but the ability to alter it depends, for Twain's characters, on temperament; ultimately we respect King Arthur for his rigid no-

bility more than we do Tom Driscoll, who learns obsequious-
ness so readily.

The language of command characterizes the "power figure" in Twain's work, a recurrent figure whose career James L.
Johnson has traced.[6] Power figures can be as courtly as King
Arthur or as bluff and vernacular as Captain Ned Wakeman in
his various incarnations. They have in common no regional or
class variety of speech but rather the assumption that language is an extension of the self that compels others to act.
For better or for worse, the language of command transforms
others into manipulable objects—even into prey, as evident in
the phrase that both a ship's captain and a former slave apply
to men who have fallen into their power: "You are my meat!"[7]
Yet as *Pudd'nhead Wilson* shows, once an entire group has become identified with mastery or servility, its manners and language tend to become ipso facto markers of social standing,
independent of the speakers who employ them. From its association with slavery, black vernacular is taken to be inherently inferior. Thus to Valet de Chambre, revealed as Judge
Driscoll's true heir, the white man's parlor holds nothing but
terror because he speaks "the basest dialect of the negro
quarter." *Pudd'nhead Wilson* marks Twain's increasing awareness that the "empowered Self" is not self-created, relying as
it must on the authority of the social group to which it belongs.

David Wilson, the "college-bred" lawyer who emigrates from
New York to small-town Missouri, is the only character in the
novel who speaks consistently in Standard English. Yet on the
day of his arrival the town's citizens deny him the authority
his discourse ought to confer on him, because of his "fatal remark" about a yelping dog:

> "I wish I owned half of that dog."
> "Why?" somebody asked.
> "Because, I would kill my half."
> The group searched his face with curiosity, with anxiety
> even, but found no light there, no expression that they could
> read. . . . One said—

"'Pears to be a fool."
"'Pears?" said another. "*Is*, I reckon you better say."

(*PW*, 5)

The villagers puzzle over Wilson's "folly": if he killed half a dog, the other half would die, too, and he would be responsible for the entire dog. The "jury" submits its findings: Wilson is a lummox, a "labrick," a "dam fool," a "perfect jackass":

"And it ain't going too far to say he is a pudd'nhead. If he ain't a pudd'nhead, I ain't no judge, that's all."
Mr. Wilson stood elected. . . . Within a week he had lost his first name; Pudd'nhead took its place. . . . That first day's verdict made him a fool.

(*PW*, 6)

Critics discussing this episode have focused on the curious misinterpretation by Dawson's Landing citizens of a witticism that was commonplace on the Southwest frontier.[8] Their literal-mindedness is no less exaggerated than Huck's, but it serves a different purpose. While Huck is merely an observer, the citizens are judges. Confronted by a form of language that is opaque to them, they determine to rule its creator out of social existence. Rejecting Wilson's ironic speech act, they assert that the normative and authoritative speech act in Dawson's Landing is the performative utterance. The first reaction to Wilson is tentative: "'Pears to be a fool." A constative utterance, one asserting a truth-value, it allows for the possibility of error; the folly predicated of Wilson exists independent of the observers, who may have erred in judging him. But the next response is ambiguous: "*Is*, I reckon you better say." On the surface it strongly affirms the existential truth of the proposition "Wilson is a fool," but it may also be taken as a declaration, "I pronounce [and thereby establish] that Wilson is a fool." By the end of the episode, the latter interpretation is dominant. Wilson is a "pudd'nhead" as a result of the performative acts of naming and "electing." As "judges" of the appropriateness of names, the citizens assume the power to constitute reality according to their own conventions. The verdict of folly here is the first in a series of constitutive judgments in which "is" really means "is declared to be": Tom is guilty, Tom is a slave, Valet de Chambre is "white and free," and so on.

The speech act most closely allied to power is the command, which the citizens of Dawson's Landing value far more highly than any prestige dialect or variety of speech. It is the first language that Tom Driscoll learns to use: "When he got to be old enough to begin to toddle about, and say broken words . . . [h]e would call for anything and everything he saw, simply saying, 'Awnt it!' (want it), *which was a command.* When it was brought, he said, in a frenzy . . . 'Don't awnt it! don't awnt it!' and the moment it was gone he set up frantic yells of 'Awnt it! awnt it! awnt it!'" (*PW*, 18; emphasis mine). Baby Tom, lacking perhaps the formal English imperative mood ("Give it") invents his own by making the optative mood serve—"I want it" means "do it!" (Popular speech recognizes the connection between the two forms in the formula "Your wish is my command," which can be used nonironically only by a servant.) Tom's first recorded speech as a boy is a command to his servant Chambers: "Knock their heads off!" (*PW*, 21). More genteel but no less peremptory is the melodramatic language of command that forms the natural idiom of the Southern gentleman. "Answer me!" Judge Driscoll demands of his nephew Tom, who has responded to an insult by taking the perpetrator to court, in violation of the code of honor:

> "You have challenged him?"
> "N-no," hesitated Tom, turning pale.
> "You will challenge him to-night. Howard will carry it."
>
> (*PW*, 60)

"You *will*": the modal verb of this formal imperative reminds us that commands function by overlaying one person's will with another's. The objective correlative of the judge's power is the literal will, or testament, that he revises to disinherit Tom every time his nephew is disobedient. The command is an object of desire because it seems to be a *magical* speech form: one utters a few words, a ritual formula, and one's wish is performed. The magical view assumes that the addressee is like the ever-willing helper of a fairy tale, like the genies Tom Sawyer describes, who "belong to whoever rubs the lamp or the ring, and they've got to do whatever he says" (*HF*, 16). Huck is the one who objects that the recipients of commands may have wills of their own:

> "If I was one of them [genies] I would see a man in Jericho before I would drop my business and come to him for the rubbing of an old tin lamp."
>
> "How you talk, Huck Finn. Why, you'd *have* to come when he rubbed it, whether you wanted to or not."
>
> "What, and I as high as a tree and as big as a church? All right, then; I *would* come; but I lay I'd make that man climb the highest tree there was in the country."
>
> (*HF*, 16)

Huck and Tom's brief exchange, which may easily be read as an allegory of the antebellum Southern racial situation, expresses precisely the conflicts in *Pudd'nhead Wilson*. What happens when the magical servant rebels? refuses to serve? worse, insists that the master become the servant? Murdered, Judge Driscoll can no longer command Tom; blackmailed, Tom follows Roxy's orders. *Pudd'nhead Wilson* is about Aladdin caught by a servant and thrust into his own lamp.

Because the only requirement for speaking the language of power is that the listener acknowledge the authority of its imperatives, it is indifferent whether the speaker is "vernacular" or "genteel." For Judge Driscoll, command naturally shapes itself into the pompous diction of the melodramatic hero: "Once more you have forced me to disinherit you, you base son of a most noble father! Leave my sight!" (*PW*, 60). Tom, on the other hand, tends to employ a cross between Missouri colloquial and breezy college slang when he is feeling self-assured: "Dave's just an all-around genius, a genius of the first water, gentlemen, a great scientist running to seed here in this village . . . for here they don't give shucks for his scientifics, and they call his skull a notion-factory—hey, Dave, ain't it so?" (*PW*, 49). An elegant formal register comes to him more readily when he is in an inferior position, begging favors or justifying himself with his uncle or his mother Roxy. Roxy herself shows no desire to modify her own vernacular once she has gained power over Tom; making a former Yale student obey orders framed in the slave's dialect is part of her revenge.

A language of command entails a language of submission. The differential power relations among white speakers in Dawson's Landing become irrelevant when white speakers and black speakers converse, for theirs is by definition a dialogue of master and slave. Conversation between black and white is a zero-sum game: interlocutors cannot share power; one must gain what the other loses. Thus the only alternative the slave can imagine is a complete reversal of poles, the slave's dream becoming the master's nightmare. As the master-slave relation between Tom Driscoll and Roxy is inverted, Tom learns to speak the language of submission while Roxy learns to command. In the eighth and ninth chapters of *Pudd'nhead Wilson* Tom's discovery of his true identity reverses his and Roxy's respective positions. Tom, who has used the language of command unconsciously all his life, realizes the full humility of submission; Roxy, who knows quite well that her native dialect is servile vis-à-vis white speech, exposes the theological pretensions of the latter: "Fine nice young white gen'lman kneelin' down to a nigger wench! I's wanted to see dat jes' once befo' I's called. Now, Gabrel, blow de hawn, I's ready" (*PW*, 39). Earlier, Roxy has "approached her son with all the wheedling and supplicating servilities that fear and interest can impart to the words and attitudes of the born slave" (*PW*, 37), declaring that having seen her "Marse Tom" once again she "kin lay down and die in peace." Her speech, with its echoes of the prayer of Simeon, accurately reflects the ideology of slaveholding that maps the biblical dialogue between God and His servant man on the dialogue between master and slave. (The relevant passage is Luke 2:20–30: "Lord, now lettest thou thy servant depart in peace . . . for mine eyes have seen thy salvation" [Luke 2:29–30].) Now the triumphant Roxy mocks the rhetoric of the slave's religiosity as she requires an act of worship from her former oppressor.

That her unchanged black vernacular becomes the vehicle of command makes Tom Driscoll's humiliation all the more striking; the harder he tries to placate his mother, the more pronounced his genteel language becomes. The racial antagonism of the scene is qualified only by Tom's not being really "white" but legally a slave. Several years after *Pudd'nhead Wilson,* Twain would rework the Tom-Roxy inversion in an even starker and less ambiguous form as the climax of the unfinished novel *Which Was It?* (1899–1902), in which the former slave Jasper acquires absolute power over the respected citizen George Harrison by revealing that he alone knows Harrison to be a murderer. "Dey's a long bill agin de low-down ornery white race," Jasper tells Harrison, "en you's a-gwyneter *settle* it" (*WWD*, 415). Like Babo in Melville's "Benito Cereno," Jasper dictates a charade: Harrison is to play master when others are present, obedient slave when the two are alone. Melville and Twain show that such assumptions of power by slaves are invariably tragic. Both *Pudd'nhead Wilson* and "Benito Cereno" close with legal proceedings that restore dominance to the white community; presumably *Which Was It?* would have ended with a murder trial and the resulting exposure and ruin of both servant and master. Destitute of social sanction, black speech can retain its authority only by force of individual threat. Ultimately the usurper gains nothing, because his or her individual rebellion simply changes white for black while preserving a linguistic and social system based on inequity. The irony, as Evan Carton notes, is that "the subversive act that Roxy commits against white society is . . . a confirmatory one."[9]

In both *Pudd'nhead Wilson* and *Which Was It?*, the reversal of roles involves linguistic shifts, whose mechanism is virtually identical.[10] Initially the slave's discourse is self-effacing, characterizing its speaker as an object whose only possible act of will is supplication. The master's discourse is domineering, and its content is wholesale refusal of the slave's requests. Reversal of power becomes effective when the slave first uses the imperative mood and is complete when the former master is given a lesson in the discourse of servitude. Roxy, as I have noted, first approaches Tom in chapter 8 with a consciously assumed submissiveness, what might be called "yas-massa" speech:

> "Look at me good; does you 'member ole Roxy?—does you know yo' ole nigger mammy, honey?"
>
> (*PW*, 37)

> "Oh, Marse Tom, de po' ole mammy is in sich hard luck, dese days; en she's kinder crippled in de arms en can't work."
>
> (*PW*, 37)

Self-reference in the third person typifies servile speech. The I, or ego, of independent adult speech is replaced by a form that suggests at once the slave's status as property and the myth of familial relationships that Southern slavery fostered. (Slaves are "mammies" or "uncles" to their owners, but at the same time "children" of their benevolent and paternal masters; third-person self-reference is common to both partners in a dialogue between young children and their parents.) Meantime Tom is unleashing a string of commands that had begun when he ordered Valet de Chambre to admit Roxy: "Face the door—March!" "Send her in!" "Cut it short, damn it, cut it short!" "Clear out, and be quick about it!" Once Roxy's resentment has provoked her to open defiance, she abandons her use of the third person for good, and moves toward the imperative through an intermediary series of periphrastic commands. (Instead of directly ordering Tom to get on his knees and beg, she reminds him what will happen if he does not.) Only after Tom has performed the symbolic action of kneeling does she use the naked imperative: "Git up. . . . Come to de ha'nted house. . . . Gimme de dollah bill!" (*PW*, 39–40). Tom, in turn, assimilates some of the self-abnegating qualities of subservient speech into his otherwise genteel dialect, as when he balks at begging on his knees: "Oh, Roxy, you wouldn't require your young master to do such a horrible thing" (*PW*, 39). The reversal is complete when Roxy asserts the power of *naming* Tom, altering his identity. He is really Valet de Chambre, she tells him, and he "ain't *got* no fambly name, becaze niggers don't *have* 'em!" (*PW*, 41). Moreover, Tom must not call her Roxy, as if they were equals, because "chillen don't speak to dey mammies like dat" (*PW*, 42). Alone of all the characters in *Pudd'nhead Wilson*, Roxy is painfully aware that both the language of power and the language of slavery are learned forms of speech. Immediately after switching her child with Percy Driscoll's she reminds herself that she must thenceforth remember to call her son Marse Tom lest she make a mistake that will betray her. She spends most of the night "practicing," and is "surprised to see how steadily and surely the awe which had kept her tongue reverent and her manner humble toward her young master was transferring itself to her speech and manner toward the usurper, and how similarly handy she was becoming in transferring her motherly curtness of speech and peremptoriness of manner to the unlucky heir of the ancient house of Driscoll" (*PW*, 16). And this practice, continued throughout the boyhood of both children, in turn creates the forms of speech they employ: the false Tom, addressed with submission, learns to be peremptory, while the new Valet de Chambre is broken and harnessed to the language of reverence.

Roxy and David Wilson are the two major characters in *Pudd'nhead Wilson* who escape, momentarily, the game of power that defines language for the other inhabitants of Dawson's Landing. Before they are caught up in the events connected with the murder of Judge Driscoll, they share the ability to use language playfully, particularly in ironic humor. Moreover, Roxy is capable of innocent language, by which I mean language whose aim is to represent experience faithfully, free from the rhetorical constraints that govern language in its conative function.

David Wilson is labeled by Twain as the ironist who descends on Dawson's Landing to be met with incomprehension, but to my knowledge it has not been noted that the village has a native ironist in Roxy. She enters the novel in chapter 3, engaged in a shouted colloquy with the slave Jasper (not to be confused with the Jasper of *Which Was It?*), who is planning to come courting her. Twain describes the conversation as "idle and aimless jabber," a "friendly duel" that leaves each party "well satisfied with his own share of the wit exchanged":

> "*You* is, you black mud-cat! Yah-yah-yah! I got sump'n better to do den 'sociat'n wid niggers as black as you is. Is ole Miss Cooper's Nancy done give you de mitten?" Roxy followed this sally with another discharge of care-free laughter.
> "You's jealous, Roxy, dat's what's de matter wid *you*, you huzzy—yah, yah-yah! Dat's de time I got you!"
> "Oh, yes, *you* got me, hain't you. 'Clah to goodness if dat conceit o' yo'n strikes in, Jasper, it gwyne to kill you, sho'. If you b'longed to me I'd sell you down de river 'fo' you git too fur gone."
>
> (*PW*, 8)

Arlin Turner has complained about the "slapstick" tone of this conversation and what he perceives to be Jasper's representation of "the Negro as a simple comic figure."[11] He misses the point of the scene, which is to show two black characters conversing unconstrainedly in the absence of tension and—more important—with no whites around. Twain reinforces this interpretation in the ensuing description of Roxy: "She had an easy, independent carriage—when she was among her own caste—and a high and 'sassy' way, withal; but of course she was meek and humble enough where white people were" (*PW*, 8). A verbal duel at once "aimless" and "friendly" is impossible between slave and white, because the slave must always calculate the effect of his or her language on the master. The duel between Jasper and Roxy is actually neither slapstick nor "aimless." Its flirtatious repartee is set in the black speech genre of "signifying," at which Roxy obviously excels.[12] Jasper's jest about jealousy is uninspired, but Roxy, like David Wilson, can produce an ironic jibe about a hypothetical case of owning something undesirable. Roxy is no more serious about banishing Jasper than Wilson was about killing his half of a dog. But one element of Roxy's irony is not under her control: slave discourse can never be truly free, for the master's definition of the black condition lurks in its terms, thoroughly implicating it in the dialectics of the master-slave relation. When she mocks Jasper's blackness and his status as a possession, she falls into complicity with the categories that enslave her.

For the slave, the only exit from the prison house of the master's language is physical escape from slavery. Roxy's voice rises to its greatest power and autonomy in the evasion narrative she tells in chapter 18. It is an interlude, a brief respite from the constant necessity to order or obey orders. (Roxy indicates as much to Tom: "I's gwyne to tell you de tale, en cut it jes' as short as I kin, en den I'll tell you what you's got to do" [*PW*, 85].) The escape narrative allows the slave to exhibit all the qualities of strength, initiative, self-reliance, and judgment that must normally be concealed by docile submission. Forms of the verb *know* are predicated of Roxy five times in the three central paragraphs of her narrative, and the proportion of verbs of action is especially high. Similar observations apply to Jim's escape narrative in chapter 8 of *Huckleberry Finn*, for the craft and competence Jim discloses turn him into a character entirely different from the superstitious object of boys' pranks in the first few chapters. Neither Jim nor Roxy manages to escape permanently from slaveholding society, so both must return to more calculated forms of speech, Jim to humble submission, Roxy to control.[13] Reentering the life of Dawson's Landing, Roxy irrevocably commits herself to the antinomy of power and submission. Her next-to-last speech in the novel is a command to Tom: "Shet de light out en move along" (*PW*, 91). Her last speech, made in the courtroom following the collapse of all her designs, is a desperate prayer she utters on her knees: "De Lord have mercy upon me, po' misable sinner that I is!" (*PW*, 113). Her personal rebellion defeated, Roxy has no alternative to supplication.

The irony that initially sets David Wilson at odds with Dawson's Landing stands above and apart from the dialectic of power and submission. Hence the iconic function of the aphorisms from "Pudd'nhead Wilson's Calendar" that preface each chapter: from outside the narrative, they mock its "tragedy" with their sarcasm, performing this function long after their "creator" has become integrated into the plot in a major

nonironic role.[14] The villagers of Dawson's Landing miscon-
strue Wilson's "playful trifles" by reading them "in the solidest
earnest" (*PW*, 25), unaware that the "is" of an ironic or fictive
speech does not adhere to the same criteria of existential
truth as the "is" of a referential statement. Unappreciated as
an ironist, Wilson turns to the opposite extreme of absolute
literalism when he adopts fingerprinting as a hobby. Unlike
linguistic signs, fingerprints are indices: they signify an individual by virtue of a natural, biological, connection. By themselves fingerprints cannot lie or be ironic; they are powerless
to do anything but refer to the person who produced them.
Incorruptible, they are immune to the vicissitudes of human
languages, as Wilson implies in his courtroom speech: "Every
human being carries with him from his cradle to his grave certain physical marks which do not change their character, and
by which he can always be identified—and that without shade
of doubt or question. These marks are his signature, his phys-
iological autograph, so to speak, and this autograph cannot
be counterfeited, nor can he disguise it or hide it away, nor
can it become illegible by the wear and the mutations of time"
(*PW*, 108). Fingerprints would seem to be the novel's one innocent language. Their "is" makes no claim to power: "These
prints are Tom's" is an objectively verifiable statement, not an
evaluative judgment like "this man is a fool." David Wilson is
transformed from ironist to victim of irony precisely when he
fails to see that in moving from "these prints are Tom's" to
"Tom is guilty," he deprives the prints of their innocence and
makes them one more judgmental tool by which Dawson's
Landing maintains control over its citizens.

Wilson errs in transferring the semiotic of natural signs to
the semiotic of language, overlooking the conventionality of
the meanings of words.[15] He claims for his fingerprint collection far more than its ability to determine physical identity:
his prints will, he maintains, distinguish between the guilty
and the innocent, the free and the slave. Pudd'nhead Wilson's
final speech, the novel's most dramatic imperative, adroitly
confuses semantic categories: "The murderer of your friend
and mine . . . sits among you. Valet de Chambre, negro and

slave—falsely called Thomas à Becket Driscoll—make upon the window the finger-prints that will hang you!" (*PW*, 112). Although the fingerprints establish Tom's biological identity as the child born to Roxy and the wielder of the knife used to kill Judge Driscoll, they do *not* establish that he is a "murderer," a "slave," or even a "negro." The first two labels are verdictives, constituted by a human *evaluation* of certain facts. And the third label cannot be applied without a similar evaluation, since biologically Tom is only one thirty-second part black. Wilson's brilliant rhetorical trope that has the false Tom's own fingerprints "hang" him evades responsibility altogether with a synecdochic substitution that eliminates the role of judge and jury in relating evidence to guilt and punishment. By coalescing descriptive reference with constitutive reference ("These are Tom's prints" versus "[We declare that] Tom is a murderer/slave/negro"), Wilson affirms the legitimacy of the social conventions governing Dawson's Landing, using a language of power that operates by disguising imperatives as referential statements.[16] My reading of Wilson's language in the courtroom scene, then, allies itself with critical interpretations that locate the "tragedy" of *Pudd'nhead Wilson* in David Wilson's assimilation into the dominant culture rather than Tom Driscoll's unfortunate fall.[17] Wilson's motive for moving into the axis of power and submission is more obscure than Roxy's, largely because Wilson was conceived of less as a character than as a "piece of machinery . . . with a useful function to perform."[18] His failure to supply a morally authoritative variety of standard language in *Pudd'nhead Wilson*, however, is consistent with the disappearance of authentic moral norms that distinguishes Dawson's Landing from the Hannibal of Twain's earlier novels.

7

Toward a Chaos of Incomprehensibilities

"We are not allowed to explain the text, it would confuse its meaning."

—Mark Twain, "Three Thousand Years among the Microbes"

Conversation between two characters who fail to understand each other is a major topos in Mark Twain's work. In the classic example, the dialogue between Scotty Briggs and the parson in *Roughing It*, refined Eastern theological jargon collides with brash Western mining slang. "Scotty Briggses" occur from the beginning to the end of Twain's writing career, from "The Dandy Frightening the Squatter" in 1852 to the Mysterious Stranger manuscripts of the 1900s. In the earlier instances, incomprehension usually results from mutually unintelligible social or occupational dialects rather than from different regional dialects per se. (*Roughing It* is atypical in its stress on regional provenience, but even there the West is identified as the place where at a certain historical moment, men from all classes and walks of life were mingled promiscuously.) This incomprehension is presented not as the rule but as the exception, which occurs when two speakers from different spheres happen to be thrown together and obstinately refuse to move their speech toward a neutral region of expressions, usages, and grammar understandable to the average person. Twain never abandoned his faith in the ideal of clear, precise, and comprehensible speech and writing, in the "right word" and the plain style, as his own prose attests. He would be bothered almost as much by Mary Baker Eddy's muddled expository style as by her doctrines. Once Twain has adopted "everyone is insane" as an aphorism, however, he begins to treat incomprehensibility as potentially immanent in all communication. In addition, he begins his abortive—incomplete or unpublished—attempts to embody in fiction the incommensurability between the human and the divine (or the human's idea of the divine) that makes conversation with God impossible.

Three general stages in the evolution of incomprehensibility can be identified in Twain's work. Their boundaries are indistinct, and elements of each can be found at every point in Twain's career. Still, a rough classification helps account for the unquestionable difference between, say, the broad humor of *Roughing It* and the dark irony of the Mysterious Stranger tales. The first stage, then, is loosely congruent with Twain's Western period; the publication of *Roughing It* in 1872 provides a good cutoff date, especially since *The Gilded Age* (1873) marks a new direction. During this first stage, when Twain was primarily a humorist, he used mutually unintelligible varieties of language to provoke laughter through sheer incongruity. When the dialogues have a satirical aim, it is generally the lighthearted mockery of folly rather than the serious indictment of social ills. The second stage begins with Twain's first novel, *The Gilded Age,* and ends in 1894 with his last major published novel, *Pudd'nhead Wilson.* This is his "heteroglossic" stage, when, as Bakhtin puts it, incomprehension is polemical.[1] Different classes speak languages that reflect different experiences and worldviews, as Si Hawkins's wife implies when she urges him to move to Missouri: "You are out of your place here, among these groping dumb creatures. We will find a higher place, where you can walk with your own kind, and be understood when you speak—not stared at as if you were talking some foreign tongue" (*WMT* 5:10). In the novels of this period, breakdown in communication leads to violence or ostracism: Pap Finn's brutality against Huck, Hank Morgan's war on British civilization, the villagers' dismissal of David Wilson as a "pudd'nhead." Features of this middle period reemerge as late as the publication of *Which Was It?* in 1902. *Tom Sawyer Abroad,* published in 1894, marks Twain's entry into the linguistic absurdity of the final phase, in which the basic mechanisms of all semiosis, rather than the particularities of individual dialects, create barriers to under-standing, and interpretation becomes a guessing game.[2] Inquiries into the connection between thought and language become more and more insistent. To appreciate how misunderstanding becomes philosophically "absurd," however, we must first return to the early works to see how it begins as pure comedy.

From the beginning Twain had a Rabelaisian feel for the inherent humor of slangs and jargons. Thanks to a wide range of occupations and reading, he was able to wield convincingly the specialized vocabulary of such disparate fields as printing, piloting, sailing, gambling, mining, law, medicine, and theology. Travel to the West, especially, exposed him to the shocks of languages and cultures that occur continually in a physically mobile society. If the Scotty Briggs episode in *Roughing It* is the master enactment of this observation—and Twain in introducing the story explains that Nevada had attracted adventurers from "all the peoples of the earth" and had therefore the richest slang (*RI*, 298)—we see him preparing for it with a series of finger exercises as soon as he arrives in the Nevada Territory. The earliest of these exercises, one of the first things he wrote after arriving in the West, opens a letter, ostensibly to his mother, published in the *Keokuk Gate City* of 25 June 1862. Since the letter has not been widely reprinted, and since the mechanical self-consciousness of the joke contrasts with Twain's later ease in handling similar material, I include the relevant section in full:

> Lo! the poor Indian, whose untutored mind,
> Impels him, in order to raise the wind,
> To double the pot and go it blind,
>   Until he's busted, you know.

> I wrote the three last lines of that poem, Ma, and Daniel Webster wrote the other one—which was really very good for Daniel, considering that he wasn't a natural poet. . . . Now if you should happen to get aground on those two mysterious expressions in the third line, let me caution you, Madam, before you reach after that inevitable "Whole Duty of Man," that you'll not be likely to find any explanation of them in that

useful and highly entertaining volume, because I've got that learned author cornered at last—got the deadwood on him, Ma—and you'll get no consolation out of him, you know; for those are Poker expressions—technical terms made use of in the noble game of Poker. And poker not being a duty of man at all, is probably not even mentioned in that book; therefore, I have got him, Madam, where he can neither trump nor follow suit.[3]

Alexander Pope (the first line is from the *Essay on Man*), Richard Allestree (the author of *The Whole Duty of Man*), and Mrs. Clemens are jumbled together in an interlocutor who misunderstands the speaker of poker-ese. Before long Twain will learn how to stage less contrived clashes of dialect. Behind his burlesque is the sense that any language setting itself up as a model is bound for a fall—or, to use the appropriate figure, bound to be trumped. "Authorized" discourse like the *Essay on Man* and *The Whole Duty of Man* leaves out the game and language of poker, which is, if ungenteel, nevertheless a systematic mode of self-expression. The metaphor of language as a game will recur again and again; Twain delights in showing that people use specialized vocabularies more to impress others than to convey information. He enjoyed most the sheer gratuitousness of such slang: the technical vocabulary of a game is as far removed as possible from cultural universality and makes no claims for any adherence to outward fact. Twain created a doubly removed dialect when in 1866 he recorded the dialogue of old whaling captains playing euchre. "What in the nation you dumpin' that blubber at such a time as this for?" one demands, and Twain feels compelled to explain that "those ancient, incomprehensible whalers always called worthless odd-suit cards 'blubber'" (*LSI*, 12–13).

For Twain the obscure jargon par excellence would always be nautical terminology, whether correctly used or not.[4] He was hardly the first writer to exploit its resources, of course; incomprehensible nautical characters can be traced from Ben Pump of Cooper's *Pioneers* all the way back to the Elizabethan stage. But Ben Pump and his predecessors are dominated by a presiding "humor," so that their language is a fixed, stereotypical key to their limited repertoire of action and opinion. Some of Twain's more briefly sketched characters are humorous in this Jonsonian sense, but generally speaking, an authentic person in a carefully observed social setting can be seen at the core of his stylistic pastiche. One of Twain's 1866 letters from Hawaii was "Mrs. Jollopson's 'Gam,'" an account of the conversation of the wife of a whaling captain who talked in pure whaling slang. After giving what he claims is a transcription of her speech, Twain explains, "Every section of our western hemisphere seems supplied with a system of technicalities, etiquette and slang, peculiar to itself. [The account of the "Gam"] is intended to give you a somewhat exaggerated idea of the technicalities of conversation in Honolulu—bred from the great whaling interest which centers here, and naturally infused into the vocabulary of the place" (*LSI*, 69). In this case a narrowly specialized way of life has created an entire society, of whalers and nonwhalers alike, segregated from the wider speech community by its use of an occupational jargon inaccessible to outsiders.

Jargon or technical vocabulary does not by itself create confusion. That ensues when interlocutors persist in using registers that are wildly at variance with everyday English discourse.[5] In the first prototype of the Briggs-parson confrontation, idiosyncratic speech reinforces the point that there is no such thing as objective perception. "The Evidence in the Case of Smith vs. Jones," an 1864 newspaper sketch, is the mock report of a trial for assault and battery in which accounts of a fight differ absurdly. It is pointless for the judge to demand that witnesses stick to a "plain statement of the facts . . . and refrain from the embellishments of metaphor and allegory" (*ETS2*, 16): the "facts" are products of the language that expresses them. The witness Alfred Sowerby, a vernacular figure, frustrates the lawyer for the defense with his inability to use the precise verbal formulas that legal convention demands for expressing a physical fact:

> [WITNESS:] "I see this man Smith come up all of a sudden to Jones, who warn't saying a word, and split him in the snoot—"

LAWYER: —"Did what, Sir?"
WITNESS: —"Busted him in the snoot."
LAWYER: —"What do you mean by such language as that?
    . . . Do you mean that the plaintiff *struck* the
    defendant?"

(ETS2, 15–16)

Sowerby's vernacular humorously undermines the defense lawyer's implicit claim that only legal language can properly and authoritatively transmit evidence. But the lawyer cannot be faulted for his own discourse, since in the courtroom formal legal language is the unmarked variety and vernacular the deviant. Twain arrives at the Briggs-parson configuration only when two interlocutors meet on relatively neutral ground, in a context that calls for a common, ordinary language. In "A Rural Lesson in Rhetoric," for instance, an 1869 newspaper sketch, a temperance lecturer dismays a trio of farmers by employing florid euphemism to ask a simple question: "[I hope] that you do not indulge in intoxicating beverages? . . . That you do not indulge in the inebriating cup?" Once the lecturer finally gets his meaning across, one of the farmers provides the "lesson in rhetoric": a lecturer ought to adapt his words to the capacity of the hearers (*FW*, 133–34). Rephrased a bit, this lesson becomes the "cooperative principle" that H. P. Grice posits as the basis of rules governing conversation; this principle assumes that in a given speech community, individual linguistic repertoires intersect like the circles in a Venn diagram and that interlocutors are obliged to remain, as far as possible, in the portion of their circle common to each.[6] Twain's early burlesques present the comic vision of a centrifugal society in which speakers retreat to the outermost diameter of their circles, like toddlers playing separate games in the same room, cheerfully oblivious to one another.

Critics have disagreed over whose "side" Twain takes in chapter 47 of *Roughing It*, the discussion between Scotty Briggs and an unnamed minister about the arrangements for the funeral of the miner Buck Fanshaw. Henry Nash Smith is surely right to observe that the narrator no longer has the point of view of "one of the boys," but it is less certain that he now stands apart from them and "identifies himself with the men 'of high social standing and probity.'"[7] Kenneth Lynn reads the opposite moral into the chapter: "The conflict between two radically different styles is the enduring drama of American humor, representing as it does a conflict between two utterly different concepts of what American life should be. . . . The anecdote makes it quite clear that . . . the narrator prefers Scotty Briggs's."[8] Both readings err, I think, by taking the dialogue too seriously as a model of class conflict. A realistic meeting between high and low culture would be characterized by a negotiation for power that is absent here. "Are you the duck that runs the gospel-mill next door?" (*RI*, 299): Scotty's first speech to the parson would count under ordinary circumstances as "fighting words," a refusal to yield to the upward pull on language and manners that a minister's physical presence automatically created in nineteenth-century America. The parson, for his part, would have recalled the etiquette-guide dictum that one should never speak so as to make another person sensible of inferiority. The humor of the passage comes from a suspension of the feedback that normally corrects misfiring conversations: neither party becomes angered by the other's failure to be intelligible, and neither sees that his own obscure discourse is contributing to the problem. "Well, you've ruther got the bulge on me," Scotty says. "Or maybe we've both got the bulge, somehow. You don't smoke me and I don't smoke you." "Your observations are wholly incomprehensible to me," the parson complains. "Would it not expedite matters if you restricted yourself to categorical statements of fact?" (*RI*, 300). Obviously Twain is "blaming" both characters for acting silly. We are more sympathetic toward Scotty because he is by far the more fully realized character of the two; moreover, Twain's major object in this chapter was to create a tour de force of Western slang, the success of which is certified by his contemporaries' appreciative response.[9] But the object of satire here is language itself, which creates as much opportunity for misunderstanding as for communication. At worst, an individual's language becomes a meaningless idiomatic verbal tic. Among the miners, Twain tells us, formulas like "You bet!" and "No Irish need apply" were often repeated unconsciously, "very often when they did not touch the subject under discussion and consequently failed to mean anything" (*RI*, 298). The second phrase was the dead Buck Fanshaw's "word," as Scotty says (*RI*, 305), and thus Scotty sees no incongruity in adding it to the "Amen" at the close of the parson's funeral prayer. One's "word" as discourse and structure of thought can be exclusive and even xenophobic. This sinister potential of social dialect, barely nascent in *Roughing It*, develops into a major theme in the novels of the next two decades.

Even in *Roughing It* violence and death of a comic sort are associated with misunderstanding. (Scotty and the parson are trying to agree on the burial rites for Buck Fanshaw. Horace Greeley's uninterpretable handwriting drives one man mad and is the death of another.)[10] In the novels of the middle period, however, incomprehension is as often as not tragic, as the consequences of Pudd'nhead Wilson's "fatal remark" have shown us. Those whom we cannot comprehend—or who cannot comprehend us—pose threats, as Jim implies in *Huckleberry Finn* when he says he would assault any black man who dared to greet him with *"Polly-voo-franzy"* (*HF*, 97). If we treat Jim's hostility as simply funny we forget that Jim *has* become violent over a misunderstanding. Remember his "po' little 'Lizabeth," refusing to obey his command to close the door, deaf—unknown to her father—from scarlet fever. "O, she was plumb deef en dumb, Huck, plumb deef en dumb—en I'd ben a treat'n her so!" (*HF*, 202). His sin is small enough, as sins go; Hank Morgan treats an entire population so.

In *A Connecticut Yankee in King Arthur's Court*, the mutual incomprehension of a Yankee and sixth-century Englishmen destroys a whole society. It begins comically enough, in confusion over vocabulary. (The language of Twain's Arthurian society, deriving from Twain's familiarity with writers from Malory to the Elizabethans, is one of the book's many anachronisms.) Hank Morgan, transported back in time, wakes to the vision of a knight in full armor:

"Fair sir, will ye just?" said this fellow.
"Will I which?"
"Will ye try a passage of arms for land or for lady or for—"
"What are you giving me?" I said. "Get along back to your circus, or I'll report you."

(CY, 51)

Hank's puzzlement, here and elsewhere, defies the authority of chivalric language much as Scotty's defied that of the parson's. But in *A Connecticut Yankee* Hank's defiance quickly becomes conscious and programmatic, and it is generally met with a physical, not merely a verbal, response. Superficial linguistic differences that provoke confusion in the first chapter or two ("Prithee do not let me." "Let you *what?*" [*CY*, 61]) are soon replaced by a profounder misunderstanding that stems from ideological divergence. The rigidity of "Arthurian" society (really Twain's image of European culture as a whole) is demonstrated in the inability of its members to assimilate new concepts and the words that denominate them. In one narrative sequence, repeated many times, Hank's efforts to make someone see from his point of view are inevitably frustrated by the fixed vision of his interlocutor. Fair dialogue under these circumstances is impossible, yet Hank's rage to convince persists, gradually becoming an obsessive need to win arguments at any cost. If his opponent does not know the rules of the game, Hank's "victory" can come only from the opponent's wholesale destruction. In chapter 33, "Sixth-Century Political Economy," his anticipated victory in an argument over wages is snatched from him because the blacksmith Dowley lacks what for Hank is the pivotal awareness that economic signs are not fixed but "floating": a given monetary value is not permanently tied to a corresponding real value in commodities. So Hank turns Socratic method into an offensive weapon, manipulating Dowley into pronouncing his own death sentence, in effect, by admitting that he has committed a crime that should send him to the pillory. At this point conversation breaks down altogether; no longer able to trust Hank, Dowley and his friends soon precipitate a brawl. On a larger scale this happens at the end of the novel when Hank proclaims a republic in language meaningless to a feudal society: "The monarchy has lapsed, it no longer exists. By consequence, all political power has reverted to its original source, the people of the nation" (*CY*, 469). The result, as Hank foresees, is war to extinction. Since the knighthood massed against him cannot comprehend the power of the weaponry he controls, it is futile for Hank to send a message proposing surrender. Like the God we will shortly see Twain blame for punishing Adam and Eve, Hank Morgan attempts to compel obedience by threatening his opponents with a force they do not understand. Nor has Hank ever truly understood his foes. Ultimately, *A Connecticut Yankee* inscribes Mark Twain's own incapacity to comprehend the medieval world, the unbridgeable gap (which illustrator Dan Beard has represented iconically [*CY*, 491]) between Malory's language and his own.

The first major text to exemplify "absurd" misunderstanding, *Tom Sawyer Abroad* (1893), suggests why it is so easy to see the last two decades of Twain's writing career as a desperate, misguided retreat from realism. Although characters called Tom, Huck, and Jim appear in *Tom Sawyer Abroad*, they are disappointingly unlike the trio in *Huckleberry Finn*. The plot Twain cribs from Jules Verne is painfully fantastic. (An evil balloonist kidnaps the heroes but is lost when he falls overboard during a scuffle with Tom. The three sail over the Sahara and have adventures with lions and tigers, caravans, and bands of thieves. The tale ends abruptly when Jim returns home to fetch Tom a corncob pipe and is caught by Aunt Polly, who demands that Tom come back at once.) It is wrong, however, to evaluate the novel as if it were a continuation of *Huckleberry Finn*. Although it presumes to depict real characters in real settings, it is in fact a precursor of the dream voyages Twain would write over the next few years. The distinguishing feature of Twain's dream tales is that characters in them do not share the same reality. As a fragment of Heraclitus has it, "They that are awake have one world in common, but of the sleeping each turns aside into a world of his own."[11] *Tom*

Sawyer Abroad is one of Twain's first works to suggest that all of us may be "sleepers" in this sense, with languages that express different subjective worlds. I read it as a philosophical fable not with any desire to elevate its position in the Twain canon but to clarify its continuity with the line of development that leads to the Mysterious Stranger stories.

"In *Huckleberry Finn*," according to William Lyon Phelps, "we have three characters who are so different that they live in three different worlds, and really speak different languages, Tom, Huck, and Jim."[12] This is even more radically the case in *Tom Sawyer Abroad*. In *Huckleberry Finn*, the three "languages," although stylized, were motivated by each character's social background. In *Tom Sawyer Abroad* the original tendencies of the characters are exaggerated, so that each represents a myopic vision of semiosis. Tom, as in *Huckleberry Finn*, is the most sophisticated, meaning both that he understands vocabulary, references, and figures of speech beyond the others' grasp and that he is slippery and protean—able to shift from one semantic category or mode of evaluation to another, whereas his friends commonly apply a single standard. Huck is more than ever the literalist, whose special idée fixe is that representations must be identical with represented objects. Jim takes over Huck's previous role as a linguistic innocent suspicious of figurative language.

In the story's first chapter incomprehension still has the satiric bite it had in *Huckleberry Finn*. Tom is trying to stir up the other two to undertake a crusade, explaining that "a crusade is a war to recover the Holy Land from the paynim" (*ATS*, 260). Huck offers moral objections: if he owned a farm and another man wanted it, would it be right for that man to take it? An indignant Tom clarifies: "It ain't a farm, it's entirely different. . . . They own the land, just the mere land, and that's all they *do* own; but it was our folks, our Jews and Christians, that made it holy" (*ATS*, 260). In this case, he goes on, it is "religious" to take land away from someone. Now Jim objects: "I knows plenty religious people, but I hain't run acrost none dat acts like dat" (*ATS*, 261). After more discussion in this vein, Tom gives up in disgust: "I don't want to argue no more with people like you and Huck Finn . . . [that] ain't got any more sense than to try to reason out a thing that's pure theology by the laws that protects real estate" (*ATS*, 261–62). The misunderstanding here has less to do with differing vocabularies than with incompatible uses of words like "crusade" and "war." Semantic representations of these words as Tom understands them would each have some such component as

[+ morally sanctioned]

that would be lacking in Huck and Jim's versions. As in *Huckleberry Finn*, the reader is meant to sympathize with the naive view that the meaning of killing and theft cannot be changed by a label, no matter how widely that label is accepted.[13] Yet this is the first of a series of arguments that undermine faith in the workings of dialectic. More radically than in the "King Solomon" debate of *Huckleberry Finn*, Twain implies that Socratic reasoning accomplishes nothing when disputants are divided by dissimilar languages or conceptual systems.

Social satire has nothing to do with Huck's naive belief that the states they fly over in the balloon should be colored differently:

> "Huck Finn [Tom cries], did you reckon the States was the same color out doors that they are on the map?"
> "Tom Sawyer, what's a map for? Ain't it to learn you facts?"
> "Of course."
> "Well, then, how is it going to do that if it tells lies?—that's what I want to know."
> "Shucks, you muggins, it *don't* tell lies." . . .
> "All right then; if it don't, there ain't no two States the same color. You git around *that* if you can, Tom Sawyer."
> (*ATS*, 270)

(Later on Twain repeats the joke when he has Huck suggest that to discover where they are, they keep a lookout for the meridians of longitude on the ground.) Like some of the paradoxes in Lewis Carroll's work, Huck's error plays with fundamental categories of logic and symbolization. One critic has analyzed Huck's mistake as an instance of "confusing the map with the territory."[14] The problem, however, is more complex. Huck knows that a map is a symbolic representation that is meant to translate geographical facts into two dimensions. In most respects a map is a formal diagram in which each component corresponds precisely to either a geophysical or a political reality. But the use of different colors to keep the states distinct violates the nonarbitrary one-to-one correspondence that rules the map in all other respects. Tom explains, "It ain't to deceive you, it's to keep you from deceiving yourself" (*ATS*, 271). But Huck, like Jim, remains steadfastly suspicious of multiply layered semiotic systems.

The story abounds in instances of humor or confusion arising from the discrepancy between signs and referents. For Huck and Jim there is no distinction between natural and artificial signs—both are supposed to correspond to their referents without ambiguity. Jim cannot bring himself to imagine how time can vary according to a difference in longitude, refusing to admit that hours and days are arbitrary demarcations of an undifferentiated continuum. Tom, scanning the horizon, announces that he sees camels through the telescope. Huck takes up a glass and is disappointed: "Camels your granny, they're spiders" (*ATS*, 288); he has not learned the rules for translating small objects seen through a telescope into features of the landscape. Huck and Jim are terrified by a mirage and even more scandalized by Tom's insistence that it "ain't anything but imagination" (*ATS*, 300). A naive realist, Jim believes that the lake they see *must* be there one way or another; if it can disappear, it is the ghost of a lake, and the desert is haunted (*ATS*, 303). Tom, as usual, is able to jump from one form of validation to another without difficulty, becoming confident that the third lake they see is real because the flock of birds heading toward it is a natural sign (or index) of the presence of water.

Metaphor, says Umberto Eco, is a "scandal" for any literalistic theory of language: "It is obvious that when someone creates metaphors, he is, literally speaking, *lying*—as every-

body knows."[15] "Everybody" does not include Jim, whom
Twain allows to exhibit an incomprehension of metaphor unthinkable in a normal adult. Huck has just cornered Tom by
forcing him to admit that he does not know what "welkin"
means, even though Tom has just used the word. Tom counters
that its meaning is irrelevant:

> "It's a word that people uses for—for—well, it's ornamental.
> They don't put ruffles on a shirt to help keep a person warm,
> do they? . . . All right, then; that letter I wrote is a shirt, and
> the welkin's the ruffle on it."
> I judged that that would gravel Jim, and it did. He says—
> "Now, Mars Tom, it ain't no use to talk like dat, en moreover
> it's sinful. *You* knows a letter ain't no shirt, en dey ain't no
> ruffles on it, nuther."
>
> (*ATS*, 281)

Protest as he will that his example was a "metaphor"—Tom
himself uses the term ("that word kind of bricked us up for a
minute," says Huck)—he cannot convince Jim that it is not
"sinful" language. He pleads as precedent a saying whose
truth he expects Jim to admit, that "birds of a feather flock together," but Jim observes that bluebirds and jays avoid each
other despite their identical plumage. If Jim's incomprehension is polemical, it cannot be aimed at any particular social
group, since figurative language is universal. We sympathize
with his ignorance, because on some level we *do* believe both
that metaphor is showy and that the deviation from ordinary
language separating humans from one another results from
our "sinful" human condition. Huck, Jim, and Tom are no
longer characters tied to St. Petersburg, Missouri, but characters in a semantic morality play.[16]

The conventions customarily governing discourse have
broken down entirely in "The Refuge of the Derelicts," a late
(1905–1906) unpublished story about one Admiral Stormfield, whose home is a haven for outcasts and failures, and
George Sterling, a young poet whose desire to interest the admiral in a pet project (a monument to Adam) is frustrated by
his difficulty in communicating with the old man and his
"derelicts." Characters speak the same language, but their

particular manias lead them to misunderstand one another. Conversation is treated as the art of manipulation; logic is valued not for its consistency but for its power to bully an interlocutor into silence.

The opening of the story is unusual for Twain, who most often prefers a traditional exposition that immediately identifies setting and narrator. "Refuge" instead begins with a forceful unattributed command: "Tell him to go to hell!" The sentence is curious in less obvious ways. It suggests that the reader has been thrown in medias res, has just overheard, say, the furious conclusion of a heated exchange between antagonistic speakers. The succeeding sentence breaks this frame: "'So *that* was the message the footman brought you from the Admiral!' said Shipman, keeping as straight a face as he could, for he saw that his friend the young poet-artist was deeply wounded" (*FM*, 162). The opening sentence, it turns out, is an exclamation reported at the third remove. The admiral had conveyed it to a footman, who repeated it to the poet George, who in turn has repeated it to his friend Shipman. And this tenuous chain of reported speech is part of a narrative about the abrupt cessation of dialogue: George had called at the house of the admiral, a stranger, and had been unable to obtain an interview.

In chapter 2 George succeeds in meeting the admiral, but their dialogue becomes increasingly an exercise in frustration. The eccentric admiral so ignores rules governing pronoun reference, assumptions about shared knowledge, and conversational turn taking that in the admiral's account of his Aunt Martha, George finds himself adrift, a "derelict" among the others:

> "She's been with me twenty years; ten at sea, and ten here on land. She has mothered Jimmy ever since she was a baby."
>
> "Ever since—since—*she* was a baby?"
>
> "Certainly. Didn't I just say it?"
>
> "I know; but I mean, *which* she?"
>
> "*Which* she? What are you talking about with your *which* she?"
>
> "I—well, I don't quite know. I mean the one that was a baby. Was *she* the one?"

The Admiral nearly choked with vexation . . . :

"By God, if you say it again I'll scalp you! you've got me so tangled up that I—*say!* can you understand *this?* Aunt Martha—SHE—understand?—mothered Jimmy ever since she was a baby—ever since SHE was a baby! SHE—get it?"

The poet—still uncertain—gave up, and falsely indicated comprehension with a strenuous nod.

(*FM*, 178)

The admiral goes on to describe the two women in question. Jimmy, it turns out, is actually a young woman, Aunt Martha an old maid. Clarity lasts only briefly:

"I've been her father, Martha's been her mother. . . . Heart of gold, too, as I told you before. Sixty years old, and sound as a nut. As for the name, I thought of it myself. I gave it to her."

"Martha is a good name," suggested the poet, in order to say something, it being his turn.

"Martha? Who said anything about Martha? Can't you keep the run of the ordinariest conversation?" . . .

"Oh, I—you see—well, I understood you to say that she—"

"Hang it, what you understand a person to say hasn't got anything to do with what the person says, don't you know that?"

(*FM*, 178–79)

The admiral speaks a language that is veering toward solipsism. He expects his interlocutor somehow to get behind the opaque referentiality of his discourse to figure out which person "she" or "her" refers to at any given point. The pathos-tinged humor in this passage is different from that of the Briggs-parson dialogue. The image of the "derelict," which reappears in the dream-voyage tales, is reflected in the conversational isolation of the speakers, their inability to reach through the befuddling constructions their language provides and to penetrate one another's thought.

Conversation in "The Refuge of the Derelicts" is based on a principle Twain had enunciated a few years earlier, in what was to become book 1 of *Christian Science*, his attack on Mary Baker Eddy and her disciples. "Let us consider that we are all partially insane. It will explain us to each other" (*WIM*, 234). Because each belief system—religion, philosophy, political ideology, or whatever—requires new words for new concepts, each creates a dialect that is meaningless to the uninitiated. This insight is dramatized in chapter 2 of *Christian Science*, in a Briggs-parson dialogue between Twain and a practitioner of Christian Science whom he claims to have met in Austria; most of the words he puts in her mouth are taken verbatim or paraphrased from Mary Baker Eddy. Like the interlocutors in *Roughing It*, the practitioner offers explanations that are more confusing than the originals. Twain questions her assurance that pains are "illusions propagated by matter," asking,

> "If there is no such thing as matter, how can matter propagate things?" . . .
> "It is quite simple," she said, "the fundamental propositions of Christian Science explain it, and they are summarized in the four following self-evident propositions. 1. God is All in all. 2. God is good. Good is Mind. 3. God, Spirit, being all, nothing is matter. 4. Life, God, omnipotent Good, deny death, evil, sin, disease. There—now you see."
> (*WIM*, 220)

And the practitioner happily adds that it will be just as clear read backward, or jumbled up any way you please, for that matter. Twain has a marvelous time parodying what even sympathetic readers must admit are the obscurities of Eddy's style (and parts of the first chapters of *Christian Science* stand among the best burlesque Twain ever wrote), but beneath the humor lies a serious observation about the way thought and language mold one another. After reading *Science and Health* attentively, Twain concluded that it could be comprehensible only to someone who accepted its tenets. True dialogue between believer and nonbeliever is futile because each inhabits a closed system of interpretation inaccessible to the other. Twain condensed this estimation into a paragraph that comes close to stating a general theory of incomprehensibility:

> Of all the strange, and frantic, and incomprehensible, and uninterpretable books which the imagination of man has created, surely this one is the prize sample. It is written with a limitless confidence and complacency, and with a dash and stir and earnestness which often compel the effects of eloquence, even

when the words do not seem to have any traceable meaning. There are plenty of people who imagine they understand the book; I know this, for I have talked with them; but in all cases they were people who also imagined that there were no such things as pain, sickness and death, and no realities in the world; nothing actually existent but Mind. . . . When you read it you seem to be listening to a lively and aggressive and oracular speech delivered in an unknown tongue, a speech whose spirit you get but not the particulars; or, to change the figure, you seem to be listening to a vigorous instrument which is making a noise which it thinks is a tune, but which to persons not members of the band is only the martial tooting of a trombone, and merely stirs the soul through the noise but does not convey a meaning.

(WIM, 229–30)

For one who lives in the world of commonsense empiricism, the radical idealism of Christian Science is unimaginable. The "figures" that Twain hits upon to express the problem echo the metaphors Saint Paul uses in discussing the problem of un-interpreted glossolalia.[17] In the last decade of his life Twain's imagination was haunted intermittently by a vision of Pentecost in reverse, a world whose babble no descending Spirit would make intelligible.

Around 1905, in particular, *interpretation* becomes a key word, reappearing in a variety of shorter and longer pieces; typically Twain mulls over a text whose meaning is finally undecidable. Like other incomprehensibilities, the "mystifying text" has a long history in Twain's work and originates likewise as a purely humorous device. In 1866, for example, he published in the *San Francisco Golden Era* a piece entitled "Mark Twain Mystified," about a telegraphic dispatch so filled with typographical errors and other muddles that it is "in the last degree mysterious" (9 December 1866, *MTS*, 34). Chapter 70 of *Roughing It* is the story of a man driven mad when a handwritten letter he receives from Horace Greeley is so indecipherable that every reading produces a different nonsensical text.[18] "First Interview with Artemus Ward," published in *Sketches New and Old* (1875), recounts how Twain had been "sold" in California when Ward befuddled him with "a string of plausibly worded sentences that didn't mean anything under the sun" (*WMT* 7:338). In "Some Learned Fables," animals try to figure out the purpose of objects in a human village. A wood-louse philologist, puzzling over inscriptions like "Boats for Hire Cheap," concludes that Man had a written language "which conveyed itself partly by letters, and partly by signs or hieroglyphics" (*WMT* 7:156). These early "mystification" pieces have no wide symbolic significance, but they suggest a fascination with the playful subversion of norms in nonsense.

Twain returned to the motif of the indecipherable telegram in 1905 while writing the third and last of his Mysterious Stranger stories, "No. 44, The Mysterious Stranger." Forty-Four is explaining to his young friend that augury is no simple matter. Suppose, he asks, you receive "a telegram in the Christian Silence [*sic*] dialect, what are you going to do? Why, there's nothing to do but *guess* the best you can, and take the chances, because there isn't anybody in heaven or earth that can understand *both* ends of it" (*MSM*, 382–83). Forty-Four gives the text of the muddled telegram (one really by Eddy, taken from a Boston newspaper) and laments that its message, however important it may be, is hidden forever by a fog of "uninterpretable irrelevancies" (*MSM*, 384). He then returns to the subject of omens and prophecy, mocking the self-assurance of augurs confident that they can discover the divine meaning behind mundane occurrences. Twain treated this topic at about the same time in "As Concerns Interpreting the Deity." His point there is that if human communication is hard to interpret, signs from God are even more obscure. Hieroglyphs in both Egypt and the Americas have proved intractable to scholars. "Thus we have infinite trouble in solving man-made mysteries," he says, concluding sarcastically that "it is only when we set out to discover the secrets of God that our difficulties disappear" (*WIM*, 111). The remainder of the sketch satirizes interpreters, both medieval and modern, who have detected the hand of God in wars and disasters. If the world is a telegram from God, as the Protestant exegetical tradition would have it, might it not be either full of misprints or written in a dead language?

The ultimate case of incomprehensibility for Twain is communication between human and divine beings. If they existed, angels or gods would neither act nor speak in ways that men and women could understand. To borrow Wittgenstein's aphorism for the connection between mental horizons and language, "If a lion could talk, we could not understand it."[19] In attacking the orthodox view that man is responsible for the Fall, Twain depends on an explicit variant of the Whorfian hypothesis that language constrains thought: Adam and Eve could not have understood God's injunction because it used words standing for concepts wholly alien to their experience. This is the premise of "That Day in Eden," Satan's version of the Genesis narrative. As the sketch opens, Adam and Eve are puzzling over the words "Good, Evil, Death," and eventually they ask Satan to explain them. He is at a loss how to begin, but decides to try an analogy:

> "I will try, but it is hardly of use. For instance—what is pain?"
> "Pain? [Eve is speaking.] I do not know."
> "Certainly. How should you? Pain is not of your world; pain is impossible to you; you have never experienced a physical pain. Reduce that to a formula, and principle, and what have we?"
> "What have we?"
> "This: Things which are outside of our orbit—our own particular world—things which by our constitution and equipment we are unable to see, or feel, or otherwise experience—*cannot be made comprehensible to us in words.*"
>
> (*WMT* 29:340–41)[20]

Satan tries to explain death as an extended sleep, but Eve responds that sleep is delightful. Lacking any comprehension of the prohibition, they have no reason to avoid eating the fruit. "I have not understood any of this talk," Adam says to Eve, "but if you like we will eat it, for I cannot see that there is any objection to it" (*WMT* 29:344). Twain's God is, so to speak, a parson who has created Scotty Briggs, given him his circumscribed range of miner's slang, and then condemned him to death for failing to make any sense of polysyllabic theology.[21] Like most of Twain's insights in *What is Man?*, this one is neither original nor profound. It is significant, however, as the endpoint of a long literary engagement with the relation between thought and language; the frequency with which the insight recurs during the period of the Mysterious Stranger stories is evidence of its hold on Twain's imagination.[22]

Nearly all of the obsessive themes of Twain's late years play a part in the three Mysterious Stranger stories: dreams, doubles, the injustice of the Judeo-Christian God, the degraded condition of man's moral sense, the gap between man and other creatures (both "higher" and "lower"), and the limitations of human language. To the end Twain believed in the importance of dialogue, as shown by the form of the two long versions ("The Chronicle of Young Satan" and "No. 44, The Mysterious Stranger"), large portions of which are quasi-Socratic dialogues between a young narrator and an omniscient mysterious stranger. Paradoxically, however, what they learn in these conversations is that dialogue is illusion, a corollary of the radical skepticism that ends "No. 44": "It is all a Dream, a grotesque and foolish dream. Nothing exists but You. And You are but a *Thought*" (*MSM*, 405). "The Chronicle of Young Satan," the only Mysterious Stranger story known to the world as such for half a century, dramatizes in narrative form the philosophical positions that *What Is Man?* elaborates in a nonfictional form. The predominant incomprehension is adumbrated in the tales of Adam and Eve: the incommensurability of man and the divine that prevents either party from understanding the other. Philip Traum (or "Satan") states its logical basis: "One cannot compare things which by their nature and by the interval between them are not comparable" (*MSM*, 55). The angels and humans cannot converse about phenomena because they conceive of them in essentially different ways. An incident in chapter 2 powerfully symbolizes this gap. Philip is explaining to the boys that the angels were not affected by the Fall. "We . . . are still ignorant of sin; we are not able to commit it." Two of the tiny automata Philip has created begin an argument; Philip breaks off his speech to crush them between his fingers, then continues: "We cannot do wrong; neither have we any disposition to do it, for we do not know what it is" (*MSM*, 49). The boys are stunned at "the wanton murder he had committed—for murder it was, it was its true name." The paradox is that both angel and human are correct. The angels (like animals) lack the moral sense; because the words *wrong* and *sin* are absent from their conceptual scheme, to apply either one to their actions simply "does not count." Nor can the boys conceive of a "possible world" where unmotivated killing would *not* count as "murder"—hence Theodor's excusable Cratylan belief that murder is the "true name" (and not the culturally determined name) of Philip's action. Twain's irony is double-edged. On the one hand, he is debunking the orthodox view of a benevolent Providence, as he does throughout "Young Satan"; on the other, he is satirizing humans for believing that comprehensible communication is any more possible between God and man than between man and ant. To paraphrase Wittgenstein, if God could talk, we could not understand him.

An uneasy mixture of realism and outrageous fantasy, "No. 44" is indeed less "sustained and coherent" than its better-known predecessor.[23] Its faults may be attributed to a shift in emphasis: Twain is less interested here in satirizing orthodox Christianity than in creating fictional representations of the dream state and the split psyche. Absurd, chaotic, and melodramatic by turns, "No. 44" is an allegory of the limitations of speech, communication, and human thought, all conceived of as different aspects of a single phenomenon. When he returned to an Austrian setting ("Schoolhouse Hill," the second of the Mysterious Stranger tales, had been set in Hannibal), Twain made two important changes. In "Young Satan," the narrator was a boy without occupation who lived in the center of the village. In "No. 44," August Feldner is a printer's apprentice living in an ancient castle on a precipice overlooking the town. Both the print shop and its location function as symbols. Printing is a metonymy for communication in general, but in August's society the printers are treated as outcasts. The Church opposes "the indiscriminate dissemination of knowledge"; the townspeople lack interest: "Our villagers did not trouble themselves about our work, and had no commerce in it; we published nothing there, and printed nothing that they could have read, they being ignorant of abstruse sciences and the dead languages" (*MSM*, 230). The printer's workshop in an isolated castle issues messages that are ignored or not comprehended. Twain's description of the shop's exact location in the castle suggests a more specific symbolic identification. The castle itself was

> prodigious, vine-clad, stately and beautiful, but moldering to ruin. . . . It was a stanch old pile, and the greater part of it was still habitable. Inside, the ravages of time and neglect were less evident than they were outside. . . . By grace of the Prince over the river, who owned it, my master, with his little household, had for many years been occupying a small portion of it, near the centre of the mass.
>
> (*MSM*, 229)

> The printing-shop was remote, and hidden in an upper section of a round tower. Visitors were not wanted there; and if they tried to hunt their way to it without a guide they would have concluded to give it up and call another time before they got through.
>
> (*MSM*, 234)

Like Poe's House of Usher, the castle represents a physical shell inhabited by a rational soul, a Self residing at the center of a labyrinth. Whereas much of the action in "Young Satan" took place out of doors, almost all of "No. 44" is set inside the castle, which symbolizes the psyche whose architecture Twain explores in the story.

For several years Twain had been mulling over the theory that humans possess two distinct selves, a waking self and a dream self, with separate consciences and modes of existence, that are "wholly unknown to each other, and can never in this world communicate with each other in any way" (Notebook entry, 7 January 1897, *MTN*, 349). In the confrontation between the castle's inhabitants and the dream-self "duplicates" that Forty-Four creates, Twain discovers that he does not have to postulate an angelic interlocutor to arrive at maximum incomprehensibility: because the psyche is divided, in each of our minds the potential exists for an ultimate Briggsparson colloquy. When August and his dream self finally sit down for a face-to-face talk, the result is like the stalled conversation in "The Refuge of the Derelicts." August cannot understand his counterpart's apparent indifference to a girl whom he had been about to marry the previous day:

> "Don't you *care* whether you marry her or not?"
> "Care? Why, *no*, of course I don't. You do ask the *strangest* questions! I wander, wander, wander! I try to make you out, I try to understand you, but it's all fog, fog, fog—you're just a riddle, nobody *can* understand you!"
> Oh, the idea! the impudence of it! this to *me!*—from this frantic chaos of unimaginable incomprehensibilities, who couldn't by any chance utter so much as half a sentence that Satan himself could make head or tail of!
>
> (*MSM*, 368)

Perhaps because the restrictions of time and place that bind waking selves do not apply to dream-beings, their "discourse" seems nonsensical; the fewer their ties to mortality, the less comprehensible they are. It is as if a god and an infant were combined—as in effect they are in the mysterious stranger in each of the tales, a character that Twain perhaps first encountered in apocryphal tales of the boy Jesus.[24] As a minor character observes, "Sometimes they [the dream selves] know all languages a minute, and next minute they don't know their own, if they've got one" (*MSM*, 373). Because their experience is alien to that of the waking self, the dream selves find it difficult to convey that experience in human language. Schwarz, August's dream self,

> often dropped phrases which had clear meanings to him, but which he labored in vain to make comprehensible by me. It was because they came from countries where none of the conditions resembled the conditions I had been used to; . . . some from our sun, where nobody was comfortable except when white-hot, and where you needn't talk to people about cold and darkness, for you would not be able to explain the words so that they could understand what you were talking about.

. . . Schwarz said dream-sprites are well-disposed toward their fleshly brothers, and did what they could to make them partakers of the wonders of their travels, but it couldn't be managed except on a poor and not-worth-while scale, because they had to communicate through the flesh-brothers' Waking-Self imagination, and *that* medium—oh, well, it was like "emptying rainbows down a rat-hole."

(*MSM*, 377–78)

The language of the unconscious seems possessed of transcendent meaning, but the conscious glimpses that meaning fitfully, through large patches of nonsense. Simultaneously a threat and a promise, dream language keeps one poised on a knife-edge between ecstasy and madness. If Twain seems to anticipate Freud in his surmise that dreams and the unconscious have a language all their own, he is much less confident that it can be interpreted.

At its worst, submersion in the dream world brings absolute chaos, as when Forty-Four, for a joke, turns time backward. He and August journey around the globe to observe the effects: "Everywhere weary people were re-chattering previous conversations backwards and not understanding each other, and oh, they did look so tuckered out and tired of it all!" (*MSM*, 399–400). Ultimately, articulated language itself is found wanting. The dream, could we pierce its veil, would prove a "rainbow"; speech washes it of color. In "Young Satan" Theodor complains that "words cannot make you understand what we felt" when Satan was nearby. "It was an ecstasy; and an ecstasy is a thing that will not go into words; it feels like music, and one cannot tell about music so that another person can get the feeling of it" (*MSM*, 54). Number Forty-Four must go beyond language altogether to answer August's question, "What *are* you?":

"Ah," he said, "now we have arrived at a point where words are useless; words cannot even convey *human* thought capably, and they can do nothing at all with thoughts whose realm and orbit are outside the human solar system, so to speak. I will use the language of my country, where words are not known. During half a moment my spirit shall speak to yours and tell

you something about me. Not much, for it is not much of me
that you would be able to understand, with your limited human mentality."

(*MSM*, 318)

The feeling that language is an inadequate bridge between
minds drives Twain back into nostalgia for a form of communication that might undo the fall of Babel by transcending linguistic divisions. Just as Twain could espouse mechanical determinism and still place faith in a pseudo-scientific "mind
cure," so the sometime debunker of monoglossia would long
for a universal metalanguage that could withstand the menace
of cacophonous heteroglossia.

Twain's desire to escape the limitations imposed by natural
language is behind his interest in parapsychological phenomena, particularly "mental telegraphy" (what we call telepa-
thy). That interest goes back at least as far as the mid-1870s,
according to the essay "Mental Telegraphy," published in
1891. As Twain explained, a number of otherwise inexplicable
experiences had convinced him that minds could telegraph
thoughts to other minds. Several times, for instance, he had
been able to predict the contents of an unopened letter because it was from someone who had been in his mind during
the past few days. Repeated experiences of this sort demonstrated that "one human mind . . . can communicate with another, over any sort of a distance" (*WMT* 22:122). Twain was
enough of a materialist to hypothesize that the conveying medium was "a finer and subtler form of electricity." Should we
discover just how to harness it, we would be able to invent the
"phrenophone," a device whereby "the communicating of
mind with mind may be brought under command and reduced to certainty and system" (*WMT* 22:128). It is hard to
believe that Mark Twain the skeptic could write an essay like
"Mental Telegraphy" without tongue in cheek, yet all the evidence is that his interest in parapsychology was sincere. His
notebooks are filled with accounts of "telegraphic" experiences; in 1898 he assures Howells that "some day people *will*
be able to call each other up from any part of the world & talk

by mental telegraph" (*MTHL* 2:675). In the fantasy "Three Thousand Years among the Microbes" (1905), the narrator is able to dictate into a "thought recorder," which records the *impressions* preceding articulate thought, "and so luminous are they, and so clear and limpid and superbly radiant in expression that they make all articulated speech . . . seem dull and lifeless and confused by comparison" (*WWD*, 490).[25]

Fortunately, Twain did not compound his Paige typesetter mistake by subsidizing the development of a mental telegraph or a thought recorder. But he did make extended literary capital of an intuitively understood dream language in a sentimental sketch entitled "My Platonic Sweetheart," written in 1898 but not published until two years after his death. If stories like "No. 44" and "Which Was the Dream?" (about a nightmare that comes to seem real) represent the dark side of an ambivalent feeling about dream communication, "My Platonic Sweetheart" is the sunny obverse. It describes a recurrent dream that Twain first had, he says, when he was nineteen. Always in different places, a seventeen-year-old Twain meets a fifteen-year-old sweetheart. In each dream the lovers call each other by different names, because the semantics of dream names differs from that of our waking names.

> Agnes was not a name, but only a pet name, a common noun, whose spirit was affectionate, but not conveyable with exactness in any but the dream-language. It was about the equivalent of "dear," but the dream-vocabulary shaves meanings finer and closer than do the world's daytime dictionaries. We did not know why those words should have those meanings; we had used words which had no existence in any known language, and had expected them to be understood, and they were understood.
>
> (*WMT* 27:296)

Twain goes on to claim that in his notebook he has recorded and translated letters from his dream sweetheart in the dream language (none of his existing notebooks contain examples, although he did sometimes record dreams):

> Here is one of those letters—the whole of it:
> "Rax oha tal."
> Translation.—"When you receive this it will remind you

that I long to see your face and touch your hand, for the comfort of it and the peace."

It is swifter than waking thought; for thought is not thought
at all, but only a vague and formless fog until it is articulated
into words.

(*WMT* 27:296–97)

"Everything in a dream is more deep and strong and sharp
and real than is ever its pale imitation in the unreal life which
is ours when we go about awake," Twain says in the final
paragraph of this sketch (*WMT* 27:304). His true Platonic
sweetheart, it would seem, is thus Plato himself, for in this
sentence he virtually recreates the myth of the cave.[26] Natural
languages, imitations of some vaguely grasped ideal, all fall
short of the perfect communication that can be recaptured
only in dreams and visions. We have come full circle: if cacophony in the real world seems to fling the bricks of Babel
ever further apart, we may enter a dream world where the
tower stands intact as an Idea.

But we must not let even Plato have the last word. None of the
parabolic or doctrinal writings of Twain's last years sets forth
an ultimate position, and his practice often contradicts his
theory. The last fifteen years of his life, for example, represent
perhaps his greatest commitment to the spoken word as a
means of communication, as he undertook a round-the-world
lecture tour, delivered speeches at innumerable banquets,
and was interviewed more often than any other public figure.
While arguing for mechanical determinism and decrying the
intractability of language, Twain is typically doing his utmost
to change the world and to reach as many people as possible
with his words. In his stylistic criticism of James Fenimore
Cooper and Mary Baker Eddy he is still fighting the corruption of language as he had a generation earlier in *The Gilded
Age*. One conclusion of this study, accordingly, must be the
reaffirmation of an old critical insight, that there are "two
Twains," two contradictory personalities, an irreducible dualism inhabiting the same creative mind. In previous chapters
I have examined Twain's ambivalence about prescriptive grammar, the vernacular, and foreign languages. His alternate de-

bunking and embracing of primal, Adamic, transcendent languages, along with his wavering between delight and dread at the prospect of an infinity of tongues, is nothing more than the same pendulum swinging more widely.

The conflict between Language and languages is as old as the opposition between Parmenides' claim that Being is changeless and indivisible and Heraclitus' claim that Being is change, that "all things take place by strife." For all his wavering, in the end Mark Twain was a pupil of Heraclitus. He felt a great terror of absolute stasis, which he associated with speechlessness, the absence of dialogue. "The Enchanted Sea-Wilderness" provides us with Twain's mythical embodiments of change and stasis. Written in 1896, this is an unfinished tale about sailors lost south of the Cape of Good Hope, in a vast circular region of the ocean consisting of different rings. The outer ring is the Devil's Race-Track, "lashed and tossed and torn by eternal storms"; the inmost is the Everlasting Sunday, where there are "no winds, no whisper of wandering zephyr, even, but everywhere the silence and peace and solemnity of a calm which is eternal" (*WWD*, 76). The inmost ring is the more terrible. Becalmed there, sailors abandon their logbooks—"Where one day is exactly like another, why record them?" (*WWD*, 85)—and sit apart, brooding, speechless. When at length they hear a man cry, "A ship!" the human voice pains and distresses them; "their brains were so blunted and sodden that at first his words couldn't find their way into their understandings, all practice in talk having ceased so long ago" (*WWD*, 83). Unchanging eternity is death to language. By contrast, when in "Captain Stormfield's Visit to Heaven" Twain imagines an eternity he might consent to live in, the result is a joyful mingling of voices of every nation, race, and faith. To paraphrase Blake: dialogue is eternal delight. Whatever the cost of a divided psyche may have been, at least the two Twains do not cease to speak to one another, or to the world. Instead, they carry on in Mark Twain's writing a lifelong conversation, one that we enter into through the acts of reading and interpretation. Mark Twain's languages are ours.

Notes

Preface

1. Van Wyck Brooks, *The Ordeal of Mark Twain*, new and rev. ed. (London: J. M. Dent, 1934), pp. 199–200.
2. Mikhail M. Bakhtin, *The Dialogic Imagination*, ed. Michael Holquist, trans. Caryl Emerson and Michael Holquist (Austin: University of Texas Press, 1981), p. 262.

1. Introduction

1. In the letter of 1898 that provides the epigraph to this chapter, Twain notes that he has arrived independently at the empiricists' doctrine that the mind "is a mere machine" whose thoughts all come from the outside. Twain's letter to Adams is printed in Lawrence Clark Powell, "An Unpublished Mark Twain Letter," *American Literature* 13 (1942): 405.
2. The definitive reference work is Alan Gribben's *Mark Twain's Library: A Reconstruction*, 2 vols. (Boston: G. K. Hall, 1980).
3. Those familiar with Mark Twain criticism may catch in my opening queries and responses an echo of those that begin William M. Gibson's fine study, *The Art of Mark Twain* (New York: Oxford University Press, 1976). He finds that readers have hesitated to call Twain a true literary artist partly because he "exercised his art less consciously . . . and with less interest in theory" than novelists like Howells and James; it follows "that his art must be defined chiefly in his practice—and his best practice, at that" (p. 4).
4. David Simpson, *The Politics of American English, 1776–1850* (New York: Oxford University Press, 1986), p. 232. Simpson's book appeared when my own work was in a late stage, else I should have liked to integrate more thoroughly his forceful demonstration that for Cooper "language is always made up of different languages in conflict" (p. 252).
5. Mikhail M. Bakhtin, *The Dialogic Imagination*, ed. Michael Holquist, trans. Caryl Emerson and Michael Holquist (Austin: University of Texas Press, 1981), p. 68. (In the passage from which I quote, Bakhtin is speaking of the effect of "active polyglossia"; elsewhere

he makes it clear that parody is a principal agent of polyglossia in literature.)

6. The most wide-ranging general study of the problem of variety in language is George Steiner's *After Babel: Aspects of Language and Translation* (New York: Oxford University Press, 1975). Grounded in a more careful historical method is Hans Aarsleff, *From Locke to Saussure: Essays on the Study of Language and Intellectual History* (Minneapolis: University of Minnesota Press, 1982). For a popular treatment, see J. R. Firth, *The Tongues of Men* (London: Watts, 1937).

7. Samuel Kirkham, *English Grammar in Familiar Lectures*, stereotype ed. (New York: R. B. Collins, n.d. [1829]), p. 18. On Kirkham's importance, and the evidence that young Samuel Clemens used this text, see chapter 2, pp. 18–22.

8. Hans Aarsleff identifies 1860, the year that the Philological Society of London adopted the final plan for what would become the *Oxford English Dictionary*, as the end point of a two-generation battle between the new philology and the old (*The Study of Language in England, 1780–1860* [Princeton, N.J.: Princeton University Press, 1967], p. 4).

9. *Humanist without Portfolio: An Anthology of the Writings of Wilhelm von Humboldt*, trans. Marianne Cowan (Detroit: Wayne State University Press, 1963), pp. 335–36. For an overview of Humboldt's career and its importance to subsequent linguistics, see Aarsleff, *From Locke to Saussure*, pp. 335–55.

10. Humboldt, *Humanist*, p. 235.

11. Humboldt, *Humanist*, pp. 246–50. Russian semiotician Juri Lotman argues similarly that "noise" is essential to communication. "Non-understanding, incomplete understanding, or misunderstanding are not side-products of the exchange of information but belong to its very essence"; study of culture as a "sign phenomenon" leads to the conclusion that cultures advance as they purposefully multiply "the mechanisms which impede the process of message-transmission" ("The Sign Mechanism of Culture," *Semiotica* 12 [1974]: 302).

12. William Dwight Whitney, *The Life and Growth of Language: An Outline of Linguistic Science* (New York: Appleton, 1875), p. 4.

13. Max Müller, *Lectures on the Science of Language*, 2 vols. (New York: Scribner, 1872), 1:128.

14. William Dwight Whitney, *Language and the Study of Language: Twelve Lectures on the Principles of Linguistic Science* (New York: Scribner, 1867), p. 404.

15. Whitney, *Life and Growth of Language*, pp. 286–87.

16. See p. 101; Simpson, *Politics of American English*, pp. 63–81.

17. Bakhtin, *Dialogic Imagination*, pp. 262–63.

18. Bakhtin, *Dialogic Imagination*, p. 278.

19. George Eliot, *Middlemarch*, ed. Gordon S. Haight (Boston: Houghton Mifflin, 1956), pp. 73–74.

20. Bakhtin, *Dialogic Imagination*, p. 285.

21. Bakhtin, *Dialogic Imagination*, p. 279.

22. Twain tells in *The Innocents Abroad* how he "burst into tears" at the tomb of his kinsman Adam. Robert Gale lists over a dozen places in Twain's writings where Adam is referred to or figures as a character (*Plots and Characters in the Works of Mark Twain*, 2 vols. [Hamden, Conn.: Archon, 1973], 2:675–76). Allison Ensor discusses Twain's use of Adam and the biblical creation myth in *Mark Twain and the Bible* (Lexington: University of Kentucky Press, 1969), pp. 40–61.

23. Humboldt, *Humanist*, p. 240.

24. "The Poet," in *The Collected Works of Ralph Waldo Emerson*, ed. Alfred R. Ferguson et al. (Cambridge, Mass.: Harvard University Press, 1971–), 3:13.

25. Ralph Waldo Emerson, *Nature*, in *Collected Works*, 1:10.

26. Susan K. Harris has made a similar point, finding that Eve represents the possibility of communication, whereas "Adam's control over language expands as he comes to understand how much Eve means to him" (*Mark Twain's Escape from Time: A Study of Patterns and Images* [Columbia: University of Missouri Press, 1982], p. 124).

2. "A LOT OF RULES"

1. For two fine accounts of the role of language theory and prescriptive grammar in the history of American English, see Dennis E. Baron, *Grammar and Good Taste: Reforming the American Language* (New Haven, Conn.: Yale University Press, 1982); and Edward Finegan, *Attitudes toward English Usage: The History of a War of Words* (New York: Teachers College Press, 1980).

2. For White and Moon, see chapter 3. No titles by Whitney or Müller appear in Alan Gribben's *Mark Twain's Library*. I know of only one reference to the two grammarians in Twain's writing. Twain considered inserting in *A Tramp Abroad* a mock correspondence with several philologists concerning his theories on German grammar: "Wrote to Max Müller & Prof Whitney & J H Trumbull o[n] Phi[l]ological matters but only got offensive answers or silence" (Notebook 17, *NJ2*, 266). Trumbull was Twain's neighbor in Hartford; he contributed obscure foreign-language epigraphs to *The Gilded Age*, and his death in 1897 elicited a eulogistic essay from Twain. Twain probably knew Müller and Whitney by reputation only.

3. H. L. Mencken, *The American Language*, 4th ed. (New York:

Knopf, 1936); Robert A. Hall, *Leave Your Language Alone!* (Ithaca, N.Y.: Linguistica, 1950).

4. In 1909 Ambrose Bierce published *Write It Right: A Little Blacklist of Literary Faults,* a reactionary usage manual that crusades against "loose locutions of the ignorant" and "expressions ancestrally vulgar or irreclaimably degenerate" ([New York: Neale, 1910], pp. 5–6). We learn from Bierce that since *leave* is transitive, we cannot say "he left yesterday" and that *pants* for *trousers* is "vulgar exceedingly."

5. Richard Bridgman, *The Colloquial Style in America* (New York: Oxford University Press, 1966), p. 19.

6. Walt Whitman, *An American Primer,* ed. Horace Traubel (Boston: Small, Maynard, 1904), p. 6.

7. Henry James, *The Question of Our Speech* (Boston: Houghton Mifflin, 1905), pp. 35, 41.

8. Gould Brown, *The Grammar of English Grammars,* 10th ed. (New York: William Wood, 1851), p. 22.

9. The Mark Twain Papers owns a copy of an 1835 edition of Kirkham that appears to have been signed by the young Clemens. Alan Gribben hesitantly accepts it as authentic; he explains his doubts in *Mark Twain's Library: A Reconstruction,* 2 vols. (Boston: G. K. Hall, 1980), 2:383–84. As Gribben notes, Twain twice refers in passing to Kirkham, in *A Tramp Abroad* and in an autobiographical dictation of 1907 (2:384). That Twain has schoolmaster Ferguson refer to "about thirty" rules of grammar is good circumstantial evidence for his remembering Kirkham's prominent list of thirty-five rules of syntax. Rollo Lyman has documented that Kirkham's grammar was at the height of its popularity in the early 1840s, just when Twain was entering grammar school (*English Grammar in American Schools before 1850* [Washington: Government Printing Office, 1922], p. 83).

10. Samuel Kirkham, *English Grammar in Familiar Lectures,* stereotype ed. (New York: R. B. Collins, n.d. [1829]).

11. Kirkham, *English Grammar,* p. 9.

12. Mark Twain, *Tom Sawyer, a Play,* in *HHT,* p. 301; I have omitted the italics that Twain used to indicate vocal emphasis. In an 1887 dinner speech, he would cast himself in the Ben Rogers role: "I remember myself, and all of you old fellows probably remember the same of yourselves, that when I went to school I was told that an adjective is an adverb and it must be governed by the third person singular, and all that sort of thing—and when I got out of school I straightway forgot all about it" (*MTS,* 217).

13. Number Forty-Four knows the English grammar by heart because he has "heard [the] grammar class recite the rules before entering upon the rest of their lesson" (*MSM,* 178). Twain certainly believed that memory alone was incapable of conferring linguistic prowess. The prodigious memory of the pilot Brown, in *Life on the*

Mississippi, helps him navigate, but it cripples his aesthetic judgment and ruins him as a storyteller.

14. Mark Twain, "An Excellent School," *Virginia City Territorial Enterprise*, 12 February 1864 (*ETS1*, 345).

15. Twain's evaluation of the purpose for grammar resembles serious statements made by eighteenth- and nineteenth-century grammarians. Robert Lowth, for instance, wrote in the preface to his grammar of 1762 that a "principal design" of any grammatical treatise should be "to teach us . . . to judge of every phrase and form of construction, whether it be right or not" (*A Short Introduction to English Grammar* [London, 1762], p. x). Kirkham defines English grammar as "the art of speaking and writing with propriety" (*English Grammar*, p. 18).

16. Mark Twain, "The Facts Concerning the Recent Trouble between Mr. Mark Twain and Mr. John William Skae, of Virginia City," *San Francisco Californian*, 26 August 1865 (*ETS2*, 258).

17. Kirkham, *English Grammar*, p. 14.

18. Randolph Quirk suggests that speakers of English fall into three categories: assured, anxious, and indifferent. Speakers at the top of the social scale belong to the first group; their status is so secure that they need not worry about criticism or correction. "Their nonchalant attitude toward language was epitomised in the nineteenth century in the words of Bulwer Lytton: 'I am free to confess that *I* don't know grammar. Lady Blessington, do *you* know grammar?'" (*The Use of English* [New York: St. Martin's Press, 1962], pp. 69–70).

19. Writing to Bret Harte soon after the publication of *The Celebrated Jumping Frog*, Twain takes pride in the "handsome" appearance of his first book but complains of the "damnable errors of grammar and deadly inconsistencies of spelling in the Frog sketch" that slipped in because he was not able to read proof (letter of 1 May 1867, *MTL* 1:124). When he proposed turning his *Quaker City* excursion letters to the *Alta California* into a book, he promised Elisha Bliss that he "could weed them of their chief faults of construction and inelegancies of expression" to make an acceptable volume (letter of 2 December 1867, *MTL* 1:141).

20. In 1878, while correcting a manuscript by his brother Orion, Twain objected to an instance of this usage: "'Next came 100 people who looked *like* they had just been, &c' That wretched Missourianism occurs in every chapter. You mean, '*as if*'" (holograph MS, MTP, DV 415) (†).

21. While on his Mississippi trip Twain identified the "error" as peculiar to the region; in his notebook he records, "Here they say 'I *will* do so & so, when they mean *shall*'" (*NJ2*, 470).

22. Mencken, *The American Language*, p. 46. Mencken quotes the

editor of a Virginia newspaper who had complained of the proscription of "he don't": "Here in Virginia many men of the highest education use the phrase habitually. Their ancestors have used it for many generations, and it might be argued with some reason that when the best blood and the best brains of Virginia use an expression for so long a time it becomes correct." Twain must have heard the usage often from his Virginia-born father.

23. Henry H. Breen, *Modern English Literature: Its Blemishes and Defects* (London: Longman, 1857), pp. v, 8. During the 1860s, Dean Alford, George Washington Moon, and Edward Gould had engaged in a noisy feud over linguistic judgments and grammatical errors in one another's writing. Although there is no evidence that Twain knew any of their works until he read Moon in the 1890s, the controversy was covered widely in newspapers and periodicals on both sides of the Atlantic, so he was probably aware of the epidemic of mutual faultfinding among these critics.

24. Gribben, *Mark Twain's Library*, 1:83.

25. The extracts are from *A Tramp Abroad* (*WMT* 9:203); Contributors' Club, *Atlantic Monthly* 45 (1880): 850; *Life on the Mississippi* (1883) (*WMT* 12:222); dinner speech, 27 April 1887 (*MTS*, 226); "Comment on Tautology and Grammar," dated 1898 (*MTA* 1:173); "Remarks" at Women's Press Club tea, 27 October 1900 (*MTS*, 346–47); *Christian Science* (*WIM*, 273).

26. Dennis Baron (*Grammar and Good Taste*, pp. 145–51) and Edward Finegan (*Attitudes toward English Usage*, pp. 48, 57–59) both comment on the moralistic tone of nineteenth-century grammar texts. Lindley Murray, in his "Address to Young Students," says he wrote his grammar out of "a desire to facilitate your progress in learning, and, at the same time, to impress on your minds principles of piety and virtue" (*English Grammar* [Bridgeport, Conn., 1824; facsimile reprint, Delmar, N.Y.: Scholars' Facsimiles & Reprints, 1981], p. 306).

27. Kirkham, *English Grammar*, p. 13.

28. Kirkham, *English Grammar*, p. 15.

29. Mark Twain, "The Story of Mamie Grant, the Child-Missionary" (*SB*, 37).

30. Kenneth Lynn has observed that the "Clown" of Southwestern humor "was unselfconsciously infantile even when he was technically an adult. Whooping and hollering and jumping into the air, he behaved with childlike unrestraint in no matter what company; his vernacular speech—grotesque, drawling, ungrammatical—was a sort of baby-talk" (*Mark Twain and Southwestern Humor* [Boston: Atlantic Monthly Press, 1959], p. 133).

31. Brander Matthews, "What Is Pure English?" in *Essays on English* (New York: Scribner, 1922), p. 33.

32. Dixon Wecter, *Sam Clemens of Hannibal* (Boston: Houghton Mifflin, 1952), pp. 9–10.

33. Mark Twain, "A Gallant Fireman" (*ETS1*, 62).

34. On malapropism in American humor, see Walter Blair and Hamlin Hill, *America's Humor: From Poor Richard to Doonesbury* (New York: Oxford University Press, 1978), p. 138.

35. James M. Cox writes that Brown is "clearly modeled upon Pap" and "speaks in [his] tone if not [his] very accents" (*Mark Twain: The Fate of Humor* [Princeton, N.J.: Princeton University Press, 1966], p. 162).

36. In his version of the fight, Albert Bigelow Paine records several lines of dialogue between the two, but they seem to be merely a fictional expansion of the indirect description in *Life on the Mississippi* (*Mark Twain: A Biography*, 3 vols. [New York: Harper, 1912], 1:136).

37. Quoted in Robert C. Elliott, *The Power of Satire* (Princeton, N.J.: Princeton University Press, 1960), p. 12. In his first chapter Elliott discusses the ancient traditions of invective that precede the development of modern satire.

38. Thomas Lounsbury, *The Standard of Usage in English* (New York: Harper, 1908), p. 98. Twain owned a copy of this book; see Gribben, *Mark Twain's Library*, 1:424.

39. Mark Twain, dinner speech, 6 July 1907 (*MTS*, 573–74).

40. Brander Matthews provides our best independent evidence of the sway that linguistic respectability held over even a "liberal" in Twain's day. Before Twain's death Matthews had celebrated "the speech of the people," identifying Twain and Kipling as the two authors with the best ear for it. In 1920, however, he would eulogize his friend more cautiously by insisting that he did indeed speak and write the "best English": "In his own person . . . he refrained from [using slang], tempting as many of its vigorous vocables must have been to him. . . . He knew better than to yield to the easy allurement; and his English is as pure as it is direct and uncompromising. . . . Mark spoke his native tongue in its utmost purity, which is why every Englishman could understand him. He spoke pure English, as free from obtruded Americanisms as from obsolete Briticisms, the English current on both shores of 'the salt, unplumbed estranging sea,' the English of Defoe and Bunyan, of Franklin and Lincoln" ("Mark Twain and the Art of Writing," in *Essays on English*, pp. 244–45, 247). Matthews may have taken this line of defense in reaction to Van Wyck Brooks's just-published *Ordeal of Mark Twain*.

41. Mark Twain, Notebook 39, MTP TS, p. 39 (†).

42. Kirkham, *English Grammar*, p. 206.

43. Gertrude Stein, *How to Write* (1931; reprint, New York: Dover, 1975), pp. 144–45.

44. See p. 21.

45. Stein, *How to Write*, pp. 71–73.

46. Contributors' Club, *Atlantic Monthly* 45 (1880): 850. Twain would long remain sensitive about his adverb usage: in an 1898 notebook entry he carefully puts "only" in the formally required place ("a person who is present in your imagination only") and then adds the irritated parenthetical remark, "I wish the word '*only*' was in hell" (*MTN*, 365).

47. The 1860s witnessed a battle of the books over just this issue of adverb placement. Dean Alford, following the colloquial model, championed relatively free placement of *only*; purist George Washington Moon protested that this created ambiguity and "proved" that one of Alford's sentences could be read in no less than 10,240 different senses. "In contemplating the way in which our sentences will be understood," replied Alford, "we are allowed to remember, that we do not write for idiots" (*The Queen's English: A Manual of Idiom and Usage* [1864; reprint, London: George Bell, 1895], p. 98).

48. Matthew Arnold, *General Grant*, with a rejoinder by Mark Twain, ed. John Y. Simon (Carbondale: Southern Illinois University Press, 1966), p. 13.

49. James B. Fry, "Grant and Matthew Arnold: An Estimate," *North American Review* 144 (1887): 349–57.

50. "Use good grammar" is one of the "little" rules governing literary art that Cooper "coldly and persistently violated," according to Twain (*WMT* 22:63). While on his round-the-world voyage in 1896, Twain recorded in his notebook: "Zangwill's 'Master' is done in good English—what a rare thing good English is! and the grammar is good, too—and what a very, very rare thing that is!" (*MTN*, 267).

51. See Chester L. Davis, "Mark Twain's Marginal Notes on 'The Queen's English,'" *Twainian* 25 (1966): 1–4.

52. William Cobbett, *A Grammar of the English Language, in a Series of Letters* (1823; reprint, Oxford: Oxford University Press, 1984), p. 7.

53. Cobbett, *Grammar*, p. 4.

3. THE GILDED AGE AND THE CORRUPTION
OF LANGUAGE

1. Bolinger's penetrating analysis of verbal shamanism makes up the first chapter of his *Language—the Loaded Weapon: The Use and Abuse of Language Today* (London: Longman, 1980).

2. Leonard Bloomfield, "Secondary and Tertiary Responses to Language," *Language* 20 (1944): 45. For the influence and importance of White, see H. L. Mencken, *The American Language*, 4th ed. (New York: Knopf, 1936), pp. 61–62.

3. Richard Grant White, *Words and Their Uses, Past and Present: A*

Study of the English Language, 20th ed. (Boston: Houghton Mifflin, 1892), p. 3. (Further references in this chapter are to this edition and are incorporated in the text.) Richard Grant White (1821–1885), a critic and editor of Shakespeare, wrote on questions of language as a self-admitted amateur. Like his counterparts in our own day, he thoroughly opposed the latitudinarianism of professional linguists.

4. White writes, "The . . . confusion of *like* and *as* . . . is common with careless speakers. Thus, for instance, He don't do it like you do, instead of *as* you do" (p. 137). Twain's belief that *shall* and *will* were confused more often in the South can also be found in *Words and Their Uses:* "The distinction between these words . . . is liable to be disregarded by persons who have not had the advantage of early intercourse with educated English people. I mean English in blood and breeding; for . . . in New England it is noteworthy that even the boys and girls playing on the commons use *shall* and *will* correctly; . . . while by Scotchmen and Irishmen, even when they are professionally men of letters, and by the great mass of the people of the Western and Southwestern States, the words are used without discrimination" (p. 264).

5. Twain's copy of *Words and Their Uses* was an 1872 edition signed "Mark Twain, 1873" (see Gribben, *Mark Twain's Library: A Reconstruction,* 2 vols. [Boston: G. K. Hall, 1980], 2:762). Twain had probably seen at least a few of the original articles since he published his first article in the *Galaxy* in 1868 and became a regular contributor, over sixty of his pieces appearing there during 1870 and 1871.

6. *The Collected Works of Ralph Waldo Emerson,* ed. Alfred R. Ferguson et al. (Cambridge, Mass.: Harvard University Press, 1971–), 1:20.

7. Review of *Words and Their Uses, North American Review* 112 (1871): 470. The distrust of the "foreign element" evident in the concluding triumvirate looks forward to *The Question of Our Speech* by Henry James. Compare the scorn of a writer in the *Biblical Repository:* "Custom is undoubtedly high authority. . . . But the custom of whom do we accept as the standard? Of children? of the ignorant and uncultivated? Or does the voice even of the majority of those who are educated determine grammatical rules? Or is it the usage of the best speakers and writers? Really it seems almost childish to ask these questions" (quoted in George Washington Moon, *Learned Men's English: The Grammarians* [London: Routledge, 1892], p. 211).

8. Samuel L. Clemens, "The Curious Republic of Gondour," in *The Curious Republic of Gondour and Other Whimsical Sketches* (New York: Boni and Liveright, 1919), pp. 1, 3–4.

9. Sociolinguist William Labov has made a similar polemical charge in our own day: "Our work in the speech community makes it painfully obvious that in many ways working-class speakers are more effective narrators, reasoners, and debaters than many middle-

class speakers who temporize, qualify, and lose their argument in a mass of irrelevant detail. Many academic writers try to rid themselves of that part of middle-class style that is empty pretension. . . . But the average middle-class speaker that we encounter makes no such effort; he is enmeshed in verbiage, the victim of sociolinguistic factors beyond his control" ("The Logic of Nonstandard English," in *Language in the Inner City: Studies in the Black English Vernacular* [Philadelphia: University of Pennsylvania Press, 1972], pp. 213–14).

10. The first chapter of Edward S. Gould's *Good English; or, Popular Errors in Language* (1867) is entitled "Who Is Responsible?" (for the corruption of language). His answer: "Among writers, those who do the most mischief are the original fabricators of error, to wit: the men generally who write for the newspapers" (6th ed. [New York: Widdleton, 1875], p. 7). Gould goes on to quote Dean Alford's extensive criticism of the British press, which begins: "The language . . . is undergoing a sad and rapid process of deterioration. Its fine manly Saxon is getting diluted into long Latin words not carrying half the meaning. This is mainly owing to the vitiated and pretentious style which passes current in our newspapers" (Henry Alford, *The Queen's English: A Manual of Idiom and Usage* [1864; reprint, London: George Bell, 1895], p. 179).

11. Twain had already complained about the pretentious display of foreign words, notably in chapter 23 of *The Innocents Abroad.* The closest precursor to the scene in *The Gilded Age* is a signed sketch in the *Buffalo Express,* 4 December 1869, recounting the inanities of a pair of Americans "Back from 'Yurrup.'" They pretend to have spoken French so long that English comes "dreadful awkward," and they flounder through a conversation in "barbarous French . . . and neither one of them ever by any chance understanding what the other was driving at" (*FW*, 141–44).

12. Although the bulk of the chapter in which this passage occurs is unquestionably Twain's, the section that contains it appears on stylistic grounds to be Warner's. As a matter of fact, Laura's speech does *not* really "betray itself," in this chapter or elsewhere; even when Laura is still a girl in Missouri—in chapter 10 of the first volume, one of Twain's—her speech is elegant. The important point, however, is that Twain and Warner both mean us to understand Laura as a superbly manipulative woman who is superior to even practiced Washingtonians at establishing and maintaining a facade that will procure influence.

13. Jean-Joseph Goux, *Economie et symbolique* (Paris: Seuil, 1973), p. 182. See also Goux, *Les Monnayeurs du langage* (Paris: Galilée, 1984); and Marc Shell, *The Economy of Literature* (Baltimore: Johns Hopkins University Press, 1978), and *Money, Language, and Thought* (Berkeley: University of California Press, 1982).

14. Quoted in Goux, *Economie et symbolique,* p. 99; my translation.

15. The biblical echoes here are general, but two passages from the New Testament are especially relevant: "Lay not up for yourselves treasures upon earth . . . but lay up for yourselves treasures in heaven" (Matt. 6:19–20), and "[In God and Christ] are hid all the treasures of wisdom and knowledge" (Col. 2:3).

16. Twain had just handled the themes of inflation and wild speculation in *Roughing It.* Chapter 29, for instance, describes how miners in the Humboldt region owned a multitude of mines with impressive names whose wealth was wholly prospective. Chapter 44 describes in detail the rise and fall of stock in wildcat mines.

17. S. I. Hayakawa, *Language in Action* (New York: Harcourt, Brace, 1941), pp. 21–25.

18. "Random remarks here and there, being pieced together gave Laura a vague impression of a man of fine presence, about forty-three or forty-five years of age, with dark hair and eyes, and a slight limp in his walk. . . . And this indistinct shadow represented her father" (*WMT* 5:97).

19. John Locke, *An Essay Concerning Human Understanding,* abr. and ed. John W. Yolton (London: Dent, 1976), p. 255.

20. Locke, *Essay,* pp. 247–48.

21. George Steiner, *After Babel: Aspects of Language and Translation* (New York: Oxford University Press, 1975), pp. 473, 47.

4. "Babel Come Again"

1. Mark Twain, letter of 2 June 1878 (*MTHL* 1:232–33).

2. William Dwight Whitney, *The Life and Growth of Language: An Outline of Linguistic Science* (New York: Appleton, 1875), p. 154.

3. Frederic William Farrar, *An Essay on the Origin of Language* (London: J. Murray, 1860), pp. 86–87.

4. See "From the Prehistory of Novelistic Discourse," in Mikhail M. Bakhtin, *The Dialogic Imagination,* ed. Michael Holquist, trans. Caryl Emerson and Michael Holquist (Austin: University of Texas Press, 1981), especially pp. 61–66.

5. Juri M. Lotman, "The Future for Structural Poetics," *Poetics* 8 (1979): 505–6.

6. Henri Bergson poses a "law in accordance with which we will define all broadly comic situations in general. *Any arrangement of acts and events is comic which gives us, in a single combination, the illusion of life and the distinct impression of a mechanical arrangement*" (*Laughter* [1900], in *Comedy,* ed. Wylie Sypher [Garden City, N.Y.: Doubleday, 1956], p. 105).

7. See, for example, the letter Twain wrote Bayard Taylor from Heidelberg on 7 May 1878, when his knowledge of German was at

roughly the same point as his knowledge of French had been at the time of the "apotheke" story:

> Ich habe heute gecalled on der Herr Profesor Ihne, qui est die Professor von Englishen Zunge im University, to get him to recommend ein Deutchen Lehrer für mich, welcher he did. Er sprach um mehrerer Americanischer authors, und meist güngstiger & vernügungsvoll von Ihrer. . . .
> Ich habe das Deutche sprache gelernt und bin ein glucklicher Kind, you bet.

The letter is reproduced in John Richie Schultz, "New Letters of Mark Twain," *American Literature* 8 (1936): 47–48.

8. Bakhtin, *Dialogic Imagination*, p. 343. See also Caryl Emerson, "The Outer Word and Inner Speech: Bakhtin, Vygotsky, and the Internalization of Language," *Critical Inquiry* 10 (1983): 255.

9. Mark Twain, letter dated 20 March 1862, published in *Keokuk Gate City*, 25 June 1862, p. 1 (reprinted in *The Pattern for Mark Twain's "Roughing It,"* ed. Franklin R. Rogers [Berkeley: University of California Press, 1961], p. 39).

10. Pidgin English was used by Indians not only to speak to whites but also to conduct affairs with other racial groups. See J. L. Dillard, *All-American English* (New York: Vintage, 1976), pp. 99–111.

11. *San Francisco Morning Call,* 9 July 1864 (*CofC*, 70).

12. Ferdinand de Saussure, *Course in General Linguistics*, ed. Charles Bally and Albert Sechehaye, trans. Wade Baskin, rev. ed. (London: Peters Owen, 1974), pp. 11–13.

13. An extreme case of linguistic domination is the stock dialogue between the boot camp drill sergeant and the new recruit. When the former repeats a question, shouting, "I can't HEAR you!" the latter may not respond, "But I spoke perfectly clearly"; he has no choice but to repeat his answer even more loudly, as many times as the sergeant elicits it.

14. Mark Twain, *The Celebrated Jumping Frog of Calaveras County, and Other Sketches* (New York: Webb, 1867), pp. 58–59.

15. See Franklin R. Rogers, *Mark Twain's Burlesque Patterns, As Seen in the Novels and Narratives, 1855–1885* (Dallas: Southern Methodist University Press, 1960), pp. 21–24.

16. For James M. Cox, *The Innocents Abroad* is the record of Mark Twain's "mock-initiation" into the reality of Europe, through a process of "illusion followed by disillusion . . . so recurrent as to be the very mechanism of the narrator's behavior" (*Mark Twain: The Fate of Humor* [Princeton, N.J.: Princeton University Press, 1966], pp. 45–56).

17. The paradox is similar to the famous one in *Life on the Mississippi*. To navigate the river safely, the pilot must learn to read it as a system of signs that indicate relative danger and safety. Once the

river has become transparently semiotic, however, its romantic beauty as landscape is forever lost.

18. *The Collected Works of Ralph Waldo Emerson,* ed. Alfred R. Ferguson et al. (Cambridge, Mass.: Harvard University Press, 1971–), pp. 19–20. On Transcendentalist belief in a universal language, see Philip F. Gura, *The Wisdom of Words: Language, Theology, and Literature in the New England Renaissance* (Middletown, Conn.: Wesleyan University Press, 1981), pp. 9, 75–105, 125–26.

19. "Mark Twain in Paris," *New York Sun,* 27 January 1895, sec. 3, p. 4 (quoted in Louis Budd, "Mark Twain Talks Mostly about Humor and Humorists," *Studies in American Humor* 1 [1974]: 9).

20. George Steiner, *After Babel: Aspects of Language and Translation* (New York: Oxford University Press, 1975), p. 71.

21. Th[érèse] Bentzon, "Les Humoristes américains: Mark Twain," *Revue des deux mondes* 100 (1872): 314.

22. In her final paragraph, speaking of Twain's works in general, Bentzon writes: "Ce qui est intraduisible surtout, c'est ce qui fait le principal mérite de ces bigarrures, le style original et mordant, le tour *idiomatique,* le mélange bizarre et souvent pittoresque de néologie, de patois et d'argot qu'on appelle le *slang*" ("Les Humoristes américains," p. 335).

23. Rogers, *Burlesque Patterns,* p. 164, n. 7.

24. Translated direct discourse has the same formal appearance as ordinary direct discourse but a different ontological status. The resistance of foreign discourse to assimilation is suggested by the following paradigm (in which the asterisk and question mark represent "unacceptable" and "questionable," respectively):

Direct Discourse (original):	Pierre said, "J'ai faim."
Direct Discourse (translated):	Pierre said, "I'm hungry."
Indirect Discourse (original):	*Pierre said that il avait faim.
Indirect Discourse (translated):	Pierre said that he was hungry.
Free Indirect Discourse (original):	?Pierre stopped. Qu'il avait faim!
Free Indirect Discourse (translated):	Pierre stopped. How hungry he was!

We might call the translated direct discourse pseudo-direct. (Readers interested in the theory of represented discourse should refer to Ann Banfield's masterful study, *Unspeakable Sentences: Narration and Representation in the Language of Fiction* [Boston: Routledge & Kegan Paul, 1982].)

25. For an argument that there is no nonarbitrary distinction be-

tween direct and indirect discourse, see Meir Sternberg, "Point of View and the Indirections of Direct Speech," *Language and Style* 15 (1982): 67–117.

26. John T. Krumpelmann, *Mark Twain and the German Language* (Baton Rouge: Louisiana State University Press, 1953).

27. Albert Bigelow Paine, *Mark Twain: A Biography*, 3 vols. (New York: Harper, 1912), 2:621.

28. Paine thought the essay "one of Mark Twain's supreme bits of humor . . . Mark Twain at his best" (*Mark Twain: A Biography*, 2:669).

29. The Mark Twain Papers contains an unfinished burlesque German grammar, "German As She Is Acquired" (DV 155) (printed in David R. Sewell, "Varieties of Language in the Writings of Mark Twain," Ph.D. diss., University of California, San Diego, 1984, pp. 174–76).

30. According to a newspaper report, Twain made similar suggestions when he spoke on Italian grammar in Florence for a British Relief Fund benefit; see "Mark Twain to Reform the Language of Italy," *New York Times*, 10 April 1904, sec. 2, p. 1.

31. Mark Twain, "Italian without a Master," *Harper's Weekly*, 2 January 1904, 18–19.

32. Lewis Carroll, *Through the Looking Glass*, in *The Annotated Alice*, ed. Martin Gardner (New York: Bramhall House, 1960), p. 269; see also Gardner's extensive note on Humpty-Dumpty's semantic logic, pp. 268–70.

33. Twain's translation: "REVOLVERATION IN THEATER. *Paris, 27th. La Patrie* has from Chicago: The cop of the theater of the opera of Wallace, Indiana, had willed to expel a spectator which continued to smoke in spite of the prohibition, who, spalleggiato by his friends, tirò (Fr. *tiré*, Anglice *pulled*) manifold revolver-shots. The cop responded. Result, a general scare; great panic among the spectators. Nobody hurt" (*WMT* 24:240). (*Spalleggiato* means "backed" or "supported." Otherwise the translation is jovially accurate, except that *scarica* means "salvo.")

34. See Wilga Rivers and Mary S. Temperley, *A Practical Guide to the Teaching of English as a Second or Foreign Language* (New York: Oxford University Press, 1978), pp. 20–23; and R. Titone, *Teaching Foreign Languages: A Historical Sketch* (Washington, D.C.: Georgetown University Press, 1968), pp. 33–37.

35. Mark Twain, Notebook 32, MTP TS, p. 12 (†); see Alan Gribben, *Mark Twain's Library: A Reconstruction*, 2 vols. (Boston: G. K. Hall, 1980), 2:269.

36. François Gouin, *The Art of Teaching and Studying Languages*, 5th ed., trans. Howard Swan and Victor Bétis (London: George Philip & Son, 1894), p. 10.

37. Neither Gouin's name for his method nor his criticism of tra-

ditional methods was original with him. He and Twain both had been preceded by Professor John Stuart Blackie: "The time was . . . when the Latin language was taught in the natural and proper way, by talking and discoursing as well as by reading. . . . But for the most part, in this nineteenth century, Latin, and Greek also . . . are taught in a most painful and perverse manner, by grammars and dictionaries and books only, to the utter neglect of the natural method, according to which, as we have shown, the knowledge of language comes by the ear, not by the eye" ("On the Study of Languages," *Tait's Edinburgh Magazine*, n.s. 9 [1842]: 749).

5. Not All Trying to Talk Alike

1. Bernard De Voto, *Mark Twain at Work* (Cambridge, Mass.: Harvard University Press, 1942), p. 51.

2. *St. Louis Globe-Democrat*, 11 March 1885, p. 1 (quoted in Victor Fischer, "Huck Finn Reviewed: The Reception of *Huckleberry Finn* in the United States, 1885–1897," *American Literary Realism* 16 [1983]: 17).

3. Michael Egan, *Mark Twain's "Huckleberry Finn": Race, Class, and Society* (London: Sussex University Press, 1977), p. 73.

4. Henry Nash Smith, *Mark Twain: The Development of a Writer* (Cambridge, Mass.: Harvard University Press, 1962), p. 20. Smith uses no single term consistently as the antonym of *vernacular*. Instead he relies on a complex of adjectives related to language, culture, and values: *genteel, official, dominant, established, elevated, conventional, traditional, high, exalted.*

5. George C. Carrington, Jr., *The Dramatic Unity of "Huckleberry Finn"* (Columbus: Ohio State University Press, 1976), p. 23. Smith recognized that "speaking in dialect does not in itself imply moral authority" (*Mark Twain*, p. 122).

6. Though not so flagrantly, Twain himself violated the rule he charged Cooper with ignoring: "When a personage talks like an illustrated, gilt-edged, tree-calf, hand-tooled, seven-dollar Friendship's Offering in the beginning of a paragraph, he shall not talk like a negro minstrel in the end of it" ("Fenimore Cooper's Literary Offenses," *WMT* 22:62).

7. Like Mary Jane, Twain's Joan of Arc cannot abide a lie, and her purity of heart makes her, although untutored, a compelling orator: "Joan charmed [the court] with her sweetness and simplicity and unconscious eloquence, and all the best and capablest among them recognized that there was an indefinable something about her that testified that she was not made of common clay" (*WMT* 17:135).

8. Norman Page, *Speech in the English Novel* (London: Longman, 1973), p. 55.

9. Page, *Speech*, p. 98.

10. Erving Goffman, *The Presentation of Self in Everyday Life* (Garden City, N.Y.: Doubleday, 1959), p. 18n.

11. Letter of 5 February 1878, in *Mark Twain to Mrs. Fairbanks,* ed. Dixon Wecter (San Marino, Calif.: Huntington Library, 1949), p. 217.

12. Karen Halttunen discusses extensively the warnings in nineteenth-century advice manuals about hypocritical confidence men who assumed genteel habits (*Confidence Men and Painted Women* [New Haven, Conn.: Yale University Press, 1982], pp. 1–55).

13. To George Carrington, Sherburn is a "dramatist's dramatist," whose speech to the mob "is actually double-talk, impressive gibberish, a verbal drama of pure 'style'" (*Dramatic Unity,* pp. 98, 138).

14. Walter Blair, *Mark Twain and "Huck Finn"* (Berkeley: University of California Press, 1960), p. 353.

15. Some of the original forms in the manuscript are stilted. Twain revised to maintain a consistent tone of impromptu oratory throughout the speech. (The manuscript version of Sherburn's speech is reproduced in *Adventures of Huckleberry Finn: A Facsimile of the Manuscript* [Detroit: Gale, 1983], pp. 68–74 [pp. 164–65 of the holograph MS].)

16. "Preface to the Second Edition of 'Lyrical Ballads,'" in *The Poetical Work of William Wordsworth,* ed. E. De Selincourt, 2d ed. (Oxford: Oxford University Press, 1952), 2:387.

17. Richard Grant White, *Words and Their Uses, Past and Present: A Study of the English Language,* 20th ed. (Boston: Houghton Mifflin, 1892), pp. 5, 28.

18. For an example, and a discussion of the burlesque stump speech as a genre, see Robert C. Toll, *Blacking Up: The Minstrel Show in Nineteenth-Century America* (New York: Oxford University Press, 1974), pp. 55–58.

19. Richard Bridgman, *The Colloquial Style in America* (New York: Oxford University Press, 1966), pp. 32–39. In a "Comment on Tautology and Grammar" written in 1898, Twain distinguishes between justifiable and careless tautology (*MTA* 1:172).

20. David Carkeet, "The Dialects in *Huckleberry Finn,*" *American Literature* 51 (1979): 332.

21. Meir Sternberg, "Proteus in Quotation-Land: Mimesis and the Forms of Reported Discourse," *Poetics Today* 3 (1982): 148. Recently David Simpson has made the same point in relation to Cooper's *Deerslayer:* "As there are good and bad Indians [in the novel], all speaking the Ossianic language of high poetry, so there are good and bad dialect users (though no good polite speakers). No simple inference of character from speech can be made" (*The Politics of American English, 1776–1850* [New York: Oxford University Press, 1986], p. 183).

22. Richard Bridgman's *Colloquial Style in America* remains the best

account of the gradual movement of American literary prose away from the artificiality of the neoclassical models that presided over its birth. Louis D. Rubin, Jr., has identified a similar ability to draw upon the full resources of the high style and the vernacular as the essence of Faulkner's narrative art ("The Mockingbird in the Gum Tree: Notes on the Language of American Literature," *The Southern Review*, n.s. 19 [1983]: 785–801).

23. One exception is Lee Mitchell, for whom the paragraph signifies the "universe of discourses [that] compete in the novel" and undermine any belief that "language might achieve transparency, or attain some privileged relation to experience" ("'Nobody but Our Gang Warn't Around': The Authority of Language in *Huckleberry Finn*," in *New Essays on "Adventures of Huckleberry Finn*," ed. Louis J. Budd [Cambridge: Cambridge University Press, 1985], p. 97). In arguing for the fluidity of linguistic categories in the novel, Mitchell's fundamentally post-structural essay differs from my own structural account on many points; it should be consulted by any reader pleased that critics are not all trying to talk alike, either.

24. Noah Webster, *Dissertations on the English Language* (Boston: Isaiah Thomas, 1789), pp. 19–20. Cf. Simpson, *Politics of American English*, pp. 63–81.

25. Cecil B. Hartley, *The Gentleman's Book of Etiquette, and Manual of Politeness* (Boston: J. S. Locke, 1876), p. 24. Twain owned a copy of this book; see Alan Gribben, *Mark Twain's Library: A Reconstruction*, 2 vols. (Boston: G. K. Hall, 1980), 1:300. Nowadays we might translate the prescription of the etiquette book quoted in the text into a sociolinguistic rule: Avoid metalinguistic comments in an informal setting. H. P. Grice's well-known "maxims of conversation" differ surprisingly little from the rules in the old etiquette books; see his "Logic and Conversation," in *Syntax and Semantics*, vol. 3 of *Speech Acts*, ed. Peter Cole and Jerry L. Morgan (New York: Academic Press, 1975), pp. 41–58.

26. Among the "many genres of speech activity" that linguistic anthropologist Dell Hymes says an ethnology of speaking must take into account are "oath taking, verbal dueling, praying, cursing, and punning" (John J. Gumperz and Dell Hymes, eds., *Directions in Sociolinguistics* [New York: Holt, Rinehart & Winston, 1972], p. 180). All genres but the last are tremendously important in Tom and Huck's world.

27. James M. Cox, for instance, has said that Huck's role is to invert "all [the] controls, which are really *conventions*, [that] exist outside the novel" (*Mark Twain: The Fate of Humor* [Princeton, N.J.: Princeton University Press, 1966], p. 169). I disagree only in finding important traces of normative convention *within* the novel as well.

28. "Style shifting" is one of the five methodological axioms for

sociolinguistics posited by William Labov: "As far as we can see, there are no single-style speakers. Some informants show a much wider range of style shifting than others, but every speaker we have encountered shows a shift of some linguistic variables as the social context and topic change" ("The Study of Language in its Social Context," in *Sociolinguistic Patterns* [Philadelphia: University of Pennsylvania Press, 1972], p. 208).

29. For Louise K. Barnett Huck is a "picaro as linguistic outsider," whose adversarial relation to society is part of Twain's "satiric treatment of language as a social instrument." In Barnett's view, Huck differs from "society" in not having assimilated the accepted labels that impose values on social activities: "grace" for a mumbled prayer, "property" for a black slave, "gentleman" for a Sherburn or a Grangerford ("Huck Finn: Picaro as Lin[g]uistic Outsider," *College Literature* 6 [1979]: 221).

30. James M. Cox writes that "Tom's play *defines the world as play*," that Tom is an incarnation of the pleasure principle, and that in *Tom Sawyer* "the imagination represents the capacity for mimicry, impersonation, make-believe, and play" (*Mark Twain*, pp. 140, 148). Huck understands simple physical and aesthetic pleasures, but not the *plaisir du texte* in which Tom glories. Fittingly, his one mode of joking, before Jim shames him out of it, is the *practical* joke.

31. Brook Thomas has made a similar point; see his "Language and Identity in the Adventures of Huckleberry Finn," *Mark Twain Journal* 20, no. 3 (1980): 20.

32. Roman Jakobson's six functions of language are based on a communication-theory model of addresser, addressee, and message. Each of the six functions is oriented toward a corresponding linguistic "factor": (1) the referential function is the denotative orientation to the context of the message; (2) the emotive or "expressive" function focuses on the attitude and feelings of the addresser; (3) the conative function seeks response or action from the addressee; (4) the phatic function is concerned with mere contact between the interlocutors; (5) the metalingual function is focused on the linguistic code itself; and (6) the poetic function is the "focus on the message [*form* rather than its content] for its own sake" ("Closing Statement: Linguistics and Poetics," in *Style in Language*, ed. Thomas A. Sebeok [Cambridge: M.I.T. Press, 1960], pp. 353–57).

33. Emile Zola, *L'Assommoir*, in *Oeuvres complètes*, ed. Henri Mitterand (Paris: Cercle du Livre Précieux, 1967), 3:599; my translation.

34. Richard Bridgman has observed that whereas an adult is "tainted with stylistic original sin," Huck's style is "prelapsarian in its innocence and single-minded directness" (*Colloquial Style*, p. 10).

35. Roy Harvey Pearce, "Yours Truly, Huck Finn," in *One Hundred Years of "Huckleberry Finn": The Boy, His Book, and American Culture*,

ed. Robert Sattelmeyer and J. Donald Crowley (Columbia: University of Missouri Press, 1985), p. 323.

6. Languages of Power and Submission

1. Leslie Fiedler, "As Free As Any Cretur," *The New Republic*, 15 August 1955, 17.

2. George Steiner, *After Babel: Aspects of Language and Translation* (New York: Oxford University Press, 1975), p. 33.

3. Eberhard Alsen, "Pudd'nhead Wilson's Fight for Popularity and Power," *Western American Literature* 7 (1972): 143.

4. Twain's language notes are included in *PP*, 351–64. One clearly marked distinction between languages of submission and command in sixteenth-century English, the difference between "thou" and "you," is used inconsistently in Twain's historical fiction. The dialogue in *The Prince and the Pauper* shows a general understanding that "you" was for superiors and "thou" for inferiors. In practice, however, Twain often muddles the distinction: Tom Canty addresses the prince as "thou" in chapter 3, a solecism repeated in chapter 14 in the whipping boy's speech to "King" Tom.

5. Evelyn Schroth has pointed out that in *A Connecticut Yankee* Twain attempted only sporadically to differentiate among classes on the basis of dialectal differences; see "Mark Twain's Literary Dialect in *A Connecticut Yankee*," *Mark Twain Journal* 19, no. 2 (1978): 26–29.

6. James L. Johnson, *Mark Twain and the Limits of Power* (Knoxville: University of Tennessee Press, 1982).

7. The two characters are Ned Blakely in *Roughing It* (*RI*, 322), and Jasper in *Which Was It?* (*WWD*, 410).

8. See Kenneth Lynn, *Mark Twain and Southwestern Humor* (Boston: Atlantic Monthly Press, 1959), p. 262; and Martha McCulloch Williams, "In re 'Pudd'nhead Wilson,'" *Southern Magazine*, February 1894, 101.

9. Evan Carton, "*Pudd'nhead Wilson* and the Fiction of Law and Custom," in *American Realism: New Essays*, ed. Eric J. Sundquist (Baltimore: Johns Hopkins University Press, 1982), p. 85.

10. The structure of the dialogues in each case follows this scheme:

Black initiative	*White response*
(1) Self-effacing request for attention	Irritated response
(2) Plea of physical and other hardship	Angry response
(3) Despairing request for aid/sympathy	Firm refusal
(4) Final query and request for aid	Angry dismissal
(5) Veiled threat of retaliation	Fear, puzzlement
(6) Disclosure of threat	Attempted conciliation

(7) First commands   Grudging obedience
(8) "Manners lesson"   Crushed submission

A reader who compares the two passages (in *PW*, 36–42, and *WWD*, 407–16) will find that *Which Was It?* echoes not only narrative structures but even specific phrases from *Pudd'nhead Wilson*.

11. Arlin Turner, "Mark Twain and the South," *Southern Review* 4 (1968): 514.

12. On signifying, see Thomas Kockman, ed., *Rappin' and Stylin' Out: Communication in Urban Black America* (Urbana: University of Illinois Press, 1972); and Geneva Smitherman, *Talkin and Testifyin: The Language of Black America* (Boston: Houghton Mifflin, 1977).

13. Harold Beaver has gone so far as to argue that Jim designedly crafts his sentimental speech to Huck to influence Huck's actions and secure his own liberty ("Run, Nigger, Run: *Adventures of Huckleberry Finn* as a Fugitive Slave Narrative," *Journal of American Studies* 8 [1974]: 339–61).

14. James M. Cox's view of the aphorisms as above and outside the narrative is similar to mine (*Mark Twain: The Fate of Humor* [Princeton, N.J.: Princeton University Press, 1966], p. 238).

15. As Evan Carton has it, Wilson's fingerprints "collapse the distinction between biology and convention, for they represent biology in the service of convention" ("Fiction of Law and Custom," p. 92).

16. All classificatory statements implicitly assert the speaker's power or right to classify; hence no classificatory statement can ever be ideologically innocent. See "Classification and Control" and "Utterances in Discourse," in Gunther Kress and Robert Hodge, *Language as Ideology* (London: Routledge & Kegan Paul, 1979), pp. 62–102.

17. Richard Chase, *The American Novel and Its Tradition* (Garden City, N.Y.: Doubleday, 1957), pp. 149–56; Cox, *Mark Twain*, pp. 233–45; and Alsen, "Pudd'nhead Wilson's Fight," *passim*.

18. Mark Twain, letter to Olivia Clemens, 12 January 1894, in *The Love Letters of Mark Twain*, ed. Dixon Wecter (New York: Harper, 1949), p. 291.

7. Toward a Chaos of Incomprehensibilities

1. "Stupidity (incomprehension) in the novel is always polemical . . . always implicated in language, in the word: at its heart always lies a polemical failure to understand someone else's pathos-charged lie that has appropriated the world and aspires to conceptualize it, a polemical failure to understand generally accepted, canonized, inveterately false languages with their lofty labels for things and events" (Mikhail M. Bakhtin, *The Dialogic Imagination*, ed. Michael

Holquist, trans. Caryl Emerson and Michael Holquist [Austin: University of Texas Press, 1981], p. 403). Several recent studies have explored this aspect of Twain's fiction, concentrating especially on *Huckleberry Finn*. See Louise K. Barnett, "Huck Finn: Picaro as Lin-[g]uistic Outsider," *College Literature* 6 (1979): 221–31; Janet H. Mc-Kay, *Narration and Discourse in American Realistic Fiction* (Philadelphia: University of Pennsylvania Press, 1982), chap. 4; and Brook Thomas, "Language and Identity in the Adventures of Huckleberry Finn," *Mark Twain Journal* 20, no. 3 (1980): 17–21.

2. Walter Blair and Hamlin Hill make a similar point about the evolution of Twain's use of nonsense. His earlier fiction contains wordplay that is "traditionally funny because . . . incongruous in a world that is sane." But "some of the linguistic humor in later works like 'The Great Dark' . . . stands somewhere between the verbal gymnastics of the literary comedians and the verbal nihilism of contemporary absurdist humor" (*America's Humor: From Poor Richard to Doonesbury* [New York: Oxford University Press, 1978], p. 360).

3. Reprinted in Franklin R. Rogers, *Mark Twain's Burlesque Patterns, As Seen in the Novels and Narratives, 1855–1885* (Dallas: Southern Methodist University Press, 1960), p. 35.

4. Twain used the nonsensical collocation of nautical terms as a comic device as early as 1868 ("The Story of Mamie Grant, the Child-Missionary") and as late as 1898 ("The Great Dark").

5. In 1898 Twain records a memorandum concerning an ambitious use of jargon in a projected story: "In next story the sailors must talk sailor-talk, the doctors doctor-talk, the carpenter carpenter-talk &c—everybody must be glibly & easily technical" (Notebook 40, MTP TS, p. 50) (†). Following the word "doctors" Twain subsequently inserted "astronomer, chemist lawyer, midwife barber." The story was apparently never written, but elements surface in works like "The Refuge of the Derelicts."

6. H. P. Grice, "Logic and Conversation," in *Syntax and Semantics*, vol. 3 of *Speech Acts*, ed. Peter Cole and Jerry L. Morgan (New York: Academic Press, 1975), pp. 41–58.

7. Henry Nash Smith, *Mark Twain: The Development of a Writer* (Cambridge, Mass.: Harvard University Press, 1962), pp. 61–62.

8. Kenneth Lynn, *Mark Twain and Southwestern Humor* (Boston: Atlantic Monthly Press, 1959), p. 168.

9. William Dwight Whitney singled out the conversation as an "instructive" literary example of the extent to which a jargon can "be made to go in figurative substitution for ordinary speech" (*The Life and Growth of Language: An Outline of Linguistic Science* [New York: Appleton, 1875], p. 112).

10. I am indebted to my former student Alan Spring for drawing to my attention the morbid undercurrent in these passages.

11. Heraclitus, frag. 95, in *Selections from Early Greek Philosophy*, ed. Milton C. Nahm, 3d ed. (New York: F. S. Crofts, 1947), p. 93. Other fragments make it clear that the "world in common" here is a figure for the divine *logos*, or wisdom, that may be identified with the Adamic language lost to fallen humanity.

12. William Lyon Phelps, "Mark Twain, Artist," *Review of Reviews* 41 (1910): 703.

13. Compare Huck's well-known passage on the semantics of "borrowing" watermelons and other produce: "Pap always said it warn't no harm to borrow things, if you was meaning to pay them back, sometime; but the widow said it warn't anything but a soft name for stealing, and no decent body would do it" (*HF*, 80).

14. Jack Matthews, "Mark Twain, 'Cartographer,'" *ETC: A Journal of General Semantics* 23 (1966): 479–84.

15. Umberto Eco, *Semiotics and the Philosophy of Language* (Bloomington: Indiana University Press, 1984), p. 89.

16. A more farcical and less effective version of this debate over metaphor occurs at the end of chapter 31 of "No. 44, The Mysterious Stranger" (*MSM*, 394).

17. "And even things without life giving sound, whether pipe or harp, except they give a distinction in the sounds, how shall it be known what is piped or harped? For if the trumpet give an uncertain sound, who shall prepare himself to the battle? So likewise ye, except ye utter by the tongue words easy to be understood, how shall it be known what is spoken?" (1 Cor. 14:7–9).

18. As a reporter for the *San Francisco Call* in 1864 Twain had been less amused by mystifying handwriting. In the newspaper published 1 October 1864 he reported the case of a doctor's patient who had recovered damages from two druggists who had put up the wrong prescription for him. The blame in cases like this, Twain editorialized, usually "lies with the prescribing physicians who, like a majority of lawyers, and as many preachers, write a most abominable scrawl, which might be deciphered by a dozen experts as many different ways, and each one sustain his version by the manuscript" (*CofC*, 192).

19. Ludwig Wittgenstein, *Philosophical Investigations*, trans. G. E. M. Anscombe (New York: Macmillan, 1958), p. 213. Richard Macksey comments: "The philosopher is clearly not talking about 'cracking the code' of lions or dolphins, but of the impossibility of apprehending any language unless we have some access to the speaker's *Lebensform*" ("Lions and Squares: Opening Remarks," in Richard Macksey and Eugenio Donato, eds., *The Languages of Criticism and the Sciences of Man: The Structuralist Controversy* [Baltimore: Johns Hopkins University Press, 1972], p. 13). Macksey cites G. C. Lichtenberg and

Leibniz, both of whom speculated that God and the angels might be able to entertain propositions that are absurd to humans, such as that two times two equals thirteen.

20. It is not necessary to look forward to the anthropologist Benjamin Lee Whorf for an analogue to Twain's theory, since the theory is already implicit in John Locke's epistemology. Thus Locke says that the names of simple ideas cannot be defined because they are indivisible; the first framers of language borrowed from "ordinary known *ideas* of sensation," which come either from "sensible objects without, or what we feel within ourselves" (*An Essay Concerning Human Understanding*, abr. and ed. John W. Yolton [London: Dent, 1976], p. 206).

21. As early as 1882 Twain had handled this very scenario, in a dialogue between two blacks he claims to have overheard on a steamboat. The first speaker states the theme: "Wanted to send message to His Chillen, & didn't know no way but to sen' it in read'n & writ'n, w'en he know'd pow'ful well dey warn't no niggers could read it—& wouldn't be 'lowed to learn, by de Christian law of de Souf—& more'n half er de white folks! Ki-yi-yi-yi! (derisive laughter)—if 'twas a man dat got up sich a po' notion, a body'd say he sick er he can't invent worth shucks; but bein' its *Him,* you got to keep yo' mouf shet" (*NJ2,* 493). The speaker goes on to maintain that since man's capacity for sin came from God, God is responsible for sin.

22. The first appearance of the idea that I have found is in *A Connecticut Yankee.* Hank Morgan is training the disguised king to act like a peasant by describing the sufferings and deprivations they undergo. "But lord, it was only just words, words,—they meant nothing in the world to him. . . . Words realize nothing to you, vivify nothing to you, unless you have suffered in your own person the thing which the words try to describe" (*CY,* 324–25). The admiral in "The Refuge of the Derelicts" expounds the theory in several jocular paragraphs: "How was [Adam] going to know what 'surely die' meant? *Die!* He hadn't ever struck that word before . . . there hadn't ever been any talk about dead things, because there hadn't ever *been* any dead things to talk about" (*FM,* 209). Versions in "Letters From the Earth" and "Papers of the Adam Family" follow closely the model of "That Day in Eden" (*WIM,* 415; *LE,* 76).

23. James M. Cox, *Mark Twain: The Fate of Humor* (Princeton, N.J.: Princeton University Press, 1966), p. 271.

24. See *MSM,* p. 16, for a discussion of Twain's familiarity with the Apocryphal New Testament.

25. In one of his early letters to Livy, Twain had quoted his friend Joseph Twichell to the effect that "we *didn't* always think in words—that our . . . most brilliant thoughts were far beyond our capacity to

frame into words" (quoted in Susan K. Harris, *Mark Twain's Escape from Time: A Study of Patterns and Images* [Columbia: University of Missouri Press, 1982], p. 147).

26. For Susan K. Harris, because "My Platonic Sweetheart" is Twain's "most formal statement of belief that he has an ideal alternative life divorced from concrete time," this text is central for a theme that she calls "the imagination of escape," which runs through his work (*Mark Twain's Escape from Time*, p. 141).

Selected Bibliography

Aarsleff, Hans. *The Study of Language in England, 1780–1860.* Princeton, N.J.: Princeton University Press, 1967.

Alford, Henry. *The Queen's English: A Manual of Idiom and Usage.* 1864. Reprint. London: George Bell, 1895.

Alsen, Eberhard. "Pudd'nhead Wilson's Fight for Popularity and Power." *Western American Literature* 7 (1972): 135–43.

Arnold, Matthew. *General Grant.* With a rejoinder by Mark Twain. Edited by John Y. Simon. Carbondale: Southern Illinois University Press, 1966.

Ayres, Alfred. "A Plea for Cultivating the English Language." *Harper's* 103 (1901): 265–67.

Bakhtin, Mikhail M. *The Dialogic Imagination.* Edited by Michael Holquist. Translated by Caryl Emerson and Michael Holquist. Austin: University of Texas Press, 1981.

————. *Problems of Dostoevsky's Poetics.* Edited and translated by Caryl Emerson. Minneapolis: University of Minnesota Press, 1984.

Banfield, Ann. *Unspeakable Sentences: Narration and Representation in the Language of Fiction.* Boston: Routledge & Kegan Paul, 1982.

Barnett, Louise K. "Huck Finn: Picaro as Lin[g]uistic Outsider." *College Literature* 6 (1979): 221–231.

Baron, Dennis E. *Grammar and Good Taste: Reforming the American Language.* New Haven, Conn.: Yale University Press, 1982.

Bentzon, Th[érèse]. "Les Humoristes américains: Mark Twain." *Revue des deux mondes* 100 (1872): 313–335.

Berthold, Dennis. "The Conflict of Dialects in *A Connecticut Yankee.*" *Ball State University Forum* 18, no. 3 (1977): 51–58.

Blair, Walter. *Mark Twain and "Huck Finn."* Berkeley: University of California Press, 1960.

————, and Hamlin Hill. *America's Humor: From Poor Richard to Doonesbury.* New York: Oxford University Press, 1978.

Breen, Henry H. *Modern English Literature: Its Blemishes and Defects.* London: Longman, 1857.

Bridgman, Richard. *The Colloquial Style in America.* New York: Oxford University Press, 1966.

Brooks, Van Wyck. *The Ordeal of Mark Twain.* New and rev. ed. London: J. M. Dent, 1934.

Brown, Gould. *The Grammar of English Grammars*. 10th ed. New York: William Wood, 1851.

Budd, Louis J. *Mark Twain: Social Philosopher*. Bloomington: Indiana University Press, 1962.

Carkeet, David. "The Dialects in *Huckleberry Finn*." *American Literature* 51 (1979): 315–32.

———. "The Source for the Arkansas Gossips in *Huckleberry Finn*." *American Literary Realism* 14 (1981): 90–92.

Carrington, George C., Jr. *The Dramatic Unity of "Huckleberry Finn."* Columbus: Ohio State University Press, 1976.

Carton, Evan. "*Pudd'nhead Wilson* and the Fiction of Law and Custom." In *American Realism: New Essays*, edited by Eric J. Sundquist. Baltimore: Johns Hopkins University Press, 1982.

Cobbett, William. *A Grammar of the English Language, in a Series of Letters*. 1823. Reprint. Oxford: Oxford University Press, 1984.

Cox, James M. *Mark Twain: The Fate of Humor*. Princeton, N.J.: Princeton University Press, 1966.

Davis, Chester L. "Mark Twain's Marginal Notes on 'The Queen's English.'" *Twainian* 25 (1966): 1–4.

De Voto, Bernard. *Mark Twain at Work*. Cambridge, Mass.: Harvard University Press, 1942.

———. *Mark Twain's America*. Boston: Little, Brown, 1932.

Dillard, J. L. *All-American English*. New York: Vintage, 1976.

Eco, Umberto. *A Theory of Semiotics*. Bloomington: Indiana University Press, 1976.

———. *Semiotics and the Philosophy of Language*. Bloomington: Indiana University Press, 1984.

Egan, Michael. *Mark Twain's "Huckleberry Finn": Race, Class, and Society*. London: Sussex University Press, 1977.

"The English Language in America." *North American Review* 91 (1860): 507–28.

Ensor, Allison. *Mark Twain and the Bible*. Lexington: University of Kentucky Press, 1969.

Farrar, Frederic William. *An Essay on the Origin of Language*. London: J. Murray, 1860.

Finegan, Edward. *Attitudes toward English Usage: The History of a War of Words*. New York: Teachers College Press, 1980.

Firth, J. R. *The Tongues of Men*. London: Watts, 1937.

Fitzgerald, Joseph. "Anarchism in Language." *Harper's* 104 (1902): 597–600.

Fowler, Roger. *The Languages of Literature: Some Linguistic Contributions to Criticism*. New York: Barnes & Noble, 1971.

———. *Linguistics and the Novel*. London: Methuen, 1977.

———. "Anti-Language in Fiction." *Style* 13 (1979): 259–78.

———. "Preliminaries to a Sociolinguistic Theory of Literary Discourse." *Poetics* 8 (1979): 531–56.

Freimarck, Vincent. "Mark Twain and 'Infelicities' of Southern Speech." *American Speech* 28 (1953): 233–34.

Fry, James B. "Grant and Matthew Arnold: An Estimate." *North American Review* 144 (1887): 349–57.

Gardner, Joseph H. "Gaffer Hexam and Huck Finn." *Modern Philology* 66 (1968): 155–56.

Gibson, William M. *The Art of Mark Twain*. New York: Oxford University Press, 1976.

Goffman, Erving. *The Presentation of Self in Everyday Life*. Garden City, N.Y.: Doubleday, 1959.

———. *Forms of Talk*. Philadelphia: University of Pennsylvania Press, 1981.

Gouin, François. *The Art of Teaching and Studying Languages*. 5th ed. Translated by Howard Swan and Victor Bétis. London: George Philip & Son, 1894.

Gould, Edward S. *Good English; or, Popular Errors in Language*. 6th ed. New York: Widdleton, 1875.

"The Great American Language." *Cornhill Magazine*, n.s. 11 (1888): 363–77.

Gribben, Alan. *Mark Twain's Library: A Reconstruction*. 2 vols. Boston: G. K. Hall, 1980.

Grice, H. P. "Logic and Conversation." In *Syntax and Semantics*. Vol. 3, *Speech Acts*, edited by Peter Cole and Jerry L. Morgan, pp. 41–58. New York: Academic Press, 1975.

Gura, Philip F. *The Wisdom of Words: Language, Theology, and Literature in the New England Renaissance*. Middletown, Conn.: Wesleyan University Press, 1981.

Hall, Fitzedward. *Modern English*. New York: Scribner, Armstrong, 1873.

———. "Retrogressive English." *North American Review* 119 (1874): 308–31.

———. "English Rational and Irrational." *Nineteenth Century* 8 (1880): 424–44.

Halliday, M. A. K. *Language as Social Semiotic*. Baltimore: University Park Press, 1978.

Harris, Susan K. *Mark Twain's Escape from Time: A Study of Patterns and Images*. Columbia: University of Missouri Press, 1982.

Hartley, Cecil B. *The Gentleman's Book of Etiquette, and Manual of Politeness*. Boston: J. S. Locke, 1876.

Hill, A. S. "Colloquial English." *Harper's* 78 (1889): 272–79.

Howells, William Dean. *My Mark Twain*. New York: Harper, 1910.

Humboldt, Wilhelm von. *Humanist without Portfolio: An Anthology of the Writings of Wilhelm von Humboldt*. Translated by Marianne Cowan. Detroit: Wayne State University Press, 1963.

James, Henry. "The Novel of Dialect." *Literature* 3, no. 1 (9 July 1898): 17–19.

————. *The Question of Our Speech.* Boston: Houghton Mifflin, 1905.

Johnson, James L. *Mark Twain and the Limits of Power.* Knoxville: University of Tennessee Press, 1982.

Kirkham, Samuel. *English Grammar in Familiar Lectures.* Stereotype ed. New York: R. B. Collins, n.d. [1829].

Klett, Ada. "'Meisterschaft'; or, The True State of Mark Twain's German." *Anglo-German Review* 7, no. 2 (1940): 10–11.

Krapp, George Philip. "The Psychology of Dialect Writing." *The Bookman* (New York) 63 (1926): 522–29.

Krumpelmann, John T. *Mark Twain and the German Language.* Louisiana State University Studies, Humanities Series, no. 3. Baton Rouge: Louisiana State University Press, 1953.

Labov, William. *Language in the Inner City: Studies in the Black English Vernacular.* Philadelphia: University of Pennsylvania Press, 1972.

————. *Sociolinguistic Patterns.* Philadelphia: University of Pennsylvania Press, 1972.

"Language and Grammar." *London Quarterly* 12 (1859): 387–424.

Locke, John. *An Essay Concerning Human Understanding.* Abridged and edited by John W. Yolton. London: Dent, 1976.

Lotman, Juri. "The Sign Mechanism of Culture." *Semiotica* 12 (1974): 301–5.

————. *The Structure of the Artistic Text.* Translated by Gail Lenhoff and Ronald Vroon. Ann Arbor: [Dept. of Slavic Languages and Literatures], University of Michigan, 1977.

————. "The Future for Structural Poetics." *Poetics* 8 (1979): 501–7.

Lounsbury, Thomas. *The Standard of Usage in English.* New York: Harper, 1908.

Lowth, Robert. *A Short Introduction to English Grammar.* London, 1762.

Lyman, Rollo Laverne. *English Grammar in American Schools before 1850.* Department of the Interior, Bureau of Education Bulletin, 1921, no. 12. Washington: Government Printing Office, 1922.

Lynn, Kenneth. *Mark Twain and Southwestern Humor.* Boston: Atlantic Monthly Press, 1959.

McKay, Janet H. *Narration and Discourse in American Realistic Fiction.* Philadelphia: University of Pennsylvania Press, 1982.

Marsh, George P. *Lectures on the English Language.* New York: Scribner, 1860.

Matthews, Brander. *Parts of Speech: Essays on English.* 1901. Reprint. Freeport, N.Y.: Books for Libraries Press, 1968.

————. *Essays on English.* New York: Scribner, 1922.

Matthiessen, F. O. *American Renaissance: Art and Expression in the Age of Emerson and Whitman.* London: Oxford University Press, 1941.

Mencken, H. L. *The American Language.* 4th ed. New York: Knopf, 1936.

Mitchell, Lee. "'Nobody but Our Gang Warn't Around': The Authority of Language in *Huckleberry Finn.*" In *New Essays on "Adventures of Huckleberry Finn,"* edited by Louis J. Budd. Cambridge: Cambridge University Press, 1985.

Moon, George Washington. *Learned Men's English: The Grammarians. A Series of Criticisms on the English of Dean Alford, Lindley Murray, and Other Writers on the Language.* London: Routledge, 1892.

Müller, Max. *Lectures on the Science of Language.* 2 vols. New York: Scribner, 1872.

Murray, Lindley. *English Grammar. Adapted to the Different Classes of Learners.* [9th ed.] Bridgeport, Conn., 1824. Facsimile reprint. Delmar, N.Y.: Scholars' Facsimiles & Reprints, 1981.

Page, Norman. *Speech in the English Novel.* London: Longman, 1973.

Paine, Albert Bigelow. *Mark Twain: A Biography.* 3 vols. New York: Harper, 1912.

Pearce, Roy Harvey. "'Yours Truly, Huck Finn.'" In *One Hundred Years of "Huckleberry Finn": The Boy, His Book, and American Culture,* edited by Robert Sattelmeyer and J. Donald Crowley. Columbia: University of Missouri Press, 1985.

Quirk, Randolph. *Charles Dickens and Appropriate Language.* Durham: University of Durham, 1959.

————. *The Use of English.* New York: St. Martin's Press, 1962.

Rogers, Franklin R. *Mark Twain's Burlesque Patterns, As Seen in the Novels and Narratives, 1855–1885.* Dallas: Southern Methodist University Press, 1960.

Rubin, Louis D., Jr. "Mark Twain and the Language of Experience." *Sewanee Review* 71 (1963): 664–73.

————. "The Mockingbird in the Gum Tree: Notes on the Language of American Literature." *The Southern Review,* n.s. 19 (1983): 785–801.

Salomon, Roger B. *Twain and the Image of History.* New Haven, Conn.: Yale University Press, 1961.

Saussure, Ferdinand de. *Course in General Linguistics.* Edited by Charles Bally and Albert Sechehaye. Translated by Wade Baskin. Rev. ed. London: Peters Owen, 1974.

Schroth, Evelyn. "Mark Twain's Literary Dialect in *A Connecticut Yankee.*" *Mark Twain Journal* 19, no. 2 (1978): 26–29.

Simpson, David. *The Politics of American English, 1776–1850.* New York: Oxford University Press, 1986.

Smith, Henry Nash. *Mark Twain: The Development of a Writer.* Cambridge, Mass.: Harvard University Press, 1962.

Spitzer, Leo. *Linguistics and Literary History: Essays in Stylistics.* New York: Russell & Russell, 1962.

Steiner, George. *After Babel: Aspects of Language and Translation.* New York: Oxford University Press, 1975.

Sternberg, Meir. "Proteus in Quotation-Land: Mimesis and the Forms of Reported Discourse." *Poetics Today* 3 (1982): 107–56.

Tanner, Tony. "Samuel Clemens and the Progress of a Stylistic Rebel."

Bulletin of the British Association for American Studies, n.s. 3 (December 1961): 31–42.

———. *The Reign of Wonder: Naivety and Reality in American Literature.* Cambridge: Cambridge University Press, 1965.

Thomas, Brook. "Language and Identity in the Adventures of Huckleberry Finn." *Mark Twain Journal* 20, no. 3 (1980): 17–21.

Webster, Noah. *Dissertations on the English Language.* Boston: Isaiah Thomas, 1789.

Wecter, Dixon. "Mark Twain as Translator from the German." *American Literature* 13 (1941): 257–63.

———. *Sam Clemens of Hannibal.* Boston: Houghton Mifflin, 1952.

Wheeler, Benjamin Ide. "Language as Interpreter of Life." *Atlantic* 84 (1899): 464.

White, Richard Grant. *Words and Their Uses, Past and Present: A Study of the English Language.* 20th ed. Boston: Houghton Mifflin, 1892.

———. "The Quest for English." *Galaxy* 3 (1867): 62–70.

———. "English in England." *Atlantic Monthly* 45 (1880): 374–86.

Whitney, William Dwight. *Language and the Study of Language: Twelve Lectures on the Principles of Linguistic Science.* New York: Scribner, 1867.

———. "Darwinism and Language." *North American Review* 119 (1874): 61–88.

———. *The Life and Growth of Language: An Outline of Linguistic Science.* New York: Appleton, 1875.

"Words and Their Uses." *North American Review* 112 (1871): 469–76.

Index

Compositor: G&S Typesetters, Inc.
Printer: Braun-Brumfield, Inc.
Binder: Braun-Brumfield, Inc.
Text: 10/12 Palatino
Display: Palatino